AMERICANS REMEMBER
THEIR CIVIL WAR

Recent Titles in
Reflections on the Civil War Era

The Civil War at Sea
Craig L. Symonds

Politics and America in Crisis: The Coming of the Civil War
Michael S. Green

The Confederacy: The Slaveholders' Failed Venture
Paul D. Escott

The Black Experience in the Civil War South
Stephen V. Ash

The Civil War in the East: Struggle, Stalemate, and Victory
Brooks D. Simpson

Civil War Journalism
Ford Risley

The Civil War in the Border South
Christopher Phillips

American Civil War Guerrillas: Changing the Rules of Warfare
Daniel E. Sutherland

The Civil War and the West: The Frontier Transformed
Carol L. Higham

Veterans North and South: The Transition from Soldier to
Civilian after the American Civil War
Paul A. Cimbala

Food and Agriculture during the Civil War
R. Douglas Hurt

The Northern Home Front during the Civil War
Paul A. Cimbala and Randall M. Miller

AMERICANS REMEMBER
THEIR CIVIL WAR

BARBARA A. GANNON

Reflections on the Civil War Era
John David Smith, Series Editor

An Imprint of ABC-CLIO, LLC
Santa Barbara, California • Denver, Colorado

Library of Congress Cataloging-in-Publication Data

Names: Gannon, Barbara A., author.
Title: Americans remember their Civil War / Barbara A. Gannon.
Description: Santa Barbara, California : Praeger, 2017. | Series: Reflections on the Civil War era | Includes bibliographical references and index.
Identifiers: LCCN 2017007776 (print) | LCCN 2017009527 (ebook) | ISBN 9780275985721 (alk.paper : alk. paper) | ISBN 9780313049002 (ebook)
Subjects: LCSH: United States—History—Civil War, 1861–1865—Influence. | United States—History—Civil War, 1861–1865—Social aspects. | Collective memory—United States.
Classification: LCC E468.9 .G365 2017 (print) | LCC E468.9 (ebook) | DDC 973.7/1—dc23
LC record available at https://lccn.loc.gov/2017007776

ISBN: 978-0-275-98572-1
EISBN: 978-0-313-04900-2

21 20 19 18   2 3 4 5

This book is also available as an eBook.

Praeger
An Imprint of ABC-CLIO, LLC

ABC-CLIO, LLC
130 Cremona Drive, P.O. Box 1911
Santa Barbara, California 93116-1911
www.abc-clio.com

This book is printed on acid-free paper ∞

Manufactured in the United States of America

In Memory
Cynthia Graham Hurd
Susie Jackson
Ethel Lance
Rev. DePayne Middleton-Doctor
Rev. Clementa Carlos Pinckney
Tywanza Sanders
Rev. Daniel L. Simmons Sr.
Rev. Sharonda Coleman-Singleton
Myra Thompson
They went home together, one summer night
in Charleston, June 2015.

CONTENTS

Series Foreword   ix

Acknowledgments   xi

Introduction   xiii

Chapter One: The Lost Cause: Remembering a Failed Nation   1

Chapter Two: The Union Cause: Remembering Union and Freedom   19

Chapter Three: "The Legend of the Lost Cause Has Served the
                    Entire Country Very Well": Civil War Memory
                    and America's Rise to World Power   37

Chapter Four: Battle Cry of Freedom: Civil War History
                    and Memory in the Civil Rights Era   61

Chapter Five: Landscape Turned White: The Civil War
                    in Public Memory   85

Chapter Six: Romance or Reunion: The Civil War in Popular Memory 99

Contents

Chapter Seven: The Republic of Suffering: Civil War Memory
at the Beginning of the Twenty-First Century   113

Notes   133
Bibliographic Essay   155
Index   163

SERIES FOREWORD

"Like Ol' Man River," the distinguished Civil War historian Peter J. Parish wrote in 1998, "Civil War historiography just keeps rolling along. It changes course occasionally, leaving behind bayous of stagnant argument, while it carves out new lines of inquiry and debate."

Since Confederate general Robert E. Lee's men stacked their guns at Appomattox Court House in April 1865, historians and partisans have been fighting a war of words over the causes, battles, results, and broad meaning of the internecine conflict that cost more than 620,000 American lives. Writers have contributed between 50,000 and 60,000 books and pamphlets on the topic. Viewed in terms of defining American freedom and nationalism, western expansion and economic development, the Civil War quite literally launched modern America. "The Civil War," Kentucky poet, novelist, and literary critic Robert Penn Warren explained, "is for the American imagination, the great single event of our history. Without too much wrenching, it may, in fact, be said to *be* American history."

The books in Praeger's *Reflections on the Civil War Era* series examine pivotal aspects of the American Civil War. Topics range from examinations of military campaigns and local conditions to analyses of institutional, intellectual, and social history. Questions of class, gender, and race run through each volume in the series. Authors, veteran experts in their respective fields, provide concise, informed, readable syntheses—fresh looks at familiar topics with new source material and original arguments.

"Like all great conflicts," Parish noted in 1999, "the American Civil War reflected the society and the age in which it was fought." Books in *Reflections on the Civil War Era* interpret the war as a salient event in the hammering out and understanding of American identity before, during, and after the secession crisis of 1860–1861. Readers will find the volumes valuable guides as they chart the troubled waters of mid-nineteenth-century American life.

John David Smith
Charles H. Stone Distinguished Professor of American History
The University of North Carolina at Charlotte

ACKNOWLEDGMENTS

A book has one author, but so many individuals contribute to its completion. First and foremost, I would like to thank John David Smith for signing me up for this project and being with me every step of the way as I completed it. This book is materially better because of his contribution. I would be remiss if I did not acknowledge Michael Millman of Praeger for his encouragement and patience as this project took longer to finish than planned. Partly, this book took more time because it synthesizes the work of so many fine historians, living and dead; I hope I did justice to their scholarship. Moreover, I wanted to convey one idea in these pages; these studies are all correct. Confederates hid in the attic, they paraded down main street. Union soldiers revered their former foes and rejected their comradeship. Americans forgot slavery and remembered emancipation; honored the union and sacralized disunion. The past is neither dead, past, nor unitary.

While I am grateful to all who have contributed to this volume, I must single out some of those whose kindness and support have meant a great deal to me in my career including William A. Blair, Gary W. Gallagher, Caroline E. Janney, Christian B. Keller, Kevin M. Levin, Anne E. Marshall, Brian Craig Miller, Mark E. Neely, Nina Silber, Andrew L. Slap, Elizabeth R. Varon, Joan Waugh, LeeAnn Whites, and Jim Weeks, who is with us only in memory. I would also like to recognize David W. Blight, for his body of work and his kindness to me as a young scholar, at least in academic years. Finally, to my sister Mary, and my brother Michael, your faith in me made all things possible.

INTRODUCTION

In June 2015, the waning days of the Civil War sesquicentennial, the governor of South Carolina, an Indian American woman, asked the legislature to approve measures that would remove the Confederate flag from State House grounds. The Civil War began in South Carolina more than 150 years before, and it would be gratifying to think the battle for Civil War memory ended there when the flag came down a few weeks later. This victory seemed hollow; nine African American men and women lay dead—pastors, grandmothers, and others—gunned down as they prayed in a historic Charleston church; that single act prompted this request. The accused shooter's social media accounts demonstrated his devotion to white supremacy and the Lost Cause—Confederate Civil War memory. In response to his actions, other states rejected Confederate symbols. The Lost Cause came under attack in places as varied as Stone Mountain, Georgia, home to the largest statuary of the Lost Cause, and Bowdoin College in Maine with its Jefferson Davis Prize. A new phase in the contest over Civil War memory between the Lost Cause and the Union Cause—how federal supporters remembered the Civil War—had begun.[1]

When Nobel Prize–winning author William Faulkner proclaimed that "the past is never dead. It's not even past," he might have been speaking about how Americans remember the Civil War. Nothing else can explain why Americans contest the Civil War and its memory one hundred and fifty years after the war ended. To understand how Americans remembered a war they cannot remember, you must understand memory. Memory is about what individuals remember of their lived experiences, it is about how men and women come together to make sense of what they remember, and finally it is about how people with no lived experience of an event remember. Since the Civil War ended one hundred and fifty years ago, what today is called Civil War memory represents the views of those who have no individual memory of the conflict.[2]

Everyone has experience with individual memory; however, this study is about how groups remember. Both those whose members experienced what they are remembering—collective memory—and groups whose members have no individual memory because they were not witnesses to the events they are remembering—historical memory. Though sometimes used interchangeably, for the purpose of this study these terms represent distinct types of memories. Similarly, scholars defined other important aspects of Civil War memory, public and popular memory, in many different ways. In this book, public memory refers to memory in public spaces, including monuments and battlefields. Similarly, popular memory denotes memory in popular culture, including movies and television.[3]

All memory, individual, collective, historical, public, or popular, represents the past in the present, if for no other reason than a memory involves past events recalled in the present. What happened to an individual has its roots a single, definite event with a point in time: its interpretation affected by the conditions of the individual's life and society when he or she recalls the specific episode. An American who lived through the Civil War remembers events from that period, but their current circumstances shaped and influenced their memory. An amputee's physical infirmity defined his or her battlefield memories; a widow framed the wartime home front in light of her economic struggles in the postwar world. Moreover, all memory is shaped by the social and cultural contexts of those who remember, both before the war and how society changed in its aftermath. The same soldier recalled his wartime experiences limited by his ability to describe the agony he suffered because of his idea of what a man should endure without complaining defined by society before the war; the widow in light of what society believed a woman can and should be. These men and women's memories reflected their antebellum social and cultural context, but the war and its aftermath challenged some of these ideas. After the war, women engaged in public acts related to memory; before the war society defined their place as at home in the domestic sphere. A society that demanded men to be whole changed its idea of what a man should be in a postwar world with thousands of amputees. When this amputee joined a veterans' organization and the widow a women's organization, they helped create a collective memory of the Civil War. As part of their legacy, the men and women who supported the Blue (Union Cause) and the Gray (Lost Cause) created a collective memory of the Civil War, one that they shared with people who had not lived through this conflict, and this became the historical memory for successor generations.[4]

These same processes affected historical memory—the memory of those who did not live through the war: in this case, their present, far removed from the war they were remembering. Not surprisingly, historians played a critical role in creating historical memory, acting as referees among the competing collective memories of the conflict. Making this task more challenging, Confederate supporters understood that they were part of an ongoing contest over memory and created extensive archives to chronicle their recollections, a material edge in the battle for historical memory. Reinforcing the role of collective memory, the first professional historians in the late nineteenth century, who started the process of articulating the Civil War's historical memory, echoed the disparate views of the Civil War generation. Later generations with no direct connection to the war, including historians and the broader public, responded to life in their present, including anxieties about wars won and lost, union and nation, and the changing landscape of race in the United States.

Imagine a World War I soldier who found inspiration in former Confederate soldiers' memoirs, even if his grandfather fought for the Union. His president, Woodrow Wilson, a professional historian, born into a family of Confederate supporters, advanced efforts to honor Confederate soldiers as heroic Americans in his popular historical studies. The soldier's son questioned the value of a war for Union if the industrial nation that emerged from this bloodletting accepted the gross inequities that culminated in the Great Depression. Decades later, the soldier's granddaughter applauded the end of segregation during the civil rights movement and remembered a war that ended slavery but not inequality. When she wrote a book on the Civil War, it chronicled Civil War women, a subject previously ignored by a predominantly male academic community because she came of age in an era when women rejected their exclusion from the historical narrative. Eventually, the woman's daughter observed the ongoing struggle for racial justice in the twenty-first century and wondered: did the Civil War solve anything? As a result of the relationship between the past and the present, Civil War memory continues to evolve long after the men and women who remembered it have passed into memory.

As part of this survey on how Americans remember the Civil War, or Civil War memory, I will attempt to answer a few important questions. First and perhaps foremost, why do Americans remember the war differently? It is certainly not for want of material to study and form a consensus; there are tens of thousands of books written about the Civil War; many of these volumes were by the men and the women who witnessed the war. Moreover, there have been winners and losers in the battle for Civil War memory. In contrast to the well-known saying that winners write the history, for a very long time, the losers won the memory battle. Why was the Lost Cause so much more successful, more memorable, than the Union Cause? When and why did the Union Cause finally make an impression on Americans' Civil War memory? Finally, does the evolution of Civil War memory in the past tell us about its future? It may seem odd talking about the future of memory, but it certainly is astonishing that at this late date, at the end of the sesquicentennial, Americans still do not agree on how they remember the Civil War.

There is no one way Americans remember their Civil War. The Civil War generation experienced the war differently and had distinct individual memories of these events. As a result, these men and women created opposing collective memories—a Confederate and Union Cause. Moreover, even when they lived through the same events, they perceived them differently. A Confederate supporter remembered the U.S. government's wrong-headed effort to stop peaceful secession. If slavery mattered, it was about radical abolitionists' attempts to interfere with this beneficial institution. Confederates recalled a defensive struggle to establish an independent nation in the face of a savage Union assault. When this failed, they rejected any notion that they were wrong; the memory of an honorable defeat against overwhelming odds sanctified their memories and justified their wartime losses. Similarly, federal supporters looked back on a war that suppressed a rebellion, preserved the Union, and freed the slaves. Union victory validated their cause and their wartime sacrifices. When the men and women of the Civil War generation passed, succeeding generations selected aspects of these collective memories that resonated in their present. In the first half of the twentieth century, the Lost Cause met the needs of contemporary times; in the second half, the civil rights movement and challenges to the racial status quo meant that more Americans rediscovered the Union Cause. Ultimately, what Americans remember about their Civil War past is more about the challenges of the present suggesting that Civil War memory will continue to evolve in the twenty-first century.

For the men and women for whom the war was a lived experience, it was the postwar era that cemented these different memories. Confederate and Union supporters organized separate groups that created the war's collective memories; some formed veterans' organizations, others women's groups. Not surprisingly these men and women did not articulate a memory that included any idea that their respective causes were wrong or that their generation's sacrifices were meaningless; there should be no expectation that they would do so. Though defeated during the war, and their slave society destroyed, Confederate supporters still believed that they were right on many of the war's issues. In their mind, brave men and women persevered in a noble cause against overwhelming odds for independence and states' rights, a cause that had nothing to do with slavery. Memory was not only about the past but the present, particularly for Confederates, who used their collective memory—the Lost Cause— to rebuild their shattered society. Similarly, loyal Unionists felt that victory validated their efforts and their cause. In their mind, brave men and women persevered in a noble cause for Union and freedom, a cause that had everything to do with slavery. African Americans of the Civil War generation participated in the efforts and created their own collective memory that would be "remembered" later when racial attitudes changed.

Ironically, while white and black Unionists emerged victorious in the real war, federal supporters lost the war in memory. Successive generations who did not live through the war remembered the war by fashioning a historical memory based on selectively emphasizing specific collective memories of the Civil War generation and forgetting others. In this instance, the Lost Cause won the contest over Civil War memory during the first half of the twentieth century. Initially, it appealed to Americans facing the social and cultural strains of a transition to an industrial society at the end of the nineteenth century. Later, the needs of a nation that had risen to world power status, and the subsequent wars of the twentieth century, prompted Americans to embrace Lost Cause notions emphasizing Americans of both sections' courage and military prowess. Ironically, the people who rejected American militarism, particularly after World War I, accepted aspects of the Lost Cause arguing that the Civil War was not worth the sacrifice in blood and treasure. Similarly, Americans in the first half of the twentieth century who disparaged the industrial nation that emerged after the Civil War praised the agrarian society destroyed by Union victory. Race mattered in both cases. First, white Americans saw no moral issue with slavery because they agreed that racially inferior African Americans benefited from this institution. Second, some Americans renounced a war that cost white American lives that destroyed an idealized agrarian society. In contrast, African Americans who rejected the notion of slavery's benevolence and the Lost Cause kept the Union Cause alive, even when many white Americans had forgotten it.

After World War II, it was African American actions that shaped Civil War memory; in this case, it was about contemporary times and the civil rights movement. Ironically, the critical turning point occurred during the Cold War when the state of the Union led some Americans to promote a more unitary Civil War memory to unite Americans against the threat of communism, which supported the Lost Cause. At the same time, the civil rights movement challenged the racial status quo and prompted some Americans to examine the racial assumptions that facilitated the acceptance of the Lost Cause, including the morality of slavery. When the present changed, the memory of the past did also. Once Americans began to accept the notion that slavery was wrong, the Union Cause and the effort to destroy this institution resonated in some Americans' memory. As time passed, historians realized that the Lost Cause was more memory than history, consciously created by Confederate supporters. Despite this awareness, a generation passed before historians began to broaden Civil War history and memory to include African Americans, women, immigrants, and others as part of a broader challenge to traditional Civil War memory.

It took a long time for historians, and anyone else, to understand the difference between history and memory and even longer for people to understand how the Civil War in public spaces shapes memory. Many of the issues surrounding the aftermath of the Charleston shooting involve public memory, such as the flag at South Carolina's Statehouse. In many ways, public memory is a bridge between collective and historical memory. The Civil War generation created material artifacts, such as the monuments and preserved battlefields as part of their collective memory efforts. John Bodnar in *Remaking America: Public Memory, Commemoration, and Patriotism in the Twentieth Century* (1992) made a critical distinction that explains the Civil War in public memory. He identified two types of public memory, vernacular (local grassroots) and official (state/nationally sanctioned) memory. Civil War public memory originated in the local grassroots actions of Confederate and Union supporters. Initially, people built monuments for the dead who never returned home, partly to assuage the grief of those who survived memorializing a particular cause, be it the Confederacy's Lost Cause, or the Union's Won Cause. The failure to build monuments to black soldiers seemed to reinforce amnesia about their wartime efforts. Once the Civil War generation passed away, the next generation continued to build monuments; the United Daughters of the Confederacy led Lost Cause efforts. These women's actions reflected their present. Women wanted to play a more active role in politics, and turn-of-the-century social convention limited women's roles; defending the Lost Cause represented an acceptable way to engage public issues. In contrast, battlefield preservation efforts occurred decades after the war ended, partly because the idea of commemorating the dead seemed more urgent than preserving where they died. Eventually, the federal government managed many of these sites and used them in an attempt to create an official Civil War memory; however, this has not always been successful due to the strength of sectionalism in vernacular memory. Recent efforts to introduce the idea that slavery caused the war met resistance at national battlefield parks by those who remember a Lost Cause that had nothing to do with owning human beings.[5]

People who remembered the Lost Cause have little to complain about in popular memory. Here too, the Lost Cause seemed more successful than the Union Cause for much of the twentieth century. Since many more people saw movies or television programs about the Civil War than visited battlefields, this may constitute their most vivid memory of the conflict. Partly, the success of the Lost Cause reflected its broader success in American memory; however, the Confederate cause often resonated in popular culture. *Gone with the Wind*'s (1939) success as a best-selling novel and one of the most popular movies of all times may have been as much about its popularity as a romantic melodrama than its portrayal of the Lost Cause version of Civil War memory. It place in memory may be about what happened after millions of American saw this movie. To these men and women that became their Civil War memory. In contrast, the first movie that portrayed the African American Civil War experience, *Glory* (1989), debuted almost one hundred and twenty-five years after the war ended suggesting that the Lost Cause dominated popular memory long after the civil rights movement challenged the memory of the Lost Cause.[6]

The television documentary *The Civil War* made the war more popular in the last decade of the twentieth century; its emphasis on race and slavery, reunion and union, captured the state of Civil War memory at the end of the twentieth century. In the twenty-first century, at the Civil War's sesquicentennial, the emergence of the Internet and social media allowed more Americans to weigh in on the subject making a unitary memory of the Civil War impossible. Among the present issues affecting how Americans remember the Civil War are discontent against wars on terror, distrust of the federal government, and dismay over the election of the first black president. More recently, the Charleston shooting began a new phase in Civil War memory wars when more Americans reject the Lost Cause and its symbols in public spaces. In response, supporters of the Lost Cause rallied to their colors as officials removed their flag and other Confederate icons. Since the Civil War is a mirror in which people see themselves and their times, this is not the last word on Civil War memory.[7]

Identifying how Americans remember the Civil War is a complex process particularly since this study covers almost one hundred and fifty years of American memory. Initially, I studied memory theory to identify the types of memory relevant to the discussion of the Civil War; making this theory more accessible represents one goal of this study. Later, I examined scholarly studies on Civil War memory, a recent development in the study of this era. Chapters 1 and 2 reflected my assessment of scholarly studies on the Civil War generations' collective memory. While there has always been an effort to reduce memory to Northern and Southern, this study assesses it based on the memory of Confederate and Union supporters. The presence of federal supporters in the South and Confederate sympathizers in the North explains why this book describes how the partisans of the Confederate and federal government remember. When historians assess memory, they feel compelled to say that all Northerners or all Southerners did not agree on the memory of the war, why would they? They did not agree during the war. Therefore, it would be surprising if they did in its aftermath. Especially problematic, the unity of white Confederate supporters has been translated as a unity among Southerners and conflated with Southern identity; this is true only if African Americans born in southern states are not considered Southerners.

Starting in Chapter 3, and continuing in Chapters 4 and 7, I explored historical memory—a narrative shaped by the present based on one of the streams of the Civil War's collective memory. In some cases, I relied on what historians found about Civil War memory; in others I assessed scholarly studies as memory acts; scholars made choices about the subjects they studied and the sources they used, for example, a generation that desired national unity focused on reconciliationist narratives from the Civil War generation. In Chapter 4, scholars lead the way in questioning the racial assumptions that allowed such an uncritical acceptance of the Lost Cause in American Civil War memory. This sensitivity manifested itself in a number of ways including a renewed interest in African American military units. Chapters 5 and 6 relied on a recent explosion of studies that assessed what and how Americans remember the Civil War in public and popular memory.

Public memory brings us back to a Charleston church on a summer night. It was likely no coincidence that the church assaulted by the Charleston gunman played a major role in fighting black slavery and advocating black freedom in the decades before the war and since. Perhaps the way Americans should remember the Civil War, one beyond causes either won or lost, is that these nine Americans were only the latest victims of the failure to remember the Civil War, the nation's greatest cataclysm.

ONE

THE LOST CAUSE: REMEMBERING A FAILED NATION

Robert E. Lee looked out upon his defeated army at Appomattox and knew he needed to send them a final message. While each Confederate soldier had an individual memory, Lee started shaping their collective memory with the last order he gave to his army. In Lee's farewell address to his troops, he explained the defeat of his army—an explanation that resonates today in many Americans' minds. Lee contended that his army "after four years of arduous service, marked by unsurpassed courage and fortitude . . . has been compelled to yield to overwhelming numbers and resources." While partly this represented a way of justifying the surrender, it will become enshrined as the fundamental explanation for defeat and the beginning of the notion that the Confederate military effort was more admirable than the Union effort. If Fort Sumter was the first shot of the war, this was the first shot in the battle for Civil War memory. Robert Penn Warren reflected on the legacy of the Civil War 100 years later and pinpointed Appomattox as critical to the confederacy's legacy. "We may say that only at the moment when Lee handed Grant his sword was the Confederacy born; or to state matters another way, in the moment of death the Confederacy entered upon its immortality." Surprisingly, it was neither Lee, nor any other soldier, but a civilian who coined the term "Lost Cause" to encapsulate Confederate Civil War memory. Edward A. Pollard, who edited the *Richmond Examiner*, published a book in 1866 entitled *The Lost Cause: A New Southern History of the War of the Confederates* (1866). In contrast, scholars will not even begin to formulate the idea that there was a Union Cause until the beginning of the twenty-first century. Ironically, the Lost Cause won the battle of Civil War memory for much of the first one hundred years after the war ended.[1]

Broadly speaking, scholars agree on the fundamental principles of the Lost Cause. First, Confederate supporters remembered a Civil War for states' rights, not slavery, though they contended there was nothing wrong with slavery, as demonstrated by the many faithful slaves who served their masters during the war. Instead of slavery, the war was about secession as a constitutional right, or about the divorce between two sections that were culturally distinct and at odds. Despite the fact that slavery did not cause the war, supporters of the Lost Cause argue that abolitionists initiated the war to free slaves who did not want to be freed, but would have eventually been freed because slavery was dying in the South. In fact, Southern society was better than Northern society because of slavery, and this superiority explained the many military successes of their army and its leaders—men such as Robert E.

Union forces celebrate their victory at the fourth anniversary of Fort Sumter's Surrender, Charleston, South Carolina, April 14, 1865. (Library of Congress)

Lee and Thomas "Stonewall" Jackson, though both men were portrayed as antislavery. The Union only beat these great men and their soldiers because of its material advantages in men and equipment. Since their superior society had been a product of the slave society, even though the war was not about slavery, Confederate supporters refused to apologize for this institution. (Despite the war not being about slavery, Lost Cause supporters seemed obsessed with an institution that had nothing to do with the war.). As a result, Confederate soldiers, along with the military and civilian leadership of the former Confederate states, refused to accept any notion that they were at fault. It would be unlikely that Southern supporters would have ever created a Lost Cause that they remembered as the wrong cause.[2]

Confederate supporters' Lost Cause followed the same pattern as other collective memories; on the one hand, their memories were about the past, and on the other hand about their postwar present. Further, their wartime memories were filtered through a social and cultural context largely formed in antebellum society. Some scholars have emphasized the Lost Cause as a product of Southern romanticism; others its religiosity; and still others the need to rationalize defeat, ensure elite white rule, and rebuild Southern white identity. When examined carefully, in light of what is known about memory, all of these interpretations are correct. Antebellum romanticism and religiosity represented the social and cultural context that shaped the Lost Cause. During the war, individuals understood their experience through these frameworks. After the war, white Southerners focused on maintaining white supremacy above almost all else; the Lost Cause supported this critical contemporary need. The only question to keep in mind when considering the link between the Lost Cause and white supremacy is, how important was Civil War memory to this effort? Would white Southerners have acted any differently if they remembered the Civil War in another way? Would any memory have prompted these men and women to support a racially egalitarian society? Given these factors, the Lost Cause may not so much have represented a conscious construction of Confederate supporters; instead, it may have reflected an almost inevitable product of men and women coping with defeat, the destruction of their social order, and the need to reimagine their Southern white identity.

The first historians to assess the Lost Cause with the idea that this was something more myth than fact appeared to have different views on the origins of this memory; however, a closer examination of their findings demonstrated that they were describing how social and cultural context shapes collective memory. Thomas Connelly and Barbara L. Bellows, in *God and General Longstreet: The Lost Cause in the Southern Mind* (1982), identified antebellum romanticism as the root of the Lost Cause. "The origins of the phrase are easier to understand. Southern Romanticism of the early nineteenth century had thrived upon Sir Walter Scott's accounts of the lost cause of Scotland in its quest for independence." Given the nature of collective memory, it comes as no surprise that antebellum romanticism shaped Confederate Civil War memory. Similarly, Rollin G. Osterweis's *The Myth of the Lost Cause 1865–1900* (1973) maintained that just as antebellum "romanticism . . . was the force behind the movement for southern independence," the Lost Cause "represented the postbellum adjustment of the old chivalric concepts and the old idea of Southern cultural nationalism to the traumatic experiences of devastation, defeat, poverty, and humiliation." To some extent, the romanticism associated with the Lost Cause explains its popularity in historical memory.[3]

Romanticism reflected the secular mind-set of a religious antebellum society. Charles Reagan Wilson in his study *Baptized in Blood: The Religion of the Lost Cause 1865–1920* (1980) examined Confederate memory as a religious phenomenon, in this case as a function of "civil religion" that included "a set of ideological beliefs, ritualistic practices, and organizational structures that seeks transcendent meaning in the nation." As Wilson explained, the Lost Cause represented "the afterlife of a redeemer nation that died. The nation was never resurrected, but is survived as a sacred presence, a holy ghost haunting the spirit and actions of post-Civil War Southerners." According to Wilson, when the Confederacy as a "political nation was not to be . . . the dream of a cohesive Southern people with a separate cultural identity replaced the original longing." As a result, "the cultural dream replaces the political dream . . . [and] religion was at the heart of the dream." Ultimately, he concluded "the lost cause was the story of the use of the past as the basis for a Southern religious–moral identity, an identity as a chosen people." Similarly, W. Scott Poole in his study *Never Surrender: Confederate Memory and Conservatism in the South Carolina Upcountry* (2004) suggested that "devotion to the Confederacy became a religious value for South Carolinians who sought to shape a southern sacred world" that "provided a paradigm for regenerative change amid the ruins of the Old South." Religious people created a collective memory that reflected their religious worldview to rebuild their shattered society.[4]

Rooted in the past, the Lost Cause reflected the present needs of postwar Confederates. Gaines M. Foster in *Ghost of the Confederacy: Defeat and the Lost Cause and the Emergence of the New South* (1987) concluded that the celebration of the Lost Cause "offered a memory of personal sacrifice and a model of social order that met the needs of a society experiencing rapid change and disorder." Foster understood that collective memory originated in individual memory. As he explained, the Lost Cause "developed out of and in turn shaped individuals' memory of the wars." Memory theorists recognized that there is an iterative process by which individual memory is the source of collective memory, but as time goes on collective memory shapes how individuals remember. Foster focused on groups including the "postwar Confederate organizations: the memorial associations, the Southern Historical Society, the United Confederate Veterans, the United Daughters of the Confederacy (UDC), and others" collective memory efforts because "more Southerners formed an under-standing of their past through the ceremonial activities or rituals conducted by these groups than through anything else." Because of the intensive effort to create a collective memory, individual memory may have become subsumed into a larger narrative.[5]

Foster included women's groups among these critical organizations; in fact, women in memorial associations articulated many of the Lost Cause's enduring notions at cemeteries and commemorations for the Confederate dead. In addition to women, elite white men like Pollard, Lee, and other prominent Confederate leaders formulated the Lost Cause in its early years. In contrast, rank-and-file veterans groups cited by Foster, such as the United Confederate Veterans, organized only after other men and women framed Confederate collective memory. Because the elite articulated the Lost Cause, some scholars argued that Confederate Civil War memory reflected their need to rationalize both the decision for secession and their wartime defeat, while ensuring that they continued to rule in the postwar world. These scholars view the Lost Cause as fundamentally political, a tool to establish the old order and its racial and social hierarchies. More recently, scholars found that because its supporters had different wartime experiences and sometimes competing postwar interests the Lost Cause was not monolithic as it has been portrayed. Regardless of divisions among former Confederates, these men and women would have been gratified that their version of Civil War memory did so well when they had passed from the scene and the next generation formulated the Civil War's historical memory.

One profound difference between the collective memory of the Unionists and Confederates is women's prominent role in constructing the latter's narrative. The first memory task of Confederates supporters was not about the past, but the very real present, burying the dead. Confederate supporter's articulated the first and most resonant statements of the Lost Cause at the many commemorations that honored the Confederate dead. As John R. Neff in *Honoring the Civil War Dead: Commemoration and the Problem of Reconciliation* (2004) explained, "In the processes associated with mourning and memorializing, it was incumbent, upon the living to interpret and render sensible the sacrifice of those no longer among them." When they did so, they made sure it was clear that their death was in a worthy cause. "Soldiers lost their lives as 'martyrs,' as a 'sacrifice,' especially on the 'altar of the nation,' language that each side used to ennoble both the dead and their separate causes." It would be impossible to imagine Confederate supporters doing anything but proclaiming the rightness of a cause, even if they did not believe this to be so; who can tell a father, mother, or a widow that their son or husband died in vain for an unworthy cause?[6]

The need to bury and memorialize the dead created some of the most critical divergences in Civil War memory. While the inescapable fact that the dead were dead because the other side killed them mattered, it was also the different needs of each side to bury and commemorate their dead. In the North, the federal government and the states organized and funded these burials; in the South, the local community interred the dead. Because Northern troops occupied these communities, or later Republican governments dominated by black and white Southern Unionists ruled, local Confederate supporters took care of the Confederate dead. Since Confederate men's organizations represented a political threat to occupiers, the widows and mothers of the former Confederate States buried their own dead.[7]

While much of the attention on Confederate women focused on the UDC, it was their predecessors, the Ladies Memorial Associations (LMAs), who shaped the collective memory of this conflict. Like all Civil War memory, the memory of women's deeds was about the present; awareness of the important role of women in society in the late twentieth century made scholars more sensitive to the role of women in history. Once scholars examined the Lost Cause with an awareness of women's role in history, they understood what was obvious to people of the time: the critical role played by women in the construction of the Lost Cause. Caroline E. Janney in her study *Burying the Dead but Not the Past: Ladies' Memorial Associations and the Lost Cause* (2008) examined how these women's groups in Virginia composed of "middle- and upper-class southern white women came to shape the public rituals of Confederate Memory, Reconstruction, and reconciliation." While these women's roles seemed forgotten, contemporary Confederate supporters understood the critical role these women played in the postwar era. "They understood that it had been the Ladies, not Confederate veterans, former politicians, or even the Daughters (UDC) who had established Confederate cities of the dead [cemeteries] and had organized elaborate Memorial Day celebrations where they might gather to mourn their failed cause." As a result, these organizations remade "military defeat into a political, social, and cultural victory for the white South." Women played these critical roles because immediately after the war women seemed less of a threat to the Union military. "Memorial activities lay clearly within the province of female mourning and posed no threat to sectional reunion." Ironically, Janney described this work as "intensely political" and began Southern women's postwar political development. Ladies Memorial Associations allowed women to go beyond antebellum ideas of women's role in the public sphere and laid the foundation for modern Southern women's organizations.[8]

As part of this study, Janney summarized her view of what constituted the Lost Cause centering it in the present needs of former Confederates. "The rhetoric and traditions of the Lost Cause developed in the postwar climate of economic, racial and gender uncertainty" as a result of the end of slavery and the challenges of reconstruction. To address these issues, former Confederates "romanticized the 'Old South' and the Confederate war effort, often factually and chronologically distorting the way in which the past would be remembered." These men and women filtered the past and their memories through preexisting social and cultural ideas and language, such as romanticism. According to Janney, the memory of slavery was a victim of both romance and contemporary political reality. "The nostalgia for the past accompanied a collective forgetting of slavery, while defining Reconstruction as a period of 'Yankee aggression' and black 'betrayal.'" In many ways, the Lost Cause represents the perfect example of the relationship between the present and the past filtered through the social and cultural ideas and language of those who were remembering.[9]

While Janney focused on Virginia, Lee Ann Whites examined these commemorations as part of a larger examination of Augusta, Georgia, in the Civil War era. In her study *The Civil War as a Crisis in Gender: Augusta, Georgia, 1860–1890* (1995), she identified memorialization activities as central to the postwar reconstruction of Southern men and women's gender roles. As scholars became aware of the role of women, they also came to understand that more than biology was at work. Instead, how society believed women should act, how women themselves believed they should act—their gender identity—had to be examined. According to Whites, "Confederate men, rather than having fought the war in defense of their right to dominate those household dependents—the slaves—who were now lost to them, were reenvisioned as having loyally stood for the defense of those household dependents—their women and children—who in the postwar era continued to stand loyally by them." Whites, like Janney, viewed women's role in reshaping Civil War memory as politically transformative. "White Women, especially elite white women, acquired a new kind of public voice and a public cultural power by virtue of their special role and status in articulating and celebrating the reconstruction of white southern manhood." In contrast to this newly empowered status "the new freedpeople were rendered mute in this remembering of the war effort": or were they?[10]

Antoinette G. Van Zelm examined both black and white women's participation in Southern memorialization activities and decided that black women spoke at these commemorations. While white women memorialized the Confederate cause, African American women commemorated the Union Cause. Van Zelm in "Virginia Women as Public Citizens: Emancipation Day Celebrations and Lost Cause Commemoration, 1863–1890" (2000) found that while both types of commemorations "ultimately confirmed male authority within their postemancipation communities, these women clearly shaped the orchestrated transition from slavery to freedom within civic space." While she found that black and white women engaged in these postwar observances, there were significant differences. Not surprisingly, Van Zelm found that white women had "more resources at their disposal and appear to have been more likely to initiate their commemorations." Despite originating these observances, "white women . . . did so as reluctant citizens, animated by a vision not of the future but of the past." In contrast, "African American women participated in Emancipation Day ceremonies as eager citizens, impatient to bring the new reality of freedom closer to its ideal and determined to protect their newly acquired rights." One key difference she cited: African American women were more likely to speak at the commemoration than white women at their observances. Ideas of how white men thought white women should act may explain their silence at these observances. Formerly enslaved African American women did not have the same constraints.[11]

In contrast, some white women used a gendered idea of what they should do, be romantically courted by Confederate soldiers, to situate themselves in the larger Lost Cause narrative. As Victoria E. Ott explained in her essay "Love in Battle: The Meaning of Courtships in the Civil War and Lost Cause" (2012), after the war "young women, now adults, remained devoted to the traditional values and offered up their own version of the southern experience in hope of venerating the region but also to advocate a return to the gender ordering of the antebellum era." These women harkened back to antebellum ideas to reframe their memory of the war as an era of romantic courtship to deal with the unsettled and unsettling present. Similarly, women used their participation in Lost Cause commemorations to justify what might be considered unwomanly behavior. Michele Gillespie chronicled, in "Peddling the Lost Cause: A Southern White Women at Work" (2011), the story of Mary Ann Harris Gay, who was not married but lost her brother during the war and supported his family in its aftermath. She worked as a traveling Bible saleswoman to support her family, something that would have been considered unwomanly behavior before the war. She published books to make money, including a *Life in Dixie* (1892), a popular memoir of Confederate life on the home front that advanced the Lost Cause. While this is only one story, Gillespie claimed that her life "suggests [that] some white women were at least as invested in peddling the memory of the Civil War dead to serve their own very real needs, as in romanticizing the white past to secure cultural authority, perpetuate racist ideology, and pursue political ends."[12]

Ms. Gay was an anomaly; it was elite white men who wrote the books that articulated the Lost Cause. Former Confederate officials and other elite civilians needed to rationalize their actions that led to secession before the war, their failures during the war, and justify their elite status in the postwar era. Not surprisingly, former military leaders of the Confederate army played a prominent role in these efforts. Gary W. Gallagher in *Lee and His Generals in War and Memory* (1998) chronicled former Confederate major general Jubal Early's "efforts to bequeath a written legacy favorable to Lee and Jackson and the nascent republic for which they fought." According to Gallagher, "Early understood almost immediately after Appomattox that there would be a struggle to control the public memory of the war. He worked hard to helped shape that memory and ultimately enjoyed more success than he probably imagined possible." Early argued that "his Army of Northern Virginia set a standard of valor and accomplishment equal to anything in the military history of the Western world until finally, worn out but never defeated, they laid down their weapons at Appomattox." Gallagher suggested that because of his reputation as a "crabby anachronism," men and women of the next generation rejected his conservative ideas and elitism. Despite this short-term failure, Early and others had a "long-term impact on the ways in which Americans understood the Civil War," particularly his efforts to "foster a heroic image of Robert E. Lee and the southern war effort. Many of the ideas . . . became orthodoxy in the postwar South, [and] eventually made their way into the broader national perception of the war, and remain vigorous today."[13]

Early succeeded because Lee was an outstanding soldier who won in the face of great odds. As Gallagher maintained in a related essay (2000), "The distortion came when Early and other proponents of the Lost Cause denied that Lee had faults or lost any battles, focused on Northern numbers and material superiority while ignoring Confederate advantages, denied Grant any virtues or greatness, and noticed the Confederacy outside the eastern theater only when convenient to explain Southern failures in Virginia." In addition to canonizing Lee, Early demonized his subordinate James Longstreet. He destroyed Lee's senior lieutenant's reputation because he criticized Lee's actions at Gettysburg. As William Garrett Piston contended in his study *Lee's Tarnished Lieutenant: James Longstreet and His Place in Southern History* (1987) it was Longstreet and his "alleged slowness and obstinacy in Pennsylvania" that lost the battle and the war. As a result, Longstreet became a "scapegoat for the Confederate defeat." None of Lee's associates dared to criticize Lee after observing Longstreet's fate. In fact, Longstreet was for many years the lost Confederate general, only "found" in a twentieth-century novel *Killer Angels* (1974). The author, Michael Shaara, portrayed Longstreet as opposed to the ill-advised attacks at Gettysburg including Pickett's charge.[14]

Richard Starnes documented other efforts by elites to shape Civil War memory; however, he focused on the institution they created—the Southern Historical Society. Starnes in "Forever Faithful: The Southern Historical Society and Confederate Historical Memory" (1996) described the *Southern Historical Society Papers* as "second only to the *War of the Rebellion* records" representing "the largest collection of battle accounts, unit rosters, and other primary materials about the southern armies during the Civil War." Despite the value of this archive, Starnes emphasized the *Papers'* role in shaping historical memory. "The articles that appeared in the *Papers* were carefully selected by the Society's editors to achieve one overriding goal: The acceptance by white southerners of the Lost Cause as the explanation of southern defeat." Starnes linked the efforts to shape the past to present needs. "Accepting this historical memory not only rationalized Confederate defeat, but also strengthened a sense of solidarity among white southerners of all classes. Such acceptance, moreover, could translate into political, economic, and social power for those who were able to evoke such recollections." Leaders of the Society demonstrated a sophisticated understanding of how to shape the collective and historical memory of an epoch when they preserved select Confederate manuscripts that might be used by future scholars. As a result, "many historians . . . adopted the Society's Confederate historical memory as

a true record of events." The *Southern Historical Society Papers* also remained important because of their longevity; they continued in print until 1959. Starnes's article
documented the memory work performed by elites and how this reflects a larger
truth about memory. As Starnes explained, "Historical memories do not represent
the past as it occurred, but rather the past as it is perceived. Such perceptions do not
arise spontaneously. Instead, they are created, and often bear the stamp of the times
during which they were constructed."[15]

One of the most influential and successful efforts to shape historical memory
involved Robert E. Lee. James C. Cobb answered the question: "How did Robert E.
Lee become an American Icon?" (2011). According to Cobb, "Lee's death at age
sixty-three actually left his would-be canonizers free both to invoke him as they
pleased and to ensure that his reputation remained immaculate by dispelling the lingering questions about his leadership at Gettysburg." The Southern Historical Society proved "critical to sacralizing the historical and personal reputation of the man
who would become not just an embodiment of the highest ideals of the Lost Cause,
but one whom succeeding generations of northern and southern whites alike found
both admirable and inspiring." Michael A. Ross examined "The Commemoration of
Robert E. Lee's Death and the Obstruction of Reconstruction New Orleans" (2005)
and found that Lee "became the flawless 'marble man' that generations of white
Southerners would embrace as the symbol of the virtues of the Old South. Although
Lee in life could be cold, testy, and stubborn, in death, he became the perfect Christian gentlemen, an ideal husband, father, patriot, and military leader whose army lost
because it was numerically and materially overwhelmed." The acceptance of Lee as
an American hero revered by Southerners and Northerners alike will be discussed in
the next chapter.[16]

The place of Lee in Confederate memory reflected another bias: honoring their
military effort in the eastern theater as opposed to the western theater. Thomas L.
Connelly studied the main Confederate armies in the West and Robert E. Lee's place
in Civil War memory and identified a relationship between disinterest in the western
theater and devotion to Lee. In his study of the *Army of the Heartland: The Army of
Tennessee, 1861–1862* (1967), he explained that "the history of the Army of Tennessee . . . has been rather badly neglected." In contrast, he protested that "Robert E.
Lee and the Army of Northern Virginia have been deified." While his two-volume
study of the Army of Tennessee represented a critical evaluation of a neglected topic,
his reference to the deification of Lee relates to his best-known and most controversial work, *The Marble Man: Robert E. Lee and His Image in American Society* (1977).
In contrast to the "Marble Man" created by Lost Cause advocates, Connelly emphasized Lee's human frailties and described him as "a troubled man, convinced that he
had failed as a prewar career officer, parent, and moral individual." While some have
suggested that Connelly's devotion to the Army of Tennessee made him less than

objective about Lee, his books were an important corrective to eastern bias in Civil War memory. Early's success in minimizing a theater in which so many Confederate soldiers fought suggests that the Lost Cause represented an elite effort reflecting the views of those who had the resources to produce Confederate histories.[17]

In addition to Lee, Thomas J. "Stonewall" Jackson was a member of the Confederate pantheon. Unlike others, such as his colleague James Longstreet, he did not live to be reassessed by postmortems. He was, in so many ways, the perfect Lost Cause Hero—extraordinarily religious, extraordinarily able, and extraordinarily dead. Wallace Hettle in his study *Inventing Stonewall Jackson: A Civil War Hero in History and Memory* (2011) identified one of his wartime staff officers, Robert Lewis Dabney, as critical to creating this postwar image that encompassed "two competing themes—the sacred nature of Jackson's martyrdom and the ethic of professionalism central to the nineteenth-century military." While Dabney made Jackson his life's work, Hettle emphasized the evolving nature of Jackson image. His widow authorized Dabney's works and later wrote her own biography that "established a new image of Jackson, that of a thoroughly domestic family man, a picture at odds with his sometimes harsh wartime image as a religious fanatic." Still other advocates emphasized Jackson the military genius; British army officers seemed particularly passionate in their devotion to the valley campaign. Hettle ended his examination with a discussion of a twenty-first-century movie, *God and Generals* (2003) that portrayed Jackson as all of these characters, religious zealot, military genius, and family man. The nature of collective memory allowed some people who knew Jackson in life to create an image that has been transmitted to people who had not.[18]

In contrast to its military leaders, Jefferson Davis, former president of the Confederacy, fared poorly in Confederate memory. Donald Collins in his study of Jefferson Davis, *The Death and Resurrection of Jefferson Davis* (2005), identified the ups and downs of Davis in historical memory. While Davis was viewed with sympathy by his comrades because he was jailed after the war for treason, he had not been popular as Confederate president. He had made some enemies because he had a prickly personality for a politician; after the war, some blamed him for defeat. Despite his rather ambiguous status in Confederate memory, he became one of the architects of the Lost Cause—a spokesman for what Collins termed the "'die-hards' historical interpretation." Advocates of this strand of memory rejected the notion that the war was a rebellion and blamed Northerners' actions for secession and the coming of the war. As a result of these efforts, at the time of his death, he had returned to an honored place in memory as demonstrated by the three-year struggle by Southern cities to host his final resting place. While he became a member of the Confederate pantheon, Northerners never embraced him the same way they did Lee or Jackson. Treason may only be odious for civilian officials and presidents and not so much for military figures and generals.[19]

Where there are saints, there must be villains; if there was a candidate for Lost Cause villainhood, it is William Tecumseh Sherman who marched through Georgia and, in memory, left nothing in his wake. Ironically, in the immediate aftermath of the war, when the memory of his campaign would have been strongest, Sherman's treatment of surrendering Confederate forces and his political conservatism tempered former Confederate's attitudes. According to Carol Reardon in her essay "William T. Sherman in Postwar Georgia's Collective Memory, 1864–1914" (2009), he was not "remembered" at all because many Georgians believed that Reconstruction was worse than anything that happened during the war. Once Reconstruction passed, the focus returned to the war. In response to a number of Unionist histories that glorified Sherman and his March, the usual architects of Lost Cause memory created the memory of Sherman popular today. "By the late 1870s" Reardon explained, "Sherman's place in Georgia's past had begun what appeared to be a steady spiral down to demonization." Sherman's reputation never recovered. Later, Georgia-based New South advocates tried to ignore Sherman's actions, as part of their focus on reconciliation; however, this effort was not always successful because more traditional elements of the Lost Cause maintained their hold over Georgians' minds.[20]

While this essay examined one place and time, Edward Caudill and Paul Ashdown, in *Sherman's March in Myth and Memory* (2008), chronicled its memory in different eras. Not surprisingly, Confederate supporters vilified his memory and Northerners embraced him as a hero. According to Caudill and Ashdown, his heroism reflected not just his military accomplishments during the war but how "his conduct of war was akin to a well-managed factory, a symbol of progress in Gilded Age America." Reinforcing the importance of the past in the present, Caudill and Ashdown contented that "the postwar era, the empirical-industrial age, was the foundation for the national memory of Sherman." Beyond the United States, Sherman was remembered; European armies and their leaders studied his campaigns. Ultimately it was B. H. Liddell Hart, a British World War I veteran and military theorist, who made Sherman internationally famous among a broader audience. Not surprisingly, Sherman's ability to move across hundred of miles of territory with few casualties garnered the admiration of a man who lived through the disastrous stalemate on the Western Front in World War I.[21]

Sherman's march received another extensive examination in Anne Sarah Rubin's study *Through the Heart of Dixie: Sherman's March and American Memory* (2014). Rubin did not address this as part of Lost Cause memory, but as part of all Americans' Civil War memory including white Northerners, Sherman's men, and African Americans who were affected by the march. As one can imagine it is much more complex when examined from these various viewpoints. According to Rubin, this campaign was "the most symbolically powerful aspect of the Civil War, one that has a cultural dominance perhaps disproportionate to its actual strategic importance."

Much of this symbolic importance represents it status in historical memory, for example, when it was used to explain American involvement in Vietnam, or describe burnt-out urban areas or in popular culture images of Sherman in music and film. The evolution of Sherman's March in memory represents a valuable case study in the transition between historical and popular memory.[22]

The creation of Northern villains reflects a critical truth about Civil War memory, the eradication of Southern villains. Today, when people discuss Civil War memory or forgetting, the focus is on slavery as the root of villainy; however, to most federal supporters Confederates committed treason, a greater sin in their world view. As William A. Blair found in his study *With Malice Toward Some: Treason and Loyalty in the Civil War Era* (2014), Northerners certainly understood the war in that way since "treason pervaded the public discourse. It represents a challenge for a researcher to find a Northern newspaper or periodical during any day of the war in which the words 'traitor' or 'treason' *do not* [italics in the original] appear as a characterization of the rebels." Blair identified the complex reasons that Northerners did not charge Confederates with treason after the war, such as the difficulty of proving this charge; however, how was the very idea of treason forgotten?[23]

Not surprisingly, Lost Cause advocates worked hard to distance themselves and their comrades from this charge. Alexander Stephens had been the Confederate vice president; after the war he was charged with treason though, like so many others, he was released. Stephens has been castigated by historians because he articulated the notion that slavery was the Confederacy's cornerstone during the war and he forgot its centrality in its aftermath. He described slavery as a "*minor question*" in his two-volume justification of secession—*A Constitutional View of the Late War between the States* (1868). Instead, Stephens argued that the war came because of "different and opposing ideas as to the nature of what is known as the general government. The contest was between those who held it was to be strictly federal in its character, and those who maintained it was thoroughly national. It was a strife between the principles of federation, on the one side, and Centralism or Consolidation on the other." Stephens suggested that some states supported a stronger central government and others did not; the war was between these states and not a rebellion against central authority. Stephens explicitly rejected the notion that Confederates committed treason arguing that the Constitution described this as a crime against a state and not the federal government. More practically, he cited the failure of the federal government to convict Confederate leaders of treason, "notwithstanding all that is said about the *treason* [italics in the original] of the Confederates, about 'traitors,' about the 'Insurrection' and the 'Atrocious rebellion,' so-called, the Authorities at Washington have not put that issues before Judicial Tribunals." While Stephens's long and legalistic explanation on succession's constitutional basis would never be as popular as others histories, the notion that the Civil War was a war between the states and not a rebellion against federal authority endured long after his death in 1883 because it reflected an ongoing debate about the relationship between the federal govenrment and the states.[24]

Albert Taylor Bledsoe, a well-known theologian, political theorist, and defender of slavery before the war, echoed the same themes. Terry A. Barnhart in *Albert Taylor Bledsoe: Defender of the Old South and Architect of the Lost Cause* (2011) described his postwar activities as a "stalwart vindicator of southern slavery, the constitutional right of secession, and the 'Lost Cause' of southern independence." Bledsoe's most influential work defended Jefferson Davis rejecting the notion that he committed treason. Barnhart believed that even if you disagree with Bledsoe's arguments "nowhere are the divergent views of the origin, nature, and meaning of the American Union and the causes of the Civil War more clearly delineated than in the meticulously argued" defense of the Confederate president. While Bledsoe authored many books on related issues defending the failed Confederate nation, he also founded the *Southern Review*. "Bledsoe's significance as an architect of the Confederate interpretation of the conflict is second to none. His exonerations of the Lost Cause did much to shape the collective memory about the war among former Confederates." While elites like Bledsoe, Stephens, and Early seem well suited to articulate the Lost Cause, one does wonder when the common soldiers who fought and suffered so much were allowed to have their say.[25]

Surprisingly, rank-and-file veterans established organizations only after many of the principal tenets of Confederate collective memory had been established by elites. Initially, Confederates created veterans' organization that reflected their unit affiliations, for example, the Association of the Army of Northern Virginia. In 1883, the Robert E. Lee Camp formed in Richmond, and this group attempted to create a state-wide organization as did Confederate veterans in Tennessee and Louisiana. It was not until 1889 that veterans met in New Orleans to establish a truly national organization, the United Confederate Veterans (UCV). This group grew steadily; by 1896 it had 850 camps, local organizations, and it doubled the number of camps by 1903. It was never clear how many veterans actually belonged; one estimate suggests that there were 80,000 members in 1903. According to Gaines M. Foster's calculation, based on comparing these numbers to census figures, between one-quarter and one-third of all Confederate veterans belonged to this group in the early twentieth century.[26]

Like most aspects of collective memory, the veterans' magazine documented their contribution to Civil War memory. Steven E. Sodergren in "'The Great Weight of Responsibility': The Struggle over History and Memory in *Confederate Veteran* Magazine" (2013) assessed this journal's role in creating collective memory. Sodergren concluded that while historians have paid more attention to the *Southern Historical Papers*, the *Confederate Veteran* had more influence. The magazine, which had over 20,000 subscribers in 1902, was likely read by more people since it was passed around in UCV camps and among veterans' families. Like the *Southern Historical Papers*, this journal was a conscious effort to document the collective memory of this generation for the future. According to a report by the United Sons of Confederate Veterans', an allied organization, historical committee, "We know that tens of thousands of boys and girls are growing up into manhood and womanhood through the South, with improper ideas concerning the struggle between the States, and with distorted conceptions concerning the causes that led up to the tremendous conflict." What history did these young people need to know? After assessing the contents of these articles, Sodergren believed that the "'truth' of history . . . was a repeated refrain in the pages of the *Veteran* and familiar to students of the Lost Cause: secession was justified, the North waged an unjust war, and the South had been victimized ever since. Thus the 'truth' of history could only reach one conclusion: the South was right." He argued that there was little change in the content of this journal over the decades of its existence. "The vehemence and structure of how contributors articulated their view of history appeared in 1932, just as they had in 1893," the first year the magazine published. In some ways, this constancy itself reveals a great deal about memory. By the early 1890s the collective memory of Confederate supporters had already been articulated: the *Confederate Veteran* merely transmitted this to the next generation. Despite this unanimity, Sodergren identified some dissent and "a certain level of hostility beneath the placid surface of Lost Cause memory" concerning the "aristocratic campaign to dominate the historical memory of the war." If there is a way forward, in Confederate memory studies it may be to determine if there were any challenges to the Lost Cause version of history among its supporters.[27]

An examination of various former Confederate states, Florida, South Carolina, and Virginia, supports the principle of the Lost Cause as a way of unifying whites around a particular candidate or ideology. Seth Weitz identified the importance of the Lost Cause in politics in "Defending the Old South: The Myth of the Lost Cause and Political Immortality in Florida, 1865–1968" (2009). He found that the Lost Cause that formed in the 1860s was critical to understanding Florida politics up to 1960s. For almost a century, North Floridians used the Lost Cause to justify the political process by which they dominated other areas of the state. "In the decades following the end of the Civil War, the proponents of the 'Lost Cause' were determined to do everything in their power to defend the 'Old South' value system [;] . . . conservatives continued to defend this system close to a century later . . . [to] maintain the order and stability they felt necessary to protect their culture and worldview as the demographics of the state underwent radical change." W. Scott Poole examined "Religion, Gender, and the Lost Cause in South Carolina's 1876 Governor's Race: 'Hampton or Hell!'" (2002) and found that conservatives employed the Lost Cause to advance their political interests. "South Carolina Conservatives used the Lost Cause to publicly represent their worldview, to express continued defiance

toward the government of the United States despite their military defeat, and to sta-
bilize the boundaries of their racial and gendered hierarchy in the topsy-turvy world
of the postbellum, post-emancipation south." In contrast, Rod Andrew Jr. identified
something more personal than political in his essay "'My Children in the Field':
Wade Hampton, Biography, and the Roots of the Lost Cause" (2010). In his view
the Lost Cause represented, to Hampton and others, "a persistent, deeply felt need to
find validation and meaning in all that he had suffered, and in all that his beloved
had given for the Confederate Cause" including his son and brother. He witnessed
his son's death and held him as he died on the battlefield. Andrew maintained that
"the experience of war was so deeply engrained in Hampton's mind that it influenced
his understanding of postwar political and social issues. It was not the other way
around." Given the truly horrific nature of the Civil War experience, it may be time
to look at the Lost Cause and the Union Cause as a response to the trauma and grief
experienced by the Civil War generation.[28]

When scholars found some crack in a unified Confederate memory, it tended to
be about politics. Charles Holden assessed Wade Hampton's downfall in an essay
entitled "'Is Our Love for Hampton Foolishness?': South Carolina and the Lost
Cause" (2000) and found that "rival political factions introduced war memories to
sharpen the divisions among white voters." Some former Confederates employed
Civil War memory to challenge elite rule. Ben Tillman—a Democrat with populist leanings—and his followers used the memory of rank-and-file enlisted soldiers'
service in a revolt against Hampton and the conservative, aristocratic, rule in South
Carolina. Similarly, Kevin M. Levin examined "William Mahone, the Lost Cause,
and Civil War History" (2005); Mahone led a black and white coalition of Republicans and Democrats, the "readjustor" movement in postwar Virginia. This movement was not popular with the conservative elite and other Southerners who rejected
a biracial coalition. According to Levin, Mahone used his service as a major general
and commander at the "Crater" at Petersburg in 1864 to advance his career. This
narrative was a two-edged sword; his opponents attacked his military record to
undermine his political efforts. As Levin explained, "Mahone was forced to deal with
continued attacks on his war record by former Confederate officers outraged with
his decision to align himself with the Republican Party." Eventually, another Confederate general, Fitzhugh Lee, defeated Mahone. Levin concluded that "Mahone's
postwar difficulties . . . undermine the notion that white southerners—especially
Virginians—were in agreement over who could claim rightful ownership of their
past" suggesting that a unitary memory of the past may have relied more on a unified
view of the present.[29]

Another former Confederate soldier, William C. Oates served as a state governor
and participated in the collective memory efforts. Glenn W. LaFantasie in *Gettysburg
Requiem: The Life and Lost Causes of Confederate Colonel William C. Oates* (2006)

assessed this complex figure: on the one hand an unreconstructed rebel and on the other a brigadier general of volunteers in the U.S. Army in the Spanish-American War. As part of this study, LaFantasie articulated the relationship between individual and collective memory. "Collective memories—are constructed by individuals who see their own [individual] memories as matching or resembling the memories of others." This general statement is particularly true in the case of the Lost Cause. According to LaFantasie, "In the postwar South, the Lost Cause provided Oates and other white supporters with a theater of memory that allowed them to search their own individual memories in an effort to substantiate what they came to believe was the *truth* [italics in the original] of the Lost Cause by drawing on their own recollections of experiences during the war as evidence." As a result, LaFantasie believed that "public and private memory merged for many, if not most, white southerners in the decades after the Civil War." LaFantasie used Oates as a model because despite the link between individual and collective memory, "he seems . . . to have confronted the past more honestly, more straightforwardly, more doggedly, than many of his contemporaries had done or were willing even to try." As a result, his wartime memoirs seemed at odds with other former Confederates. Taking this one step further, one might examine the extent to which Confederate supporters' individual memory was distinct from their collective memory. By examining individuals outside the mainstream of the Lost Cause, including non-elites, scholars might identify any divergence between these two types of memories.[30]

When Americans remember the non-elite, common soldier of the Confederacy they probably recall a native-born Protestant American; however, immigrants and Catholics also supported the Confederacy—including the Irish. An Irish priest, Father Abram J. Ryan penned the best-known poem honoring the confederacy and its cause. According to Robert E. Curran in his essay "The Irish and the Lost Cause: Two Voices," (2013), Ryan's "1865 poem 'The Conquered Banner' may be said to have launched the Lost Cause movement." In Curran's view, this poem represented a "primordial expression of the Lost Cause literature comforting the region's white people, the poem provided religious meaning for their horrific war experience and a veritable sanctification of the Cause." While Father Ryan's loyalty was unquestioned, rank-and-file Irishmen had a more complex relationship with Confederate memory. According to David Gleeson, in *The Green and the Gray: The Irish in the Confederate States of America* (2013), the Irish embraced the Lost Cause, partly because they "knew their own 'lost causes' from Ireland and found it easy to embrace the southern one." When Irish veterans dedicated their own memorials, such as the Irish Volunteer Memorial in Charleston, the ceremonies were both Irish and Confederate. According to Gleeson, "They had intertwined very successfully their Irishness with their Confederate experience." While they may have embraced the Confederacy after the war, Gleeson questioned their devotion in wartime; Irish units experienced a high rate of desertion from the Confederate army. Despite this wartime reality, support of the postwar Lost Cause allowed Irish Confederates to "banish memories of their ambiguous support for the cause and remember only the 'glories.'" Once again, the needs of the present including assimilation into broader Southern society shaped past memories of wartime events.[31]

While Irish soldiers were welcome by Lost Cause advocates, guerillas and insurgents might not have been. As John C. Inscoe found in *Race, War, and Remembrance in the Appalachian South* (2008), the Lost Cause had "no room for any mention of divided loyalties, for internal dissent, or for guerrilla warfare. Such ambivalence or complexity in Southern wartime behavior would have seriously undermined the basic, clear-cut interpretation of regional solidarity to the Cause in which white Southerners so wanted, indeed needed, to believe." As Matthew C. Hulbert asserted in his essay "Constructing Guerrilla Memory: John Newman Edwards and Missouri's Irregular Lost Cause" (2012), this is partly historians' fault because they "have generally presented white southern efforts to explain the war and culturally restore the region as a linear movement that revolved around a monolithic narrative." Much of this narrative focused on conventional warfare in Virginia and the eastern theater with little place for western states such as Missouri, and even less for guerilla war. Hulbert described the effort of one man, John Newman Edwards, to create an "irregular Lost Cause . . . defined as both a literal guerrilla movement within the broader context of a conservative Lost Cause (aimed at both cultural *and* political reclamation) and as a counter-narrative strain of Civil War memory that revolved around the Missouri bushwhacker." According to Hulbert, in this narrative, "The Missouri bushwhacker had fought hardest for the cause and had never been defeated—that despite their state's failure to secede and despite its paltry slave population, a very select group of Missouri guerrillas had been the most confederate all along." The memory of a guerrilla war has been buried until very recently; it will be discussed as an aspect of historical memory that reflects how people remember in our present as Americans fight guerrilla wars and insurgencies overseas.[32]

Hulbert also points to another way forward and a significant gap in looking at the Lost Cause: what about states that fought in the west? How did they respond to this eastern focus, sometimes the Virginia focus of the Lost Cause? Hulbert is correct; historians have accepted the hegemony of Lost Cause memory, studying the Lost Cause and memorialization in Virginia and other eastern Confederate states more than in other places. It may be appropriate to carefully examine other Confederate states, particularly those in the west—the stepchild of Confederate Civil War memory. Despite this neglect of one theater, the subject of the next chapter is the real "Lost Cause" of Civil War memory—the Union Cause.

Two

THE UNION CAUSE: REMEMBERING UNION AND FREEDOM

The three different names—Union Cause, the Cause Victorious, and the Won Cause—used by scholars to describe federal supporters' collective memory emerged as concepts in the first years of the twenty-first century. Before that, no one bothered to systematically examine what federal supporters might have remembered about their wartime experiences. Even today, no comprehensive examination focusing on the Union Cause in the decades after the war exists. As a result, this book pieces together a variety of scholarly studies to describe federal Civil War memory. Despite this lack of interest, men and women who supported the federal government and survived the Civil War formulated their collective memories of this conflict. The following represents my summary of the Union Cause based on my study of Union Civil War memory.[1]

Federal supporters remembered the war as an attempt to destroy the Union and to preserve slavery that failed because of their generation's suffering and sacrifice. Many Union supporters, though not all, believed that ending slavery was central to the memory of what they accomplished. First, they remembered the fact that the secession crisis was the culmination of decade's of agitation over the status of slavery. Second, they recalled slaveowners seceded because they assumed that Lincoln and the Republicans wanted to end slavery. Third, they recalled a war that was successful only when ending slavery became the war's central aim. Men and women who supported the federal government linked Union and emancipation together because the former could not have been saved without the destruction of the latter. While some scholars suggested the Civil War generation forgot both slavery and its role in the coming of the war and the securing of emancipation as a consequence of that war, the single most overlooked Unionist Civil War memory remains the notion that war was treason against the U.S. government. Union veterans, in particular, refused to forget that leaving the Union and the subsequent attack on federal facilities, including Fort Sumter, constituted treason. Finally, Union supporters reject the notion that their enemies were better soldiers. Victory was not merely a matter of overwhelming numbers. Instead, it was the righteousness of the Union Cause and its heroic volunteer soldiers that saved the Union and freed the slaves.

The actions of soldiers represented a critical aspect of the Union Cause because veterans and their organizations, including the largest Union army's veteran's organization, the Grand Army of the Republic (GAR), articulated the Union Cause. There is no comparison between women's role in shaping the Union Cause and Confederate women's memory efforts; federalist women were involved but were, at best, bystanders. Similarly, Union men wrote the history of the war. Federal supporters, like their Confederate counterparts, documented their wartime experiences and created their own heroes; in this case, they glorified Grant and Lincoln and not Lee and Jackson. Among these heroes, African American soldiers, who along with the rest of the black community, played a major role in shaping the collective memory of the Union Cause. Surprisingly, black women seemed to play a more critical role in these efforts than white women. Because black women and men had a common individual memory of slavery and emancipation, they partnered in collective memory efforts.

While the black and white Americans, men and women, who supported the federal government agreed on many aspects of their Union Cause, they often disagreed on emancipation. Partly, this was because during the war some Unionists rejected emancipation as a war aim. Many of the same federal supporters who fought emancipation during the war still rejected it in the aftermath, including Northern Democrats and citizens from border slave states. Both anti-emancipationist groups embraced critical tenets of the Lost Cause because it seemed more appropriate to their postwar present in which they actively rejected black civil rights. These divergences had consequences. Confederate supporters left a stronger, more unified Civil War memory, one that may be more reflective of future generations' present. For much of the twentieth century, white Americans embraced the notion that the fight for Union succeeded best when the fight to free slaves was forgotten. While the federal Civil War generation rejected this emancipationist amnesia, it eventually passed into memory and, ironically, the memory of the Union Cause lost.

It is hard to understate the extent to which Union memory of the war was forgotten; it was not until the twenty-first century that scholars recognized any aspects of federal collective memory that emerged in the Civil War's immediate aftermath. Most studies that discussed the idea of a distinct Union Cause were written in the last two decades. One of the first scholars to address the Union Cause was John R. Neff in *Honoring the Civil War Dead: Commemoration and the Problem of Reconciliation* (2005). Like the Lost Cause, the Union Cause began in the graveyards of the dead, where the living came together to commemorate the sacrifice of the dead. According to Neff, "the commemoration of the war's dead provided the quintessential forum for engaging—and, most important, expressing—the war's meaning." The simple fact that each side buried their dead separately in different places, and commemorated them in separate ceremonies, represented the first step in creating a distinct Confederate and Union Cause. Establishing a specific day dedicated to the Union war dead and not all war dead—Memorial Day—both facilitated federal commemoration efforts and provided a platform for the Union Cause. While the day's origins remain disputed, officially it began in 1868 when the GAR commander-in-chief promulgated an official order declaring May 30th of each year as a time to place spring flowers on soldiers' graves. As John Neff explained, "The order also recounted the central elements of the Northern nationalist myth: 'their soldier lives were the reveille of freedom to a race in chains, and their deaths the tattoo (final call) of rebellious tyranny in arms.'" From the very beginning, Union veterans placed Union and emancipation on equal footing when remembering the war.[2]

While the Memorial Day Order reflected the central principles of the Union Cause, it does not necessarily establish which belief was more important than the other. A closer examination of the federal supporters' memory demonstrated the primacy of Union over emancipation. Neff argued that this primacy represented these men and women's present; in their minds, the Union ended slavery; in contrast, reestablishing the Union remained an ongoing postwar process. In Neff's view, the "Cause Victorious" asserted the achievement of national union long before it was actually accomplished. "The initial assertions of the Cause Victorious were usually more strident than accurate, for the essential character of the mythology was to describe in carefully coded language a nationality reunited in imagination long before reconciliation had been actually accomplished." Caroline E. Janney in *Remembering the Civil War: Reunion and the Limits of Reconciliation* (2013) agreed that the central dilemma of the Unionist Civil War generation revolved around this question: "How would a nation that had been so divided that it went to war move forward as a truly *United* States of America?" [italics in the original] While Northerner's war generation remembered, and even valued emancipation, "reunion was the Union cause."[3]

While Janney's study covered a broader swath of memory, the author's study, *The Won Cause: Black and White Comradeship in the Grand Army of the Republic* (2011), assessed on segment of Unionist—the Grand Army of the Republic (GAR) members and their female auxiliaries. Founded in the immediate aftermath of the Civil

War, the GAR was not only a veterans' organization but also a political one. It often worked closely with the Republican Party. Despite Republican electoral success, by the middle of the 1870s, the GAR almost disappeared from the national scene and even ceased to exist in some states. This organization experienced a renaissance in the 1880s when it became less of a partisan organization and more of a social and patriotic organization dedicated to three primary principles—fraternity, charity, and loyalty. Despite the GAR's less partisan focus, in 1890, after a successful campaign to expand veterans' pension, its membership reached its pinnacle—400,000 belonged to this organization. From this date, its membership declined because the GAR only accepted former Civil War soldiers as members; when the last Union veteran died in 1956, so did the GAR.[4]

As part of an examination of black and white members of this organization, I found that this organization, unlike all other social organizations in this era, welcomed black and white members in all-black posts, or local groups, and in integrated posts. This unprecedented acceptance was a product of their Civil War memory. White GAR members remembered that black veterans had suffered and sacrificed in the war, even if they had not served at their side because racial segregation prevailed in Civil War units. As a result, GAR members recognized all Union soldiers, regardless of their race, as comrades. While these memories involved the past, after the war

Parade of the Grand Army of the Republic, at their twenty-sixth national encampment (meeting), Washington, D.C., September 1892. (Library of Congress)

former Union soldiers still suffered from wounds, both physical and mental, and endured the legacy of chronic diseases from their military service; for these men, the war was still in their present. The relationship between memory of the past and the pain of the present reinforced the GAR's interracial comradeship.[5]

The need to find some type of meaning for their generation's suffering led the men and women affiliated with the GAR to articulate their own "Won Cause," just as Confederate supporters had formulated their own Lost Cause. GAR members and their supporters remembered a war that both preserved the Union and freed the slaves. They recalled a dual cause of Union—preserving the nation—and Liberty—ending slavery because the Union could not have been preserved without ending slavery since slavery caused secession. Many of these Unionists took this one step further rejecting the idea of saving a Union with slavery intact because emancipation gave meaning to the sacrifices of their generation. When these men and women passed from the scene, the next generation constructed a historical memory of the Civil War that omitted the Unionist generation's commitment to emancipation. The GAR's Won Cause was a Lost Cause in memory.[6]

Similarly in a more focused study of veterans, Robert Hunt in *The Good Men Who Won the War: Army of the Cumberland Veterans and Emancipation Memory* (2010) also found these emancipationist memories. After examining the memoirs of former members of the Army of the Cumberland, an important Western army, he argued that veterans "incorporated emancipation and its legacy into their war by absorbing

African American members of the Grand Army of the Republic and African American women parading on Memorial Day, New York City, May 1912. (Library of Congress)

it into their search for innocence"; a state of mind that he believed was lost by the necessities of Total War—the mobilization of Northern society and the hard war policies against Southern society. While scholars still debate the issues of Civil War as a Total War, the need for men to come to terms with wartime memories, be it a loss of innocence or some other injury, was central to how and why Union veterans remembered the war. Hunt found that this interpretation resonated in later decades when "the liberation of others became understood as a critical objective for which an American military fights." Regardless of whether the United States fought Total Wars or those with more limited objectives, twentieth-century wars shaped Civil War memory.[7]

Given that Union veterans had such strong memories, one might ask why they seemed to be willing to embrace their enemies at Blue and Gray reunions. Scholars have used reunion and reconciliation between former Union and Confederate soldiers as somehow indicative of what they remembered or had forgotten about the war. These assessments focused on Union veterans and speculated that amnesia about the Union Cause, particularly emancipation, facilitated reunion and reconciliation. As early as 1937, Paul Buck in *The Road to Reunion* made note of a small number of anti-reunionist elements in the GAR that he describes as "cranks" and "irreconcilables." More recently, Janney identified more than a few veterans and other sectional partisans who refused to embrace their former enemies. These men and women refused to forget what had happened during the war making reconciliation impossible. Instead, men and women of both sides wanted reunion, which did not imply reconciliation, and the victory of their version of Civil War memory—an acknowledgment that they were right and the other side was wrong.[8]

For many Unionists, emancipation remained central to the idea of the right cause. According to Janney, federal supporters refused to forget their role in a war for freedom because in their mind union and liberty could not be separated. Unionists remembered that "the Federal Armies had saved the Union, helped to abolish slavery, and now one flag would once again wave over the *United* States." As Janney succinctly summarized, "Emancipation had been a crucial means and a happy result of Union victory." M. Keith Harris in his study, *Across the Bloody Chasm: The Culture of Commemoration among Civil War Veterans* (2014), found that while "veterans from both sides of the bloody chasm set out to craft this particular message of reconciliation from the scattered shards of disunion . . . they preserved the memories of their sectional ideals, their trials, and their respective causes." Most Union soldiers fought for Union during the war and accepted reunion afterwards; however some "former soldiers and groups of white Northern veterans singled out the sectional conflict over slavery as the fundamental origin of the war and praised emancipation as its righteous consequence." Moreover, memories also shaped veterans' willingness to reconcile. Harris cited a Union veteran who rejected reunion explain that those "whose life-blood watered the gory field [and] those who went promptly to the front when danger threatened" could not let "bygones be bygones" and forget their cause: in other words, no one for whom the war and its horrors were a lived experience.[9]

Some of those men who left their blood on the field left their limbs also. Brian Matthew Jordan studied "'Living Monuments': Union Veteran Amputees and the Embodied Memory of the Civil War" (2011) and identified these men as "both dutiful and conscious custodians of the war's historical memory." According to Jordan, because the North largely lacked a war-ravaged landscape, empty sleeves and their one-legged counterparts functioned as the foremost reminder of the Civil War's cost in human life and suffering." These men, like so many others, understood that they were part of a conscious effort to create the collective memory of the war. As a result of their efforts, Northern amputees "remain[ed] a significant thread of remembrance in post-Civil War America."[10]

In contrast, women who supported the federal cause were not. Partly, this may be due to the fact that unlike Confederate memorial activities, men were able to take the lead. Frances M. Clarke's in her essay "Forgetting the Women: Debates over Female Patriotism in the Aftermath of America's Civil War" (2011) claimed that despite the fact that during the war "Northerners agreed . . . that never before had so many women done so much to aid a war effort," these "women's war work was relegated to a footnote in Civil War history." Clarke believed "a lack of consensus among women themselves over who or what should be remembered" explained this amnesia. Battlefield service defined a man's patriotism. In contrast, women played many different roles, some closer to the battlefield than others, a hospital nurse versus home front relief workers. Moreover, women's broad agreement about the need for humility facilitated this amnesia. Ultimately, there may be a link between forgetting women's wartime activities and their secondary role in the formulation of Union war memory.[11]

Despite their lesser role, women who supported the federal government during the Civil War formed their own organizations in its aftermath; these groups aligned with the GAR. The Ladies of the Grand Army of the Republic (LGAR) claimed their status based on their relationship to a veteran. In contrast, the Woman's Relief Corps (WRC) welcomed all loyal women. Because the federal government took care of the dead, these women's groups focused on supporting the living veteran. In addition to providing relief, women played a real, if subordinate, role in postwar sectional memory battles. According to Janney, these women explicitly rejected the Lost Cause and "the memories perpetuated by the Confederate LMAs." While these women focused on the notion of loyalty, those who supported the Union, and disloyalty, those who supported the Confederacy, they also remembered slavery and emancipation. As Janney argues, Unionist "women like their male counterparts, endorsed a patriotism that vindicated the Union war effort and condemned that of the disloyal, slaveholding South." Despite the existence of two national organizations composed of Unionist women, neither group's role can be compared to that of the Ladies Memorial Associations or later the United Daughters of the Confederacy. However, these Northern organizations did something that their Southern counterparts refused to do—allowed African American women to join. Black women who championed the Union and later joined the women's auxiliary to the GAR, the WRC and the LGAR, used their status as members of these interracial groups to place the African American experience as central to the collective memory of this conflict.[12]

Black men and women, including Frederick Douglass, formulated their own collective memory of the war based on their personal memory of slavery and emancipation. David W. Blight in *Frederick Douglass' Civil War: Keeping Faith in Jubilee* (1989) chronicled his effort to fight Southerners and Northerners' amnesia about the war and its consequences. Douglass realized that the ongoing battle over memory centered on the desire to reunite the nation. Blight quotes Douglass's speech at Arlington Cemetery, Memorial Day, 1871. "We are sometimes asked in the name of patriotism to forget the merits of this fearful struggle." While Douglass understood this desire for reconciliation, he refused to "forget the difference between the parties to that . . . bloody conflict." What did Douglas want remembered? On the one side, men "struck at the nation's life," and on the other, men "struck to save it—those who fought for slavery and those fought for liberty and justice." This notion is one part of what Blight called in a later work, *Race, and Reunion: The Civil War in American Memory* (2001), the "emancipationist vision, embodied in African Americans' complex remembrance of their own freedom." Blight terms this as a vision and not a memory because it is not only about the war, but the period afterward "in the politics of radical Reconstruction, and in conceptions of the war as the reinvention of the Republic and the liberation of blacks to citizenship and Constitutional equality." African Americans' battle for Civil War memory in the postwar era demonstrates the relationship between the past and the present in the construction of collective memory.[13]

Other, lesser known, African Americans participated in these efforts at Civil War commemorations. W. Fitzhugh Brundage in *The Southern Past: A Clash of Race and Memory* (2005) chronicled African Americans' enthusiastic participation in Civil War commemorations including Emancipation Day parades. According to Brundage, "Postbellum blacks, no less than whites, appreciated the power that flowed from the recalled past." The circumstance of life in the postwar South demanded a different response than that of white Southerners. African Americans did not have the resources to build monuments. Writing books and creating archives did little for formerly enslaved men and women who had not been allowed to learn to read and write. Instead, African Americans turned to public commemorations because "such celebrations demanded neither literacy nor large sums of money, and, most important, they ensured that the black sense of the past was accessible to more than just literate, elite African Americans" including "the college trained preacher to the illiterate day laborer, from the battle-scarred veterans to the impressionable school-child." White Southerners demonstrated the importance of these commemorations by the "mocking derision that they showered on black commemorative spectacles, and the frequency of legal and extralegal harassment directed against black revelers." Despite this opposition, "black celebrations made manifest a forceful and enduring understanding of their own" and created an opposing narrative in former Confederate states.[14]

William A. Blair in *Cities of the Dead Contesting the Memory of the Civil War in the South, 1865–1914* (2004) examined African American involvement in Southern Emancipation Day celebrations. Blair found that African Americans used these "commemorations to claim the right to citizenship." Similarly, Antoinette G. Van Zelm assessed Emancipation Day commemorations in post–Civil War Virginia and observed that more black women appeared on programs for these gatherings than white women appeared in Lost Cause programs. According to Van Zelm in her examination of "Virginia Women as Public Citizens: Emancipation Day Celebrations and Lost Cause Commemorations, 1863–1890" (2000), it was not only their roles but also how they seemed to view their participation. "African American women participated in Emancipation Day ceremonies as eager citizens, impatient to bring the reality of freedom closer to its ideal and determined to protect their newly acquired rights." In contrast, "white women who organized Lost Cause commemorations did so as reluctant citizens, animated by a vision not of the future but of the past." If white Confederate women played a more prominent role in Civil War commemorations than white Unionist women, and black Unionist women took center stage more often than Confederate women, there may need to be a reassessment of what type of women played the greatest role in shaping their community's Civil War memory. Similarly, Kathleen Clark in *Defining Moments: African American Commemoration and Political Culture in the South, 1863–1913* (2005) studied Emancipation Day celebrations and realized that these observances "reflected ongoing debates among African Americans over how they could best represent themselves, debates that centered on such issues as the content and meaning of black history, class–inflected ideas of 'respectability' and 'progress' and gendered notions of citizenship." The present and its concerns shaped these commemorations even among men and women who had a significant stake in memorializing a particular past.[15]

The urgency of remembering in the present cannot always compete with the need to forget a horrific past. Mitch Kachun in *Festivals of Freedom: Memory and Meaning in African-American Emancipation Celebrations, 1808–1915* (2003) found a certain ambivalence about remembering slavery that reflected another critical aspect of memory theory—trauma and memory. Kachun understood that slavery "was for many a personally painful and degrading experience whose recollection bred collective racial humiliation and fed the continued derision of the larger society." In this case, the traumatic memory of slavery made efforts to remember it difficult. In its place, the African American Civil War generation remembered the black soldiers and sailors who ended this institution and memorialized "African Americans who served the race and the nation in that bloody conflict." Former slave and black novelist, Williams Wells Brown composed the first book on the African American Civil War experience in 1867, *The Negro in the American Rebellion: His Heroism and His Fidelity*, suggesting the importance of chronicling this experience for the black Civil War generation.[16]

Black veterans also contributed to the war's collective memory. Among the best known were Joseph T. Wilson and George Washington Williams; both men wrote histories of African American soldiers in the last decades of the nineteenth century. Joseph Wilson served as an official in the Virginia GAR and claimed that it was his comrades, both black and white, who urged him to tell the story of African American soldiers so "that posterity might have a fuller and more complete records of the deeds of the Negro soldiers than had been given in the numerous already published histories of the conflict in which they had played so important a part." Wilson understood that black soldiers' wartime service and their role in freeing their race had been omitted from other volumes. "I acknowledge it has been a labor of love to fight many battles of the war of the rebellion over again, not because of a relish for the blood and the destruction of human life, but for the memories of the past; of the bondage of a race and its struggle for freedom." Williams covered the same ground but was able to bring his greater experience as a historian to the subject. He recognized the complex relationship between memory and history. "In writing of the remote past, the historian has the benefit of sifting and winnowing to which time subjects historical data; but in writing of events within living memory it requires both fortitude and skill to resist the insidious influence of interested friends and actors, to separate error from truth with an even and steady hand." To accomplish this task, Williams relied on the *Official Records of the War of the Rebellion* and other government documents. In his effort, he was aided by Library of Congress and War Department officials suggesting that white men supported the documentation of black soldiers' wartime service. Moreover, both books sold well, demonstrating that African Americans succeeded in their efforts to shape Civil War memory in this era.[17]

White officers who commanded men like Williams and Wilson worked to remind white Americans of black service. Because only a few black soldiers earned a commission, white officers commanded African American units. After the war, these men documented their memories of their experiences, Thomas Wentworth Higginson authored the best-known memoir, *Army Life in a Black Regiment* (1870), based on his experiences with an all-black unit recruited and based in South Carolina. Other officers wrote of their service in black units; in 1891, former captain Luis F. Emilio composed the history of the most famous regiment, the Fifty-Fourth Massachusetts Infantry. Without the efforts of these black and white veterans, the story of African American soldiers would have been lost. Both Williams and Wilson held prominent positions in the GAR. The black men and women affiliated with the GAR used their status as members of interracial organizations to place their memory of slavery and emancipation as central to this conflict. In some ways, their affiliation with this group may have been one of the most effective ways they shaped Civil War memory.[18]

Williams and others availed themselves of a valuable effort to document this conflict in *The Officials Records of the War of the Rebellion*, known as the *OR*. The first volume appeared in 1881, the last volume in 1901. Initially in print, today on the Internet, this collection represents the result of a government decision to publish the records of both armies. Despite seeing the war as a rebellion, as evinced by its title, the project leaders partnered with former rebel officers. While these men assisted U.S. officials in finding Confederate records, they were also tasked to ensure that these records were "unbiased." As a result, Joan Waugh argued that these histories deemphasized "the still controversial issues of slavery and emancipation," as part of an essay on Grant as a historian (2004). She contended that this "influential publishing project's emphasis on fairness to both sides was echoed in the larger society's desire for reconciliation." These records became critical as Americans who did not live through the Civil War wrote its history. Waugh asserted that these records "encouraged a professional and nonpartisan style when writing the war's history" that supported the idea that "both sides fought for noble causes." The commitment to what its editors considered fairness meant that a key repository of the federal war effort's collective memory gave equal space to Confederate memories.[19]

Similarly, Union leaders and their Confederate counterparts penned articles for *Century* magazine's *Battle and Leaders of the Civil War* (1884–1888) series. According to Waugh, the series editors "explicitly demanded neutral contributions from their authors" to promote reconciliation. One editor explained why impartiality was so critical: "We rightly judged that articles celebrating the skill and valor of both sides would hasten the elimination of sectional prejudices and contribute toward reuniting the country by the cultivation of mutual respect." Stephen Davis assessed "'A Matter of Sensational Interest': The *Century* 'Battles and Leaders' Series" (1981) and identified another motive for this series. "*Battles and Leaders* . . . came into being not so much as a result of conscientious scholarship as of determined entrepreneurship." The editors wanted a larger share of the illustrated magazine market. So while Civil War leaders viewed these articles as a contribution to memory, the editors (of the *Century* series) focused on sales and wanted something with a more general appeal. In many ways, this foreshadows how and why some threads of Civil War memory do better than others. The Union Cause and its decidedly non-neutral, ideologically driven memories did not appeal to future generations more concerned with reunion and reconciliation.[20]

Though popular, the *Century* series failed to match the recognition of the best-known memoirs of the war; the *Personal Memoirs of U.S Grant* (1885) sold over 300,000 copies in its initial printings. This success would have been gratifying for Grant, but he did not live to see the book's reception; he finished the manuscript two days before he died. He scripted the book while he was dying of cancer to support his family after his death; poor investments claimed much of his fortune. While the story of writing these memoirs is fascinating, Joan Waugh identified Grant's critical role in creating a collective memory of the Civil War. "Grant sought actively to influence and shape the historical memory of the South's rebellion," challenging "the idea, just beginning to take hold in the 1880s, that the Northern and Southern causes were equivalent." Grant wanted Americans to remember that "the great War of the Rebellion against the United States will have to be attributed to slavery." Grant in this short statement clarifies two essential tenets of the Union Cause; the Civil War represented a rebellion in the name of slavery.[21]

His memoirs enhanced his reputation, but even before he completed this volume, Grant was the hero of the Union Cause. Joan Waugh in her study *U. S. Grant: American Hero, American Myth* (2009) characterized Grant as "a gigantic figure in the nineteenth century . . . the embodiment of the American nation [and] . . . a symbol of national identity and memory, equal in stature to George Washington and Abraham Lincoln." Waugh chronicled the rather drastic changes in Grant's memory, a story made more complex by his success in wartime as a general and his failures in peacetime as a president. According to Waugh, "Depending on one's point of view, he was either the brilliant leading U.S. military commander or the mediocre general who won the war by brutal attrition alone, either the stalwart and honest president trying to implement the northern vision of the war or the imposer of hated 'Republican Rule' on a helpless, defeated region." Ultimately, Waugh concluded that "in the long run, the image of the brutal general and inept president lingers most powerfully." While those who supported the Lost Cause contested Grant's place in American memory as part of their advocacy of Robert E. Lee, they also challenged his vision of what the North had achieved with its victory. Grant's views reflected those of many men and women who supported the Union during the war. According to Waugh, Grant believed in the "Union Cause," specifically that "the premier goal of the Civil War was to preserve the American republic and, after 1863, to fight for freedom and the destruction of slavery. To Grant, those were noble ideals worth fighting for, dying for, and remembering." Grant's fate in memory reflected that of his Union Cause: the victim of a "constant drumbeat of criticism from a small but influential group of ex-confederate partisans," and the efforts of "eager reconciliationists from the North [who] began to distort his legacy in pursuit of national unity." Northerners and Southerners allied to defeat Grant in the struggle for the Civil War's historical memory.[22]

Lee may have beaten Grant in memory, but Abraham Lincoln thrashed his Confederate counterpart Jefferson Davis. Merrill D. Peterson in *Lincoln in American Memory* (1994) observed that it was his death as much as his life that explained his place in American memory. Assassinated on Good Friday after the surrender of Lee's army, "the martyr was instantaneously deified both because of the dramatic structure of the events surrounding his death and because of public esteem for him as a man and a statesman." In some ways, over and above all other Northern officials, the president embodied the Union Cause; "the memory of Lincoln became the most treasured legacy of that conflict." Peterson identified five themes encapsulating his memory including "Lincoln as Savior of the Union, Great Emancipator, Man of the People, the First American, and the Self-made Man. Nationality, Humanity, Democracy, Americanism, and the individual opportunity which is its essence: these are the building blocks of the Lincoln image." Patterson recognized both the resilience of these themes and their adaptability. "The five themes here set forth would be developed, entwined, embellished, revised, and recast, through several generations" because "the public remembrance of the past . . . is concerned less with establishing its truth than with appropriating it for the present."[23]

Not surprisingly, Barry Schwartz, a sociologist who specializes in memory theory, identified a similar evolution. Schwartz's study, *Abraham Lincoln and the Forge of National Memory* (2000), described Lincoln's transformation "from martyr to idol." It was his "assassination [that] transformed Abraham Lincoln from a controversial president into an emblem of Northern society." Once the initial outpouring of grief diminished, Lincoln's memory became a subject of controversy, and this reassessment shaped both federal and Confederate collective memory. "Many Americans—the vast majority when white Southerners are included—questioned Lincoln's merits." This revaluation did not include all federal supporters, "the Republican party, veterans' groups, and Lincoln's personal acquaintances, created a literal cult of commemorative biography, poetry, statuary, painting, monuments, shrines, and ritual observance." Schwartz maintained that this effort was not fully successful; while "few Northerners openly disparaged this cult [,] . . . most were unwilling to embrace it." Partly, this reflects the sectional and partisan memory of people who lived through the war. Once the Civil War generation passed from the scene, the men and women who did not live through the war embraced Lincoln as an American hero, partly based on his supporters' earlier efforts.[24]

Democrats rejected the heroic Lincoln. The debate over Lincoln in collective memory reflected a basic truth; Americans, even Union supporters, did not agree during the war, and their memories reflected this disagreement. M. Keith Harris made one key distinction in his study of "Slavery, Emancipation, and Veterans of the

Union Cause: Commemorating Freedom in the Era of Reconciliation, 1885–1915"
(2007) that appears to have been lost in much of the discussion of Northern Civil
War memory. "During the War, a great number of white union volunteers opposed
all association with blacks, even those who served in the Union army, rejecting any
semblance of racial equality." It would be surprising if men or women, soldiers or
civilians, who rejected emancipation as a war goal, placed it as central to their Civil
War memory. As time passed, this partisan divide influenced the historical memory
of the war. On the one hand, the Republican Party waved a "bloody shirt" that
emphasized the war's cost and the Union Cause; on the other hand, the Democratic
Party highlighted a "laundered shirt" memory that minimized the war's price and
articulated many Lost Cause ideas. Supporting the importance of Civil War parti-
sanship in assessing Civil War memory, Elizabeth R. Varon identified how various
groups in the North and South responded to the Appomattox surrender (2013).
"Southerners who had supported the Confederacy, together with Northern antiwar
('Copperhead') Democrats who had deplored the Lincoln Administration's policies,
particularly emancipation[,] . . . believed that Grant's magnanimity was both a con-
cession to the moral rectitude of the defeated Confederates and a promise that honorable men would not be treated dishonorably." When it comes to the memory of
the war, there is no "North" because Northern free-states included men and women
who did not support the war. Just as there is no unified "South" because Southern
slave-states included black and white Americans who rejected secession and the Confederacy. Civil War memory reflected the complex nature of wartime loyalties.[25]

Anne E. Marshall in *Creating a Confederate Kentucky: The Lost Cause and Civil
War Memory in a Border State* (2010) reviewed Civil War memory in this pivotal, loyal, slave-state. According to Marshall, "In the thirty years [after] the Civil
War . . . Kentucky developed a Confederate identity that was seemingly at odds with
its historical past" as a state that supported the Union cause. Despite proving many
more volunteers to the United States than to the Confederacy, Kentuckians "built
Confederate monuments, published sectional periodicals, participated in veterans'
organizations and historical societies, and produced literature that portrayed Kentucky as Confederate, while seemingly leaving the Union Cause and the feats of its
soldiers largely uncelebrated." While the Lost Cause appeared to have triumphed in
the Commonwealth, Marshall disagreed with the view that there was a monolithic
Civil War memory in Kentucky. Instead, she found "divergent memories belonging
to many Kentuckians, which competed with one another over time for cultural primacy" revealing "an active political and cultural dialogue that included white Unionist and Confederate Kentuckians, as well as the state's African Americans." Given
the diverse nature of Kentuckians' individual wartime experiences—freed slaves on
the one hand, unionist slave owners on the other—it would have been impossible to
create a singular collective memory.[26]

Moreover, if collective memory relies on the present as much as the past, the destruction of slavery made the postwar experiences of some white Union supporters, particularly slave owners, more similar to that of their Confederate counterparts than other Union supporters. As Marshall contended, "In a postwar world where racial boundaries were in flux, the Lost Cause and the conservative politics that went with it seemed not only a comforting reminder of a past free of late nineteenth-century insecurities but also a way to reinforce contemporary efforts to maintain white supremacy." Marshall claimed that race mattered the most: "Union memory in Kentucky became too closely associated with emancipation and African American progress for white Unionists to accept it as their own." She concluded that Kentucky's experience represents a broader truth that "the way people interpreted the war often had little to do with their wartime loyalties." Much of the historical memory of the Civil War and the strength of the Lost Cause, even in states that supported the Union, demonstrate the disconnect between wartime sectional loyalties and Civil War memory.[27]

Two essays on postwar Appalachia support the notion that assessing loyalty and memory by section might be a mistake. Kentucky's neighbor Tennessee seceded from the Union, though many men and women in the eastern section of this state rejected disunion. Tom Lee studied "The Lost Cause That Wasn't: East Tennessee and the Myth of Unionist Appalachia" (2010) and found that residents who wanted to improve the region's image in Northerners' eyes created a wartime memory that emphasized residents' Unionism. While Lee agreed that many Tennesseans supported the Union, he concluded that "the image of East Tennessee Unionism . . . belied the complexities and consequences of Unionists' sentiment during and after the war." Robert M. Sandow discovered that "Grudges and Loyalties Die So Slowly" when he examined the "Contested Memories of the Civil War in Pennsylvania's Appalachia" (2010), the home of a number of men and women who refused to support the federal war effort, particularly if it meant military service. After the war, these Pennsylvanians remembered their dissent. In fact, these memories were as much about Pennsylvania's present as it was about their past. Many residents who rejected the war worked in the mines and participated in 1870s' labor struggles. Between the memory of wartime rebellion and the reality of postwar turmoil it was not surprising that when a local citizen who had shot a sheriff enforcing the wartime conscription came to trial in 1874, he was cleared of all charges.[28]

Ironically, abolitionists who supported the Union Cause during the war have been accused of forgetting slavery and emancipation. Among the best known of these men was Thomas Wentworth Higginson, who financially supported John Brown and his uprising and later commanded one of the first black army units. In a Memorial Day speech, Higginson appeared to reject the idea that the war was about slavery, asserting the "two principles of government on which men might honestly differ in opinion—the difference between states rights and the sovereignty of the nation" echoing Alexander Stephens's, the Confederate vice president's, postwar views. W. Scott Poole assessed "Memory and the Abolitionist Heritage: Thomas Wentworth Higginson and the Uncertain Meaning of the Civil War" (2005) and rejected the notion that these remarks reflected his Civil War memory. Instead, he emphasized Higginson's "disillusion about the possibilities of nationalism and his doubts about whether or not it could serve as a force for racial justice." Poole traced these views to the antebellum era when Higginson and other radical abolitionists had little faith in a federal government that protected slavery. Moreover, Higginson rejected the power of the central government, including its imperialistic actions overseas in the Spanish-American War, and this too affected how he remembered the war. Higginson's postwar views foreshadow a broader twentieth-century phenomenon; Civil War memory reflected contemporary views of the American union, including the power of the national government.[29]

Higginson was not alone; other abolitionists lived to see the postwar world, and they also shaped Civil War memory. In an epilogue to his study of the abolitionist movement, John Stauffer in *The Black Hearts of Men: Radical Abolitionists and the Transformation of Race* (2001) described an 1874 abolitionist gathering that advanced an all-white version of the Union Cause. According to Stauffer, "The principal aim of the four-day affair was to bring together reformers of all persuasions to 'relate their personal experiences of the Anti-Slavery movement,' so that future generations would learn 'what they did and endured for the cause.'" People at the time understood that this gathering represented a significant memory act; the *Chicago Tribune* covered the event in detail. Stauffer emphasized the absence of women and African American abolitions at this meeting. "The primary effect of the reunion was to characterize the abolitionist movement as a white man's movement." The collective memory of an all-white, all-male abolitionist movement resonated with future generations. In addition to ignoring the contribution of women and African Americans, this version of abolitionist memory also downplayed the radical nature of this movement; future more conservative generations prefer this version of abolitionism rather than the one that challenged the racial status quo in the antebellum era.[30]

Just as abolitionists wanted to assimilate into mainstream America life and memory, so did immigrants. One scholar suggested that Civil War memory made this more difficult for one group. Christian B. Keller in *Chancellorsville and the Germans: Nativism, Ethnicity, and Civil War Memory* (2007) identified the dual effect of Civil War memory on German immigrants' assimilation. German Americans believed they had proved their loyalty by their service; they had paid the price and claimed their American citizenship. Despite this memory, they also recalled antebellum anti-German sentiment and what Keller called the "specter of Chancellorsville" that "haunted their celebrations of the war." During the battle, German American units had been flanked by Stonewall Jackson's Confederate forces and retreated; as a result, some soldiers referred to these men as "Flying Dutchmen." Germans resented these accusations. Moreover, in the postwar present German unification and their pride in their birth nation's accomplishments made this treatment seem even more unacceptable. Ultimately, while they asserted their American citizenship, they were "reluctant to jump into the melting pot" and lose their ethnic identity because they remembered their treatment both before and during the Civil War.[31]

Germany united in the crucible of nineteenth-century wars; in contrast, the United States reunited after the Civil War, and this affected the memory of the Union Cause. Ironically, postwar reunion sometimes relied on forgetting elements of the Union Cause. Edward Blum identified this phenomenon in *Reforging the White Republic: Race, Religion, and American Nationalism, 1865–1898* (2005). Blum explored the relationship between religion and reconciliation and described the critical role played by Northern Protestants in reestablishing an American national identity based on whiteness. The Union Cause represented a challenge to their efforts because the memory of African American Unionism challenged whiteness as central to nationality and citizenship. Blum examined the life of Dwight Lyman Moody, famous evangelical preacher and chaplain for the Civil War Christian Commission. According to Blum, Moody's "sermons revealed a northern amnesia regarding the Civil War that effaced memories of the importance of slavery and racial issues in the terrible conflict." As part of his efforts to emphasize "similarities between northern and southern whites," Blum believed that "Moody invented a mythical 'War between the States' in which the fact of northern and southern soldiers' bravery and a shared experience of combat obscured the reality of their fundamentally antagonistic convictions about the essential organization of society." While representing one religious figure's views, this interpretation appealed to a broader segment of Northern society.[32]

The question of examining the memory of individuals may seem counter to identifying a collective memory; however, it is the concept of resonance, the idea that individual's memory resonated with others, that may be key to the relationship between individual memory, collective memory, and historical memory. Thomas J. Pressly in his study *Americans Interpret Their Civil War* (1962) identified how historians and others in the immediate postwar period interpreted the Civil War. Despite the fact that some of these men's views were not popular with their own generation, others who did not live through this conflict found their memories more compelling. Pressly discovered that "the peace interpretation" that blamed the war on extremists, particularly abolitionists, became an enormously influential interpretation in the twentieth century. In addition to blaming the North more than the South for the war, individuals who supported this argument asserted that the war brought about a number of undesirable outcomes including a more powerful federal government. Pressly highlighted the view of Orestes A. Brownson, the transcendentalist-turned conservative Catholic writer, who had supported the war despite his prewar proslavery and anti-abolitionist views. After the war, Brownson "still den[ied] the validity of the state sovereignty doctrine and criticiz[ed] secessionists who had fought in its defense [; however,] he now looked at the same time with disfavor upon a centralized national government based on majority rule." Brownson blamed the abolitionists, not just because they freed the slaves: instead, he claimed that they had plans for a "socialistic democracy." While these were minority opinions after the war, the conservative pushback against the revolutionary nature of emancipation might explain some of the Lost Cause's power in historical memory.[33]

Pressly identified a common truth of historical memory; what Americans remember represents a choice made among diverse collective memories based on the next generations' present needs. Americans look for and find the Civil War past they require; for a very long time, for many white Americans, the Lost Cause represented the most useful Civil War memory. The process by which the Lost Cause won and the Won Cause lost, and later how their fortunes changed, is the subject of the next chapters.

THREE

❧❧❧

"THE LEGEND OF THE LOST CAUSE HAS SERVED THE ENTIRE COUNTRY VERY WELL": CIVIL WAR MEMORY AND AMERICA'S RISE TO WORLD POWER

No historian advanced the memory of the Union war effort with greater eloquence than Bruce Catton—winner of the Pulitzer Prize in 1954 and chronicler of the Army of the Potomac, the hard-luck eastern Union army. Despite his support for the Northern war effort, when Catton reflected on the Civil War in the late twentieth century, he decided "the legend of the lost cause has served the entire country very well," supporting the notion that even strong Union supporters accepted that version of Civil War memory. As he explained, "We have had national peace since the war ended, and we will always have it, and I think the way Lee and his soldiers conducted themselves in the hours of surrender has a great deal to do with it." Catton exhibited a sophisticated understanding of the roots of Lost Cause success—its appeal to American romanticism. "The things that were done during the Civil War have not been forgotten, of course, but we now see them through a veil. . . . It is a part of American legend, a part of American history, a part, if you will, of American romance." Even well-informed Americans like Catton, who understood that the Lost Cause represented a legend or history through a veil, decided that how it served national unity was more important than how it reflected historical reality. While the Lost Cause endured for much of the twentieth century, Catton lived through events that would eventually challenge Americans' uncritical acceptance of Confederate memory. The transition occurred when the civil rights movement challenged the racial status quo.

A fundamental change in racial views propelled the American scholarly mainstream to question the uncritical acceptance of the Lost Cause in the name of reunion. Only when slavery mattered, did the Union Cause matter.[1]

Understanding the success of the Lost Cause in the Civil War's historical memory turns on interrelated ideas; among these are race and reunion, a mating created by David W. Blight in his seminal work, *Race and Reunion: The Civil War in American Memory* (2001). Blight argued that Americans forgot the centrality of the race question, that is, the struggle against slavery in the Civil War, to allow for national reunion based on permitting Southerners to discriminate against and disenfranchise African Americans. In his assessment, Blight assumed that Americans would have elevated racial issues related to the Civil War over reunion, something they did not do during the war, let alone decades after the war's conclusion. White Americans broadly agreed on black inferiority and supported discriminatory measures that reduced African American political and civil rights. Neither Northerners nor Southerners needed Civil War memory to support their racial views.[2]

Instead of concerns over race, during the last decades of the nineteenth century and the first half of the twentieth, reunion shaped Civil War memory because the question of Union and nation remained unresolved in white American minds. In contrast, other Americans believed that the United States that emerged after the war had not been worthy of the war's cost in blood and treasure. Initially, the Lost Cause appealed to Americans facing the social and cultural strains resulting from the transition to an industrial society at the end of the nineteenth century, an evolution that many tied to Union victory and Confederate defeat. The romance of reunion seemed more attractive than the rapaciousness of rampant capitalism and a salve for American's concerns about the role of men and women—gendered anxiety—and alarm over the number of immigrants arriving in the United States—nationalist anxiety. Moreover, the triumph of the United States as an industrial power occurred in tandem with the nation's rise to world power status and its involvement in many wars inherent in this new role: a transformation that prompted white Americans to embrace an imagined community of American military heroism that included the Confederate military experience—a central tenet of the Lost Cause. Ironically, the Lost Cause also served those dissatisfied with the state of the Union. In some cases, more progressive Americans repudiated the industrial capitalism associated with the Union Cause. Others rejected contemporary wars, such as World War I. In its aftermath, the antiwar impulse led to a reconsideration of the costs and benefits of Union victory. Racial views proved critical to this reassessment; racism prompted many white Americans to view slavery as a benevolent institution that served the nation, including African Americans' best interests. Not surprisingly, some Americans renounced a bloody war that ended what they perceived as a largely beneficial institution. Catton's assertion proved correct; the Lost Cause served so many diverse interests that Confederate interpretations would dominate American Civil War memory for much of the twentieth century.

The evolution of the Lost Cause in the late nineteenth and early twentieth centuries illustrates two critical ideas: first, the relationship between collective memory and historical memory and second, the idea that the latter is more about the present than it is about the past. In that period, the next generation replaced the Ladies Memorial Associations (LMAs) as custodians of Confederate memory and organized the United Daughters of the Confederacy (UDC). Karen L. Cox in *Dixie's Daughters: The United Daughters of the Confederacy and the Preservation of Confederate Culture* (2003) chronicled this organization. The UDC formed in 1894 and advocated a historical memory of the Confederacy rooted in the collective memory created by the Confederate Civil War generation, particularly the LMAs. One question that must be answered is, why did women continue to dominate Confederate memorialization in the 1890s? Union troops left former Confederate states at least two decades earlier suggesting that Confederate men were able to memorialize their dead. By that time, Confederate veterans had formed their own organizations, and they could have curtailed women's involvement in this effort. Given these circumstances, why did memory work continue to be the province of Southern women?[3]

Civil War memory remained women's work because it was as much about women's status in Southern society in 1894 as it was about their role in 1864. The generation of the 1890s included "New Women," educated women who wanted to participate in political life. The UDC offered one way that elite women realize their ambitions. According to Cox, "Membership in the UDC allowed these southern women to apply their education and leadership skills without fear of being criticized as 'unfeminine.'" These women took the tradition of the LMAs into the twentieth century by expanding women's roles in the public sphere, while maintaining traditional ideas of what was appropriate for a woman. According to Cox, this was typical of this era, across the nation, north and south. Women created organizations such as "Women's Christians Temperance Union (1874) and General Federation of Women's Clubs (1890), among others, [that] fostered women's involvement in public education and progressive reform." Southern white women belonging to these organizations had the same opportunity to be political without being considered unwomanly. In fact, because women had been so critical to creating Civil War memory in the immediate aftermath of the war, one can conjecture that Southerners perceived these duties as appropriate women's work. Since the dead had been buried, the UDC needed a new mission. According to Cox, these women focused on "building monuments, caring for indigent Confederate veterans and widows and publishing pro-southern textbooks." Ultimately, the UDC, the most successful Lost Cause memory organization, materially advanced the Lost Cause in the battle for Civil War memory well into the twentieth century.[4]

Members of the UDC at the monument to Gen. John H. Morgan, Confederate Army, erected in Lexington, Kentucky. (Library of Congress)

Shaping the Civil War in school textbooks represented one of the UDC's most critical missions; most Americans' exposure to Civil War history begins and ends in these volumes. Joseph Moreau examined the Civil War in textbooks as part of a larger work in *Schoolbook Nation: Conflicts over American History Textbooks from the Civil War to the Present* (2003). Moreau assessed the treatment of the Civil War as an illustration of pressure groups' efforts to affect the content in textbooks. This study responded to a suggestion that in the past a single, grand, unified vision of American history unfolded in school textbooks; instead, Moreau found a great deal of controversy over the nation's history in these studies. He begins his examination with texts produced by members of the Civil War generation—one written by Alexander Stephens and the other by Thomas Wentworth Higginson. Not surprisingly, when these men wrote about the war, they defended their respective causes. Stephens forgot the speech he made at the beginning of the war identifying slavery as the "cornerstone" of Confederate society; instead, he asserted the states' rights argument, as discussed in Chapter 1. Higginson emphasized emancipation and Union heroes including black soldiers. Other textbooks took up these sectional themes, particularly those written in the South. According to Moreau, "Various elements of the Lost Cause myth—fanatical abolitionists, chivalrous Southern officers, courageous White women back on the plantation, loyal slaves, vindictive Republicans—held a central place in histories used by the south at the turn of the century."[5]

James M. McPherson studied the same issue. According to McPherson, white Southerners formed committees at the turn of the twentieth century to defend their cause against "Long-legged Yankee Lies" a part of a "Southern Textbook Crusade" (2004). "These historical committees insisted on three broad themes as sine qua non of textbook acceptability: secession was not rebellion but rather a legal exercise of state sovereignty; the South fought not for slavery, but self-government; and Confederate soldiers fought courageously and won most of the battles against long odds but were finally worn down by overwhelming numbers and resources." McPherson identified some of the falsehoods that advocates labeled as the "Truths of History," including "Southern men were anxious for slaves to be free. They were studying earnestly the problems of freedom when Northern fanatical Abolitionists took matters into their own hands." Initially, these committees wrote letters encouraging authors and publishers to frame the Civil War in this way. When that effort failed, Confederate supporters pressured school boards to reject these unacceptable texts. Because state purchased texts, their efforts succeeded and Southern textbooks enshrined the Lost Cause much better than any public monument.[6]

The Grand Army of the Republic (GAR) fought to keep these notions out of textbooks used in Northern schools; however, they found this difficult because of the nature of publishing. Textbook makers could either publish different textbooks for different states or get authors who could write neutral books for a national audience. Eventually, textbooks reflected a middle ground with an emphasis on reunion and reconciliation because publishing houses wanted to sell books across the country, including in the former Confederate states. Moreau identified the popular message in 1920s' textbooks written for a national audience. "These textbooks portrayed the Civil War as a crucible of the American nation-state, which was sanctified through Anglo-Saxon bloodshed on both sides. In this national narrative, the crushing of slavery and the passage of postwar amendments [13th, 14th, 15th] played peripheral roles, and African-American soldiers perhaps no role at all." In addition to being about selling books, these textbooks reflected the popularity of a more nationalist and patriotic narrative in the aftermath of World War I. Ironically, some schools that needed these books were a product of Reconstruction; Republican governments had established the public school system in the Southern states.[7]

Many of the more forward-thinking members of the Civil War generation and their children hoped that education would allow the South to reap the benefits of industrialization that they had observed in the North and create a "new" and progressive south. Scholars have studied the idea of the "New South" as articulated in the 1880s and 1890s. Paul M. Gaston's *The New South Creed: A Study in Southern Mythmaking* (1970) believed that "the South in the generation after Appomattox was desperately poor, alternately despised, ridiculed, or pitied." In response, "optimistic young southerners" articulated an idea of a "New South" based on "harmonious reconciliation of sectional differences, racial peace, and a new economic and social order based on industry and scientific, diversified agriculture." The Lost Cause might have been problematic to New South advocates because it idealized the Old South— a preindustrial Southern past that rejected progress and modernity—if advocates of the New South had not enlisted the Lost Cause to advance its modernization efforts. Gaines M. Foster in *Ghost of the Confederacy: Defeat, the Lost Cause, and the Emergence of the New South* (1987) claimed that the New South's acceptance proved critical to the Lost Cause's endurance. In Foster's view, the Lost Cause "eased the region's passage through a particularly difficult period of social change. Many of the values it championed helped people adjust to the new order; to that extent, it supported the emergence of the New South."[8]

Ironically, Foster believed that Southerners became less interested in the Lost Cause because "after the Spanish-American War, the south received its long-desired vindication in the form of northern acknowledgment of its heroism and honor" just as Confederate veterans died, passing into memory. Perhaps, it was not the death of the Civil War generation but the success of their efforts; the dominance of the Lost Cause in Civil War memory meant that its supporters could be less strident.[9]

While some white Southerners saw hope in the promise of industrialism and modernity, some Northerners feared it and embraced elements of the Lost Cause

"The New South: The Triumph of Free Labor" cartoon by *Puck* magazine, for the Cotton States Expedition, Atlanta, Georgia, 1895. (Library of Congress)

narrative. Nina Silber studied this phenomenon in *The Romance of Reunion: Northerners and the South, 1865–1900* (1993) and found that "confronted with the haunting spectres of class conflict, ethnic strife, and alienation that their own industrialized society had produced, many northerners remained unconvinced about the benefits of industrial progress and about obliterating whatever remained of the old southern legacy; in many ways they were unconvinced as to the unqualified benefits of Union victory." As a result, Northerners of the middle and upper middle-classes welcomed reunion and the type of idealized image of the South portrayed by Lost Cause advocates. When white Americans question the desirability of the nation that emerged after the Civil War, they embraced Southern war memory. Moreover, while the Lost Cause's idealized portrayal benefited all Southerners, it particularly redeemed Northerners' view of Southern women. According to Silber, Northerners' gendered anxieties and "their fear that men had lost the independence and authority that had previously been a hallmark of their manhood and that women moved beyond their proper feminine 'sphere'" found comfort in their idealized view of "southern women, who seemed to have discovered the joys of domesticity precisely when northern women had grown weary of them." Demonstrating the effects of gender on memory, Silber assessed "romances" in which a Northern man married Southern women that "recaptur[ed] the sense of manly accomplishment" because a Northern man emerged "once again victorious, not only over the South, but also over womankind." As a result, Northerners admired Confederate women and this allowed the UDC to shape Civil War memory.[10]

Southern white men, specifically Confederate veterans, also benefited from this anxiety about masculinity. The place of Southern veterans in Southern society as exemplars of Southern manhood may not be surprising; however, the fact that in many ways, Northerners embraced these men as more manly than Northern veterans may be more remarkable. Silber cited Stuart McConnell's GAR study and many Northerners' view that Union veterans "wallowed in the past and did not contribute to the future." This judgment did not affect Confederate soldiers, because they had no future and "spent the years since Appomattox in learning to cope, manfully, with defeat." Ironically, according to Silber, "the southern soldier became a more noble warrior precisely because his cause had been lost." Romanticizing defeat represented an important factor in understanding the Lost Cause's attraction.[11]

Most politicians see nothing noble in losing; elections need to be won. The election of 1896 demonstrated how politics shaped Civil War memory. William McKinley, the successful Republican candidate, may have been a Civil War veteran but many of his supporters were not. As Patrick J. Kelly asserted in "The Election of 1896 and the Restructuring of Civil War Memory" (2004), McKinley presided over a party "led by a new generation intimately associated with the emergent corporate capitalist elite." McKinley remembered the Civil War as a lived experience; his supporters did not and their present trumped his past. As part of this election, Republicans were "eager to promote a patriotic nationalism based on the reconciliation of whites in the North and the South." The appeal of reunion reflected anxiety about social divisions. In response to the U.S. economic collapse, labor unions organized and went on strike in the cities and the Populist Party emerged to address rural economic problems. As Kelly explained, urban unions and rural populism represented an urgent present that shaped Civil War memory and led the Republican Party to emphasize its role "as the patriotic defender of the nation-state against political forces that . . . threatened to divide the country along the explosive fault lines of section and class." Republican electoral rhetoric associated class strife at the end of the century with secession in the middle of the century, suggesting that the Republican Party was better able to deal with this crisis. To facilitate reunion, Republican leaders "distanced the party from its historical role in revolutionizing U.S. race relations during the Civil War and Reconstruction"; for the first time, the Republican platform refused to support measures to ensure black voting. While this platform may have reflected a memory change, forgetting the centrality of emancipation and black rights to the party's founders, it also served the contemporary needs of the Republican Party and contemporary anxieties about emerging class and social divisions.[12]

Only two years after McKinley's election, the United States went to war with Spain after the destruction of the USS *Maine* in Havana harbor, an important milestone on the road to sectional reunion. The purported destruction of this battleship by the Spanish government in Cuba, the short-term cause of the war, followed long-term tensions between the United States and Spain over its empire in the Caribbean. In Cuba, the Spanish had been fighting an insurgency against colonial rule. The treatment of the Cuban population including the forced relocation of the population, or "reconcentration," led to tens of thousands of Cuban deaths from disease. The U.S. government, led by President McKinley, tried to negotiate with Spain about Cuba, but negotiations ended with a declaration of war in April 1898. The Cuban war terminated quickly, but not before Theodore Roosevelt charged up San Juan Heights and eventually into the presidency. While the United States won a decisive naval battle in Manila harbor led by Rear Admiral George Dewey, it fought a brutal counter-insurgency in the Philippines until President Theodore Roosevelt declared victory in July 1902. As a result of this war, the United States ruled Puerto Rico, the Philippines, Guam, and other parts of Spain's Pacific empire. The United States' rise to world power had begun.[13]

The Spanish-American War proved critical to the evolution of Civil War memory, transforming how Americans viewed Southerners. Northerners, even those who had fought in the Civil War, acknowledged that because sons of Confederate and Union soldiers served together, their common experience cemented national unity. GAR members believed that this display of national unity validated the Union Cause, particularly since this war brought freedom to the Cuban people. When some Northerners, including the Civil War generation, observed the United States at the turn of the twentieth century, they approved of a nation that brought freedom to the oppressed peoples of the world, just as their generation had freed the slaves. Unfortunately, white Unionists failed to realize that African Americans needed liberation in Southern states.[14]

"Memorial Day, 1899—Three Veterans under One Flag," *Puck* magazine, Spanish-American War veteran bringing together a Confederate and Union veteran. (Library of Congress)

"Memorial Day," *Puck* magazine, 1913, Veterans of the Blue and Gray substituting baseball for remembering. (Library of Congress)

Nina Silber identified the same use of emancipationist memory to support imperialism and other political agendas because white Americans remembered "Emancipation without Slavery" (2009). In her view, people invoked slavery and emancipation memory for alternate purposes in the early twentieth century. Imperialists used emancipation to support America's actions overseas. Anti-imperialists protested these same efforts arguing that the United States would reintroduce slavery into these new holdings. White women pointed to the emancipation and suffrage of black men and demanded the right to vote. Labor leaders maintained that wage laborers were a type of slave because workers deserved better. Similarly, reformers who fought "white slavery" or prostitution believed that white slavery constituted a greater evil; black slaves were better off than white women who had lost their virtue. According to Silber, none of these invocations challenged the Lost Cause because Americans managed "to appropriate a moral imperative from wartime abolition, while obscuring the real story of the war, emancipation, and the unfulfilled promise of black liberation." The Union Cause seemed well suited for progressive causes like women's suffrage and labor activism; this may explain its unpopularity with those advancing a more conservative agenda.[15]

Civil War memory often served conservative purposes by fostering a sense of American nationalism. Cecilia Elizabeth O'Leary's *To Die For: The Paradox of American Patriotism* (1999) identified "the development of a nationalist consciousness in the United States . . . from before the Civil War to World War I." O'Leary's thesis is central to understanding the evolution of Civil War memory in the twentieth century. "The victory of the Union in the Civil War was the *beginning* [italics in original] of a long and contentious struggle over who and what would represent the nation." Among the critical organizations contesting the nature of the Union were the GAR and the Woman's Relief Corps, the UCV and the UDC, suggesting that Civil War memory influenced this battle. Civil War memory or forgetting became central to this effort. "In the name of national unity, the struggle for black rights was all but eradicated from Civil War commemorations." As a result, O'Leary asserted, "the nation's commitment to equal rights was in full retreat." This statement suggests that at one point white Americans supported equal rights; however, the vast majority of white Southerners and Northerners rejected racial equality. Certainly, few, if any, white Americans would have placed race over reunion.[16]

Reunion mattered more in an era in which America's rise to world power and empire engendered many new wars. Caroline E. Janney's *Remembering the Civil War: Reunion and the Limits of Reconciliation* (2013) explained how these wars affected Civil War memory and contended that "ironically, the very success of the Union Cause had led to its steady demise in popular imagination. Having fought to preserve the nation, Unionists had encouraged former rebels to embrace the States and Stripes and identify themselves as Americans." Janney found that the Union Cause faded away when "during the Spanish-American War and the First World War . . . loyalty to the Union became enveloped in the national allegiance and patriotism of all Americans," an "American Cause." As a result, she claimed, "as the Union Cause became amorphous and obscure, the Confederate Cause remained distinct. Its memory and symbols continued to stand apart, suspended in time and inseparable from the war. Increasingly, it appeared as though the Confederacy *was* [emphasis in original] the Civil War." The Lost Cause served so many different present needs, particularly during the challenges facing the United States in the twentieth century, that white people equated the American cause with many tenets of the Lost Cause.[17]

While the Lost Cause seemed more memorable, there were certain elements of the Union Cause that answered the needs of the twentieth-century present, such as the memory of Abraham Lincoln. Barry Schwartz in *Abraham Lincoln and the Forge of National Memory* (2000) contended that when the Civil War generation passed from the scene Lincoln became a "national idol." He tied Lincoln's status to the progressive movement in the early twentieth century. "The surging of Lincoln's reputation and the enlargement of his symbolic role during the Progressive era" reflected the movements' members' focus on the "advancement of electoral democracy and [its] definition of new ideal of human welfare." Remembering Lincoln as a "man of the people," they took an upper-middle-class lawyer and made him a working-class rail-splitter, facilitating his use by progressives. While Schwartz correctly identified this popular portrayal, this image reflected Lincoln's close friends and associates' efforts to shape the collective memory of the sixteenth president. Progressives were not the only group that created their version of Lincoln, "socialists, conservatives, women, African Americans, immigrants, and Southerners, developed their own variations of the progressive Lincoln—the president accessible to all, embracing all." In memory, "Lincoln the war president becomes Lincoln the economic reformer, champion of labor and women's rights, friend of the black man, welcomer of the foreigner, lover of the South." When World War I came, the government found Lincoln's memory useful in its efforts to "orient, inspire, and console the people who fought in it" suggesting that the American cause identified by Janney had a place for specific Unionist elements.[18]

In the postwar era, during the Depression and World War II, men and women reimagined Lincoln to meet the needs of their contemporary crises. According to Schwartz in *Abraham Lincoln in the Post-Heroic Era: History and Memory in Late Twentieth-Century America* (2008), "His personal suffering, as the Greatest Generation perceived it, made him sympathetic to the suffering of others; and if he failed in many things he remained hardworking, resilient, and persistent. His reputation as a Man of the People, First American, and Self-Made Man, resonated with the Depression generation's economic worries." When many of these men and women went to war a decade later, the memory of Lincoln comforted them. As Schwartz suggested, "His saving of the Union exemplified the cohesion required to face a worldwide military challenge; his emancipation of the slaves symbolized his victory over foreign totalitarianism as often as racial integration at home. His identification with the common man modeled the proper relation between the state and its citizens."[19]

Similarly, Nina Silber highlighted the Civil War's contested memory during the New Deal based on her analysis of "Abraham Lincoln and the Political Culture of New Deal America" (2015). According to Silber, "In the 1930s and 1940s, Abraham Lincoln . . . became an object of intense political contention, fought over by New Deal Democrats, Republican stalwarts, black civil rights workers, and left-wing activists." It might seem natural that New Deal officials who wanted to expand federal power would invoke Lincoln; however, Lincoln was a Republican and Roosevelt a Democrat. Moreover, the Democratic Party relied on its white Southern-wing during elections and had to be careful about embracing Lincoln and emancipation given white Southerners' commitment to white supremacy. Despite any political competition over Lincoln's memory, he "achieved a cultural resonance in these years, as Americans became well-versed in the stories of his childhood hardships and youthful ambitions." Silber credited Carl Sandburg's biography and movies, such as *Abe Lincoln in Illinois* (1940), for this awareness. Resonant did not mean rigid; as the present changed, from Depression-era America to an America at war, so did Lincoln's memory. "The sixteenth president underwent a series of remarkable transformations: no longer a bland symbol of reconciliation, he emerged as a figure more firmly associated with federal power and racial justice only to change again into a singular representative of America's rebuke to global dictatorships" when war came. Lincoln's image represented one aspect of Civil War memory used for progressive political purposes; people who rejected these liberal views may have found the Lost Cause and its conservatism more palatable, though it seems odd to call rebels conservative.[20]

Robert E. Lee represented the perfect hero for a more conservative America. While Early and the Southern Historical Society sanctified Lee in collective memory, Douglas Southall Freeman deified him in historical memory. Freeman, the son of a Confederate veteran, drew inspiration from family experience and his memory of a Battle of the Crater reenactment in 1903. Neither an amateur historian nor a dilettante, Freeman had received his PhD from Johns Hopkins—the pioneering school of graduate history studies in the United States. He began his research in 1915, two years before the United States became involved in World War I, and completed his study in 1934 with his Pulitzer Prize–winning multivolume study. Freeman's Lee constituted more than just a great general; he epitomized the virtues of a great man. According to Freeman, "He was the same in his bearing to men of every station, courteous, simple, and without pretense. Of objective mind, free of any suggestion of self-consciousness, he was considerate in his dealings with others, and of never-failing tact. He made friends readily and held them steadfastly. . . . [H]e was unselfish, talked little of himself, and was in no sense egotistical." Freeman created an idealized portrait of Lee that Thomas L. Connelly called the "Marble Man." Depression-era America embraced Lee and Lincoln suggesting that when Americans desperately need heroes, they find what they need in Civil War memory.[21]

Despite Lincoln and Lee's popularity between the world wars, there seems to be less interest in Civil War memory during this period. Gaines M. Foster believed that in this era only women who belonged to the UDC and academic historians "remembered" the Civil War. While memory studies have examined women's roles, the academy's efforts have received less attention, partly because scholars often treat history and memory as distinct phenomena. However, historians chose which collective memory to use when writing about the Civil War, and these decisions reflected the present in which they live. In this period, scholarly Civil War studies that created the war's historical memory tended to support the Lost Cause version of Civil War memory. During the interwar years, a combination of economic challenges, antiwar sentiment, and a resurgent white Southern identity explained this development. These scholarly efforts, which in turn shaped Civil War memory outside the academy, contributed to the Lost Cause's success in American memory.[22]

Thomas J. Pressly in *Americans Interpret Their Civil War* (1962) analyzed how academics interpreted the war between its end and its centennial. A close reading of his analysis suggested that early efforts by the Civil War generation to "interpret" the war represented collective memory efforts and later scholarship on the Civil War represented its historical memory. He found that scholars of successor generations selected the various strains of collective memory created by the Civil War generation based on their distinct presents and needs; these, in turn, shaped historical memory. As he explained, "The attitudes toward the Civil War of historians writing in a particular chronological era seem to have reflected in some fashion the interests and the outlook of that period; as these interests and that outlook have changed so have [the] interpretations." The Civil War generation, particularly Confederate supporters, consciously created a collective memory to influence future generations' memory, including historians' interpretations. In turn, these interpretations shaped how Americans remember the Civil War.[23]

Pressly examined both the Civil War generation and their immediate successors, the "new generation." James Ford Rhodes wrote the most significant studies of this cohort, many of whom supported a nationalistic interpretation supporting reunion and reconciliation. Despite the fact he lacked academic training, his multivolume study *History of the United States from the Compromise of 1850* (1892–1922) influenced readers for decades.[24]

While it has been suggested that reunion required amnesia about slavery and race, Rhodes and other nationalists disagreed. John David Smith in his *An Old Creed for the New South: Proslavery Ideology and Historiography* (1985) identified Rhodes and cohort as opposed to the benevolent view of this institution; instead, they "disseminated a partisan, antislavery point of view—one designed to challenge the proslavery opinion so prevalent in American thought from Reconstruction through World War I." Rhodes and other nationalists believed that remembering slavery did not damage reconciliation; instead, it facilitated reunion. According to Smith, Rhodes and his cohort believed that "a thorough dispassionate understanding of slavery would not only heal the old wound but foster American patriotism, itself a nationalizing force." Rhodes explained why the memory of slavery encouraged nationalism in his landmark study. "The United States of 1877 was a better country than the United States of 1850. For slavery was abolished, the doctrine of secession was dead, and Lincoln's character and fame had become a possession of the nation."[25]

Rhodes emphasis on 1877 and not 1865 clarified his views. While he disparaged slavery and welcomed emancipation, he rejected Reconstruction-era efforts to expand the political rights of former slaves. "Universal [N]egro suffrage" resulted in "the oppression of the South by the North" that ended only with "the final triumph of Southern intelligence and character over . . . ignorance and corruption." In this retelling, he placed redeeming the South for white rule as central to American nationalism. "From 1877 on, is seen a growing marvel in national history: the reunion of hearts which gives to patriotism the same meaning at the South as at the North. Freedom and reunion were glorious achievements." A careful examination of Rhodes's study revealed that contemporary corruption shaped his memory. He cited "other legacies of the War and Reconstruction were an increase of governmental corruption and a more pronounced tendency towards bad administration." Rhodes's work suggests that accepting Southerners' efforts to impose white supremacy and their solution to the so-called race problem did not require amnesia about slavery and its end, only a strong belief in African American inferiority.[26]

Rhodes's work did not go unchallenged. Demonstrating the contested nature of Civil War and Reconstruction memory, an African American politician who served in Congress during Reconstruction rejected his assessment. John R. Lynch wrote in *The Journal of Negro History* about "Some Historical Errors of James Ford Rhodes" (1917). Unrelenting in dissecting Rhodes views, Lynch included a scathing indictment of the idea of the South being "redeemed" by whites. According to Lynch, Rhodes work "is not only inaccurate and unreliable but is the most biased partisan and prejudiced historical work I have ever read." Despite this criticism, which white scholars may not have noticed, Rhodes became the president of the American Historical Association (AHA).[27]

The AHA formed as a larger effort to professionalize historical studies in the last part of the nineteenth century. The first trained historians, at the first American graduate programs including Johns Hopkins, Harvard, and Columbia, turned their attention to the Civil War. While these men became prominent historians, Woodrow Wilson, son of a Confederate supporter, also served as president of the United States. In this position, he spoke at the Gettysburg seventy-fifth reunion in 1913. During his speech, he proclaimed, "We have found one another again as brothers and comrades, in arms, enemies no longer, generous friends rather, our battles long past, the quarrel forgotten." David W. Blight (2001) believed that his remarks "struck the mystic chord of memory that most white Americans were prepared to hear." As a historian, Wilson examined the Civil War era, in *Division and Reunion, 1829–1909* (1914), and lauded the Confederate war effort. "There is, in history, no devotion not religious, no constancy not meant for success, that can furnish a parallel to the devotion and constancy of the South in this extraordinary war." Despite his favorable view of the Confederacy, he acknowledged that slavery caused the war; however, he rejected the moral condemnation of slavery. "The charges of moral guilt for the establishment and perpetuation of slavery which the more extreme leaders of the anti-slavery party made against the slave-holders of the southern states must be very greatly abated, if they are to be rendered in any sense just." Wilson suggested that blaming Americans for slavery was unfair because "most of the colonies would have excluded [N]egro slaves from their territory, had the policy of England suffered [allowed] them to do so." Wilson portrayed slavery as a mostly benign institution that provided needed agricultural labor from slaves who "were too numerous and too ignorant to be safely set free." Because he believed that slavery benefited African Americans, he focused on Union and reunion. "In 1829 the country, homogeneous as to population, was seriously divided between geographical sections; by 1909 war, the facilities of transportation, the intricate relationships of an elaborate economic society, had conferred the unity of nationality upon a vastly more cosmopolitan United States." In a preface to *Division and Reunion*, Wilson expressed his gratitude for "the continued serviceability of the little volume, in the judgment of teachers." Using this study in school had a larger effect on Civil War memory than a single speech given, on a single day, even one delivered at an important commemoration.[28]

Fiftieth Anniversary Encampment, reunion of Confederate and Union soldiers, site of the Battle of Gettysburg, July 1913. (Library of Congress)

North Carolinians at a Confederate reunion, Washington, D.C., 1917. (Library of Congress)

His upbringing may partly explain Wilson's views; however, Northern nationalists agreed with Wilson's emphasis on reunion even when they remembered slavery. Edward Channing, a New Englander, wrote a Pulitzer Prize–winning (1926) multivolume history of the United States and popular textbooks. Hugh Tulloch in *The Debate on the American Civil War Era* (1999) highlighted Channing's influential five-volume history of the United States (1905–1925). In one volume, Channing speculated, "It is by no means improbable . . . that the slaves were often happier than their masters." No advocate of the Lost Cause could have been more articulate in defense of slavery. While Channing's multivolume history won prizes, his textbooks shaped Civil War memory more effectively than these scholarly studies. Any student reading his *Student's History of the United States* (1902) in the first decade of the century understood that slavery caused the war. Channing claimed that by 1860, Southern leaders decided that "it would no longer do for the Union merely to tolerate slavery: the federal government must cordially undertake the propagation and fostering of it, the northerners must change their sentiments and declare it to be right." If Northerners did not embrace slavery, "Southern leaders were determined to break up the Union to establish a slave republic in the South." He certainly emphasized slavery when he suggested that teachers assign the topic "Negro Slavery" to their students and include sections on fugitive slaves and the Emancipation Proclamation as part of their curriculum.[29]

Two decades after completing this school text, Channing's *A History of the United States: The War for Southern Independence* (1926) won the Pulitzer Prize. He described slavery in detail emphasizing its benign nature. In fact, he argued that nineteenth-century English schoolboys or American sailors received more brutal whippings. Ultimately, he, like Lost Cause supporters, cited the faithful slaves who stayed on plantations during the war and protected women and children as proof of slavery's benign nature. Despite his almost tacit approval of this institution, he rejected slavery because it was incompatible with Union. "Two such divergent forms of society could not continue indefinitely to live side by side within the walls of one government . . . one or the other of these societies must perish." Wilson and Channing, despite their different backgrounds, remembered the Civil War and slavery in much the same way.[30]

Much of the satisfaction felt by these men reflected their comfortable status in life. In contrast, scholars who decried contemporary poverty and inequality looked back to the Civil War with more critical eyes, though they too accepted central tenets of the Lost Cause. At the turn of the century, American efforts to reform society, the Progressive movement, affected historians. Some of these scholars hoped that a "progressive" view of history might make a difference in the present. Among the leaders of the movement, Charles A. Beard wrote one of the most influential and controversial books in American history, *An Economic Interpretation of the Constitution of the United States* (1913). While accusing historians of viewing their scholarship through contemporary lenses might insult some historians, these men and women embraced this notion. As Pressly explained, "The new movement was frankly focused upon contemporary social problems, primarily those centered ultimately in the distribution of wealth and of economic and political power among the various economic groups or classes in society."[31]

Charles and Mary Beard's *The Rise of American Civilization* (1927) articulated a progressive view of the Civil War. In this study, the Beards claimed that the Civil War resulted from economic factors and dismissed the role of slavery because no political party, including the Republican Party, advocated its end. In fact, the Beards even minimized the importance of the war itself. "The fighting was a fleeting incident" and was likely the least important aspect of a "social cataclysm in which the capitalists, laborers, and farmers of the North and West drove from power in the national government the planting aristocracy of the South." In the Beards' judgment, the war resulted from diverging economic systems that divided the nation into an agricultural and industrial society. The "so-called Civil War was in reality a Second American Revolution" that destroyed the agrarian society in the South. The fact that the agrarian society relied on slave labor and the industrial society on free labor seemed inconsequential. The Beards explicitly accepted a value-neutral assessment of emancipation. In fact, they demonstrated a degree of sympathy with slave owners, who "whatever may be the ethical view" of emancipation experienced "the complete destruction of about four billion dollars' worth of 'goods' . . . without compensation—the most stupendous act of sequestration in the history of Anglo-Saxon jurisprudence." The Beards' disdain for American industrial capitalism overcame any complaint they had against slavery, particularly because they rejected the notion that the armies fought over a moral issue.[32]

When historians like the Beards view slavery outside the context of a moral issue, they often accepted the notion that African Americans benefited from their enslavement. A college textbook written in 1931, *A History of Colonial America*, portrayed slavery as a benign institution. "Generally, when the master and slave were brought into close association, a mutual feeling of kindliness and affection sprang between them, which restrained the former from undue harshness toward the latter." This particular text remained in print into the 1960s and, even after racial attitudes had changed, continued to reject the idea that slavery was anything but beneficial. In a 1961 volume, the author continued to defend this institution. "Slavery was in some ways a blessing to the Negro himself. It taught him the rudiments of civilization and Christianity." Remembering slavery as a beneficial institution prompted Americans to question the wisdom of emancipation.[33]

These ideas originated in the work of Ulrich B. Phillips, one of William Dunning's cohort of Southern historians, men and women who rewrote the history of Reconstruction. Phillips, unlike Dunning and his colleagues, focused on slavery and the antebellum South. In *American Negro Slavery: A Survey of the Supply, Employment and Control of Negro Labor as Determined by the Planation Regime* (1918), Phillips used slave owners' sources to document the treatment of enslaved people. According to Phillips, "Severity was clearly the exception and kindliness the rule." Overall, he judged slavery as an economically inefficient way of life that benefited African Americans. According to Philips, "Plantations were the best schools yet invented for the mass training of the sort of inert people which the bulk of American [N]egroes represented." As always, this account reflected as much about the present as the past. When describing slavery, he explained that "there was . . . little of that curse of impersonality and indifference which too commonly prevails in factories of the present-day world where power-driven machinery sets the pace . . . where the one duty of the superintendent is to procure a maximum output at a minimum cost." Phillips's interpretation supported Confederate efforts to defend slavery, an unstated corollary, and it undermined the value of Union efforts to end slavery.[34]

Most of Phillips's graduate student colleagues wrote about Reconstruction as an indictment of Northern policy, mostly based on Northerners' efforts, as limited as they were, to advance the status of black Americans. Rhodes's studies demonstrated the interrelationship between Civil War and Reconstruction memory. In fact, white Southerners did an even better job of shaping Reconstruction

memory. For a long time, white Americans of both sections believed that Reconstruction was, what one journalist termed, "a Tragic Era," because black Americans
voted and served as public officials. Similarly, Massachusetts born, Harvard professor Paul H. Buck came to similar conclusions in his Pulitzer Prize–winning study
The Road to Reunion, 1865–1900 (1937) suggesting that these were not sentiments
exclusive to Southerners. White Americans in both sections cheered the loss of
African Americans' political gains after Reconstruction's end. As a result, it would
be hard to imagine white Americans embracing a Civil War memory that endorsed
efforts to free black men and women, so that these freed men and women could
rule white Americans.[35]

The specter of black rule, or at least African American voters, prompted white
Southerners to restate many Lost Cause ideals in the 1930s. The Democratic Party
seemed more open to their concerns because of black voting power in Northern
cities. Among the men leading what Pressly called the "New Vindication of the
South," Charles W. Ramsdell wrote a series of articles on the Civil War in which he
presents a more modern and effective version of the Lost Cause. Ironically, in his
1937 study, "The Changing Interpretation of the Civil War," he claimed that the
Lost Cause had lost the battle for memory before 1900. "It is enough to say that at
the end of the century the historical scholars . . . accepted the orthodox northern
version of the causes and character of that conflict." He applauded Phillips, the
Beards, and other professionally-trained historians and their revisionist views that
prompted a resurgence of interest in the Lost Cause. Ramsdell's specific contribution to Civil War revisionism involved slavery; in his view, it would have died a
natural death because it could not expand to arid Western lands, "The Natural
Limits of Slavery Expansion," and thus the war was unnecessary. "Slavery had about
reached its zenith by 1860 and must shortly have begun to decline." Ultimately, he
suggested, "the free farmers in the North who dreaded its further spread had nothing to fear. Even those who wished it destroyed had only to wait a while—perhaps
a generation, probably less." Given racial attitudes of this era and the post–World
War I antiwar sentiment, it should not be surprising that white Southerners who
argued that if there had been no war "more than half a million lives and the tens
of billions of wasted property [would have] been saved" influenced how Americans
remembered the Civil War.[36]

Another Southern vindicator, Frank L. Owsley belonged to an agrarian movement based in Tennessee espousing a critical view of modern industrial life. Owsley
participated in a symposium that published his and other essays in *I'll Take My
Stand: The South and the Agrarian Tradition* (1930). Owsley's essay addressed the
Civil War as he termed it in 1940 "The Irrepressible Conflict." This essay articulated
the Lost Cause for a modern audience, with a virulent racism that the Civil War

generation could not match. Not surprisingly, Owsley complained about emancipation because freeing slaves represented two billion dollars in lost investments. He went one step further and described "three millions of former slaves, some of whom could still remember the taste of human flesh, the bulk of them hardly three generations removed from cannibalism. These half-savage blacks were armed." Owsley viewed the war as "the irrepressible conflict, [that] was not between slavery and freedom, but between the industrial and commercial civilization of the North and the agrarian civilization of the South," echoing the Beards' views. Owsley echoed Lost Cause advocates in declaring that the South did not want slavery; it had been forced upon them by the British before the Revolution. He described "all early abolitionists—which meant most of the Southern people up until about 1800 were abolitionist only on the condition of colonization." Only when white Southerners realized that colonization was "cruel and expensive" did they resign themselves to keeping their slaves. He compared Northern abolitionists and their actions to "our recent radicals" who made slavery an issue that justified the destruction of the agrarian South. The historical usefulness of the Lost Cause to more conservative political elements partly explains its success in American memory.[37]

Among the historians affected by this general disillusionment with war were James G. Randall and Avery O. Craven, who along with other scholars that have been termed the Revisionist School rejected war and blamed the people who either advocated for it or allowed it to happen. Randall coined an important term in a 1940 article in which he assessed the Civil War generation as "the Blundering Generation." He began this article, which was also the presidential address delivered to the Mississippi Valley Historical Association (the predecessor to the Organization of American Historians), by dispelling all romantic notions of this conflict by describing the fate of the wounded, the missing, and the wretched living conditions of Civil War common soldiers. While this speech was about the Civil War, his remarks reflected the sensibilities of people who had lived through the Great War and the horror of trench life. Reflecting on this recent conflict, he noted that while "the World War produced more deaths, the Civil War produced more American deaths." Not limited to the Civil War or World War I, Randall rejected all wars. "For the very word 'war' the realist would have to substitute some such term as 'organized murder' or 'human slaughterhouse.'" Based on these views, he believed that the Civil War's genesis resulted from a "blundering generation" that "stumbled into a ghastly war." Much of the article described pacifists' inability to stop the Civil War and how propaganda made Americans "war mongers"—a very modern term. Both ideas reflected interwar Americans' rejection of World War I.[38]

Avery O. Craven agreed. In his seminal study, *The Repressible Conflict, 1830–1861* (1939), he maintained that "any kind of sane policy in Washington in 1860 might have saved the day for nationalism." He, like others in his generation, blamed fanatics on both sides; however, abolitionists, Lincoln, and the Republican Party merited the most condemnation because they prompted Southerners to defend their way of life. Some of his views were rooted in the fact that he like so many others believed slavery a beneficial institution. Craven has an entire chapter on what he calls the "peculiar institution" in his study, partly to indict abolitionists who "never had time to investigate slavery. He was too busy denouncing it." Most of the chapter is spent portraying slavery in a positive light. According to Craven, "The great majority of planters were humane; and the number who abused their slaves no greater than the number who indulged them." Craven considered indulging slaves as deserving the same type of approbation as abusing them. Like so many others, he compared enslaved American' lives to the condition of free laborers in the North, accusing these factory owners of "manifest[ing] all the attitudes of ownership toward their workers, whereas some slave master manifested few of them." Ultimately, Craven defended slavery as superior to free labor, particularly for inferior African Americans. "The Negro, because he was a Negro, required a more exacting arrangement." If race mattered, it did so because racism led to an acceptance of slavery and this, in turn, led to an acceptance of the Lost Cause.[39]

Avery O. Craven revised another seminal work *The Coming of the Civil War* in 1971 and still argued, six years after the passage of the Civil Right acts, that for the "slave there were . . . advantages and disadvantages in his lot." According to Craven, enslaved people were "relieved of all personal direction and material care." Craven restated many of the proslavery arguments popular in the antebellum era and described well-fed slaves taken care of by their masters. In an interesting and revealing remark, he addressed slave marriages. He placed the term "suffered" in quotes when he spoke of slaves' inability to choose their spouses rejecting the idea that this was a hardship. Linking his views to his present, 1971, he argued that "white comment on the slave's marital standards differs little from that current today [1971] concerning free Negro's." White angst about 1970s' African Americans, identified one hundred years after the war as merely free Negroes, and their family life, dominated his Civil War "memory."[40]

Ultimately, the dominance of the Lost Cause rested not so much on the work of amateur historians in the UDC; instead, professionals in the AHA allowed the Lost Cause to endure long after World War I. Separately, these scholars' views could not be seen as pro-Confederate; however, many of the arguments advocated by Lost Cause supporters had a great deal of support from professionally trained and "unbiased" historians. It is not surprising then that the Lost Cause even after World War II dominated the historical memory of the Civil War, since historians supported it. These historians did not forget slavery; instead, racism made its end less urgent and even undesirable. None of this changed until after World War II. After this watershed

event, some white Americans questioned the accepted notion of inherited racial inferiority because of its association with the Holocaust. Moreover, African Americans
themselves successfully challenged this racist consensus. A new generation of scholars
and Americans whose present included World War II and its end, the Cold War
between communism and democracy, and the beginning of the modern civil rights
movement began to question the racial assumptions underpinning the unchallenged
dominance of the Lost Cause. Because American memory changes slowly, it will take
decades for this to affect how most Americans remember the war.

FOUR

BATTLE CRY OF FREEDOM: CIVIL
WAR HISTORY AND MEMORY IN
THE CIVIL RIGHTS ERA

In 1988, James M. McPherson won the Pulitzer Prize for *The Battle Cry of Freedom: The Civil War Era*. For decades the book reigned as the most influential one-volume history of this landmark conflict, similar to the metanarratives described in Chapter 3. Unlike earlier narratives, he advanced the Union Cause and the emancipationist vision: what one scholar described as the neoabolitionist view. McPherson identified the principal importance of slavery's fate. "Most of the things we consider important in this era of American history—the fate of slavery, the structure of society in both North and South, the direction of the American economy, the destiny of competing nationalisms in North and South, the definition of freedom, the very survival of the United States—rested on the shoulders of those weary men in blue and gray." Because of the triumph of the Lost Cause in American memory in the first half of the twentieth century, it was inconceivable that the fate of slavery would have emerged first and foremost in an earlier Civil War synthesis.[1]

McPherson's career served as a testimony to how Civil War memory transformed over decades; in *The Negro's Civil War: How American Negroes Felt and Acted during the War for the Union* (1965), one of his first books, he collected and published primary sources that documented African American participation in the Civil War. Using their words, he emphasized that these participants rejected a passive role;

instead, they functioned as active agents of their emancipation. The evolution of racial views from this earlier volume's publication, the same year the Voting Rights Act passed, until McPherson's volume twenty-three years later, placed emancipation as central to Civil War memory.[2]

Much of this chapter considers the role of historians like McPherson in constructing Civil War memory. While this might seem to constitute an undue focus on the memory of a few well-educated Americans, as opposed to the broader society, scholars' views shaped and were shaped by historical memory. In the first half of the twentieth century, Avery O. Craven and other prominent scholars supported the Lost Cause; in the second half, academics undermined the dominant Southern version of Civil War memory. Twenty years before the publication of *The Negro's Civil War* a new phase emerged in the contest over Civil War memory. Appropriately, the new phase focused on a fight for freedom, though, like all memory, that emphasis reflected less on the past and more on contemporary freedom struggles. The idea that people remembered a war for freedom was complicated by the varied responses of Americans to contemporary wars. In the aftermath of World War I, people rejected war. In contrast, despite horrifically high casualties, World War II, the "good war" par excellence, demonstrated that something good could come from a war if it stopped a great evil. Americans, in particular, believed that the war could produce a better world, a more democratic world. Ironically, despite World War II's clear-cut victory for the United States and its allies, the war's conclusion brought no true peace, but a Cold War between communism and democracy.

The Cold War affected Civil War memory in some contradictory ways. On the one hand, the United States needed national unity in the face of what seemed to be an enduring and existential threat, and that helped the Lost Cause and reunionism. On the other hand, communists used the U.S. racial policies to attack the legitimacy of America's democracy prompting some white Americans to question the racial status quo. Ultimately breaking the racist consensus led them to question the benevolent nature of slavery and applaud efforts to end it, including the Union war effort. In addition to outside agitation, internally African Americans' decades-long freedom struggle finally achieved major successes in the decades after World War II. By the time of the Civil War centennial in 1961, the tension between race and reunion created by the Cold War and civil rights movement mired commemorative efforts in controversy. Eventually, when the civil rights movement prevailed, Civil War memory changed, though not as quickly as one might have thought given the racial revolution. Ironically, this delay resulted in some measure from the Vietnam War; once again, the long shadow of an unpopular war shaped Civil War memory. Only in the decades after Vietnam, when passions cooled, did the Union Cause finally compete with, but did not displace, the Lost Cause in American memory.

Prior to World War II, many Americans rejected war because of the experience of World War I. The attack on Pearl Harbor, Nazi Germany's declaration of war, and the four-year struggle against the Axis convinced many Americans that some wars were worth fighting supplanting the antiwar sentiments that had affected Civil War memory in the 1930s. Moreover, when the war ended, the Allies liberated concentration camps and discovered the true evil of the Nazi regime prompting some Americans to call this "The Good War." Unfortunately, the end of the war did not bring about genuine peace; the United States as the leader of the Western democracies became mired in a Cold War against communism. Between the Cold War and the hot wars of the twentieth century—Korea, Vietnam, and the Gulf Wars—the United States experienced very few years that one might consider peacetime in the twentieth century and this too shaped Civil War memory.[3]

Professional historians were no different from broader society; contemporary times affected their Civil War memory. While this was always true, in the second half of the twentieth century this might have been truer than at other times. White historians grew up in a world in which the Lost Cause dominated American memory partly because of white racism. As adults, they lived in a world in which black Americans successfully challenged the racist consensus. As a result, scholars questioned the racial assumptions that buttressed the Lost Cause. As racial views evolved, so too did the idea of union and reunion, not surprising given the unsettled nature of these decades. On the one hand, a united nation would be better able to face the existential threat of communism in both the cold and hot wars of this era by supporting sectional reunion and the Lost Cause. On the other, communists directly challenged the validity of American democracy because of American racial policies suggesting that the current racist consensus supporting the Lost Cause weakened the national Union. Despite changing racial attitudes, it would take some time to transform mainstream American memory and its allegiance to the Lost Cause.

In the academic world among historians, the new "consensus" school responded to the perceived need for national unity required for a dangerous world. John Higham in "The Cult of the American 'Consensus': Homogenizing Our History" (1959) introduced the idea by explaining its predecessors: "An earlier generation of historians . . . nurtured in a restless atmosphere of reform, had painted America in the bold hues of conflict. Sometimes their interpretations pitted class against class, sometimes section against section; and increasingly they aligned both sections and classes behind the banners of clashing ideologies"; the historians he cited included Charles and Mary Beard and their assessment of the Civil War. According to Higham, the new historiographical school "is carrying out a massive grading operation to smooth over America's social convulsions."[4]

In his analysis, Higham highlighted specific eras in American history. "The American Revolution has lost its revolutionary character"; instead it represented "a reluctant resistance of sober Englishmen to infringements on English liberties." Similarly, "Jacksonians yearned nostalgically to restore the stable simplicity of a bygone age, and that the Populists were rural businessmen deluded by a similar pastoral mythology." According to Higham, "Instead of two traditions or sections or classes deployed against one another all along the line of national development, we are told that America in the largest sense has had one unified culture. Classes have turned into myths, sections have lost their solidarity, ideologies have vaporized into climates of opinion." Only one era resisted such repaving, "the Civil War alone has resisted somewhat the flattening process." Higham posited "a significant decline . . . in the number of important contributions to Civil War history from professional scholars"; instead, Higham explained "the growing attraction of the Civil War to journalists." Partly, this might have resulted from a consensus view of history that "neutralizes some moral issues that have played a not entirely petty or ignoble part in the history of the United States."[5]

When Higham cited journalists, he most likely referred to Allan Nevins who wrote the most popular Civil War metanarrative of this era. Nevins's eight-volume study, *Ordeal of the Union*, published over twenty-four years starting in 1947, demonstrated some of the tensions in this era. Nevin's revived Rhodes and the nationalist tradition, not surprising given the need by Americans for a unifying nationalism during the Cold War. "The conflict was part of a broader movement for the unification of the nation, and for the merging of elements both varied and conflicting into a homogenous whole" that would make "unity triumph over sectionalism, homogeneity over heterogeneity." Nevins, influenced by the revisionist and the needless war schools of Civil War historiography, blamed extremists on both sides for the war. He recognized slavery as the cause but rejected both those who demanded its end immediately and those who desired its continuation indefinitely. While blaming abolitionists constituted a recurring theme in Civil War memory, castigating slave owners was new. He criticized them because they failed to accept gradual abolition because he believed that emancipation required a period of "race adjustment" based on his racial views. "The South inarticulately but clearly perceived that the elimination of [slavery] would still leave it the terrible problem of the Negro." If people saw some virtue in slavery's continuation, remembering slavery did not prompt support for the Union Cause and emancipation. As late as 1971 one reviewer complimented Nevins on his fairness and objectivity because "northern reviewers accused him of being pro-southern while reviewers from Dixie saw a Northern bias."[6]

Sadly, the year 1971 also marked the death of David M. Potter, the greatest consensus scholar of the Civil War era. His Stanford University colleague Don E. Fehrenbacher completed his masterwork *The Impending Crisis, 1848–1861*, which in 1976 won the Pulitzer Prize in history. A modern reading of this classic reveals Potter's devotion to fairness; he favored neither the Lost Cause nor the Union Cause.

Starting with the Wilmot Proviso, which attempted to keep slavery out of the territories newly acquired from Mexico in 1848, to the firing on Fort Sumter in 1861, Potter examined the complex series of events that led to war. His contribution to the consensus view of the Civil War appeared to be blaming both sides for allowing events to spiral out of control. According to Potter, it was not the weakness of nationalism, but its strength that caused the war. The triumph in the Mexican War led to a sectional division based on slavery in the territories acquired by that victory. Even though this interpretation seemed to support the centrality of slavery to the coming of the Civil War, Potter argued that slavery did not cause the war because Americans of both sections agreed on one thing—racism. "While slavery was sectional, Negrophobia was national." Instead, politics caused the war. "The slavery question became the sectional question and both became the territorial question. By this transposition, they entered the arena of politics and became subject to all the escalation and intensification which the political medium could give to them." Because of white Americans racial views, slavery mattered little in the coming of the Civil War. Instead, Potter maintained that white Americans foolishly went to war over slavery because they were unable to come to a political solution to the sectional crisis.[7]

This explanation, like so much of Civil War memory, assumed that African Americans stood by and acquiesced during the war; however, they did not. They contested any Civil War memory that suggested passivity. At the beginning of the twentieth century, African American scholars carried on this struggle; the work of Carter G. Woodson, the great pioneer of African American history, remains critical to understanding the ultimate triumph of black history and memory. Born in 1875, the son of slaves he could not "remember" slavery, but he certainly heard accounts from his parents and other community members. He received a bachelor's degree from Berea College and a Ph.D. from Harvard University, the second African American to receive that graduate degree. While working in academia, he wrote books; however, his most critical contribution might have been institutional—his efforts established the Association for the Study of Negro Life and History and the *Journal of Negro History* in 1916. The latter journal published E. R. Thomas's harsh review of Craven's *Repressible Conflict* that identified the "anti-Negro propaganda" that framed this study. Just as the Lost Cause created its institutions and periodicals, so did black Americans. In contrast, white Federalists did not. As a result, African American Unionists became the custodians of Union Civil War memory.[8]

Woodson's efforts to institutionalize African American history complemented that of another African American Harvard Ph.D., W.E.B. Du Bois, whose seminal work *Black Reconstruction in America 1860–1880* (1935) also examined the Civil War. Much of what he wrote about the black military experience was drawn from George Washington Williams and Joseph Wilson's studies, suggesting the importance of the Civil War generation's efforts to create African American collective memory. Skin color and his communist politics limited Du Bois's influence. Similarly, Du Bois's use of Marxist historical analysis also limited the reach of his study; many American scholars rejected his methodology. Du Bois described African Americans as the "Proletariat" who revolted in the Civil War, which he considered a "General Strike." Despite its limited reach, this study represented a milestone in Civil War memory: a mainstream white publisher, Harcourt Brace, issued a book in 1935 that placed African Americans and their actions as central to the war and its outcome, a mainstream interpretation of the Civil War today. Moreover, Du Bois identified the central issue in Civil War memory and its aftermath. "If [the reader] believes that the Negro in America and in general is an average and ordinary human being . . . he will read this story and judge by the facts adduced [provided]. If, however, he regards the Negro as a distinctly inferior creation . . . whose emancipation and enfranchisement were gestures against nature, then he will need something more than the facts that I have set down." No facts swayed white Americans away from their allegiance to the Lost Cause version of Civil War as long as they adhered to a racist consensus.[9]

Despite their lack of popularity in the United States, communists overseas helped overturn this racist consensus. During the Cold War, the battle between East and West, democracy and communism, encompassed a war of ideas and ideology. Communists did not hesitate to point out the hypocrisy of a nation that segregated and disenfranchised millions of its citizens as it proclaimed itself freedom's champion. In 1998, John David Skrentny identified this phenomenon in "The Effect of the Cold War on African-American Civil Rights: America and the World Audience 1945–1968" and found that people concerned about the moral legitimacy of the United States as a world leader felt this accusation keenly; others, including Southern officials, remained unaffected by this approbation over Southern racial policies. As a result, some Americans, including elites, scholars, and historians, began to rethink and challenge the racial status quo, and this might explain the broader change in American opinion cited in Skrentny's study. In 1942, only 32 percent of all Americans surveyed said that black and white children should attend the same school. By 1956 that number increased to 50 percent; in 1968, 72 percent; and in 1982, 90 percent. During these decades, attitudes toward employing African Americans and integrating public transportation demonstrated a similar improvement suggesting a change in racial attitudes among the broader public.[10]

Many of these changes that commenced in the later 1940s and continued into the 1950s had little to do with what people did or did not remember about the Civil War. African Americans had applied their political power within the Democratic Party during Franklin D. Roosevelt's administration to advance civil rights reforms even before the United States became involved in the war. The National Association for the Advancement of Colored People (NAACP) that Du Bois helped form had been critical in this effort. Among their successes, Roosevelt signed an executive order barring discrimination by defense contractors—the Fair Employment Act. During World War II the armed forces practiced segregation, though African Americans fought to expand black participation to include service as pilots. In 1948, President Harry S. Truman integrated the armed forces, once again by executive order. That same year, the Democratic Party embraced a civil rights platform, which led some white Southerners to form the Dixiecrat Party. Just after the Korean War, the first American war fought by an integrated military, *Brown v. The Board of Education* (1954) overthrew the separate but equal doctrine that had allowed racial segregation. Civil War memory did not change race relations; instead, breaking the white consensus on race affected how Americans remembered this conflict.[11]

Improved racial attitudes transformed the way Americans remembered slavery. Ironically, it was a consensus historian, Richard Hofstadter, who challenged the consensus by criticizing Ulrich B. Phillips's interpretation during World War II, when people may have been more willing to listen to this critique. He was not the first to challenge Phillips. As early as 1918, the last year of World War I, black scholars, such as Woodson and Du Bois, criticized Phillips's work. Frederick Bancroft, a white contemporary of Phillips, rejected, among other things, his assertion that parents never lost their children to the internal slave trade. By the last years of World War II, people might have been more willing to listen to this criticism. In a 1944 article in the *Journal of Negro History*, Hofstadter attacked Phillips's methodology that examined only the largest plantations in a handful of states and his neglect of owners with fewer than one hundred slaves. The vast majority of slave owners and slaves populated this neglected group. Hofstadter not only tackled his work from a methodological perspective but he also questioned Phillips's underlying attitudes and biases. Phillips's "conception of the Negro was characteristically Southern, and his version of slavery has been moderately described . . . as 'friendly.'" Hofstadter concluded that Phillips's studies "represent a latter-day phase of the pro-slavery argument." Phillips "chose to portray the Negro slave as a singularly contented and docile 'serio-comic' creature." Hofstadter cited Herbert Aptheker's study of *American Negro Slave Revolts* (1943) that documented black slave resistance criticizing Phillips's views. Both studies were published in World War II; a war against the ultimate white supremacist overseas that prompted some Americans to challenge them at home. Aptheker's membership in the Communist Party tainted his scholarship in many historians' opinions. Nevertheless, his study constituted one of the first steps in the destruction of the American consensus on slavery, which in turn shaped Civil War memory.[12]

The work of Kenneth M. Stampp, a distinguished historian of both the Civil War and slavery, demonstrated how views of slavery changed first, and later Civil War memory transformed. In this study, *And the War Came: The North and the Secession Crisis, 1860–1861* (1950), he supported a select revisionist school view that, rejecting compromise, led to a needless war. Focusing on Northerners, he highlighted what he considered their failures: one among them was Lincoln's mishandling of the resupply of Fort Sumter. Six years later, Stampp published *The Peculiar Institution: Slavery in the Ante-Bellum South* (1956), the first book-length challenge to Phillips's view of slavery. Stampp explained that his work made different assumptions than Phillips and others. "I have assumed that the slaves were merely ordinary human beings, that innately Negroes *are*, after all, white men with black skins, nothing more, nothing less." He understands that "this gives quite a new and different meaning to the bondage of black men" and that influenced his subsequent scholarship.[13]

Twenty years later, in a new edition of his Civil War study, *And the War Came: The North and the Secession Crisis, 1860–1861* (1970), Stampp rejected the contention that he supported the revisionists in the earlier volume. Instead, he believed that it was "the influence of Beard and Marx, some of whose ideas were part of the intellectual baggage I carried with me out of the 1930's" that explained his views. Reflecting on the passage of time he reconsidered his conclusion: "Twenty years after writing the decidedly negative last paragraph of this book, which emphasizes the cost in human misery and the incompleteness of Negro emancipation," he felt compelled to reassess his conclusions. "By 1860 white Americans had tolerated more than two hundred years of black slavery and still had discovered no peaceful way to abolish it. Therefore, a person is . . . entitled to ask how many more generations of black men should have been forced to endure life in bondage in order to avoid its costly and violent end." The change in racial attitudes that occurred in the two decades between the original publications of Stampp's Civil War study and this reprint changed his interpretation of the war. As part of this preface, he identified the link between Civil War memory and the value white Americans placed on black freedom. "Whether it was the worth the life of one man to give freedom to six others (and their descendants) is a moral problem that no man can answer for another." The memory of the Civil War hinged on whether black lives and freedom mattered.[14]

At the same time Stampp published his work on slavery, another contemporary historian introduced a radical notion into slavery studies. Stanley Elkins in *Slavery: A Problem in American Institutional and Intellectual Life* (1959) agreed with Stampp's rejection of slavery and racial inferiority; however, he claimed that the experience infantilized African Americans into what he termed the "Sambo" personality cited by whites who defended slavery. This controversial interpretation has been rejected by most, if not all, scholars of slavery; however, his theory demonstrated the direct relationship between the present and the past in memory studies. Elkins's analysis reflected his understanding of the concentration camps in World War II.[15]

Domestic events also affected the memory of slavery. C. Vann Woodward's *The Burden of Southern History* (1960) identified the success of this revisionism in slavery studies. As Woodward explained, "The Plantation Legend of ante bellum grace and elegance has not been left wholly intact. The pleasant image of a benevolent and paternalistic slavery system as a school for civilizing savages has [recently] suffered damage that is probably beyond repair." In addition to identifying changes in slavery memory, he discussed what he considered new lost causes suggesting that he connected Southern history and its burdens to an evolving Civil War memory. He considered the agrarianism promoted by the "I'll Take My Stand" essay writers as a "second lost cause." More recently, at least for Woodward, "segregation is a likely prospect for a third" lost cause. The idea that Southerners had many different lost causes that were not directly tied to the Civil War supported the connection between memory and contemporary needs. Despite these insights, Woodward's essays demonstrated one of Confederate Civil War memory's most subtle victories, the idea that white Southerners defined Southern identity excluding black Southerners who bore the burden of Southern history and reality.[16]

Despite the contemporary resonance of some of these revisionist arguments, these slavery studies did not lead to an immediate rejection of the Lost Cause; some time elapsed for revisionists to transform the perception of slavery. A new generation of scholars who lived through the civil rights movement and its aftermath produced landmark studies that collectively changed how Americans understood slavery. Some did so in explicit responses to Elkins's view. Eugene D. Genovese directly challenged Elkins's interpretation by describing both master's paternalism and slave's resistance and autonomy, in *Roll, Jordan Roll: The World the Slaves Made* (1974). He emphasized slave religion, something that neither Elkins nor Stampp had examined in detail. John W. Blassingame described in his study *The Slave Community: Plantation Life in the Antebellum South* (1972) and how the communal relation in the slave quarters allowed African Americans to resist slavery, and Herbert G. Gutman stressed the critical importance of familial relations in *The Black Family in Slavery and Freedom, 1750–1925* (1977). Lawrence W. Levine examined *Black Culture and Black Consciousness: Afro-American Folk Thought from Slavery to Freedom* (2007) and Albert J. Raboteau explored *Slave Religion: The "Invisible Institution" in the Antebellum South* (1978). One element omitted from these studies is women. Deborah Gray White focused on their experience in her seminal work *Ar'n't I a Woman? Females Slaves in the Plantation South* (1985). The entry of more women into the ranks of the historical profession made a profound difference to the memory of slavery and the Civil War.[17]

Modern examinations of slavery relied on formerly enslaved men and women's voices to tell their stories. During the Depression, the government established programs to employ Americans under the Works Progress Administration (WPA). One of these projects recorded aspects of American folklife, including African American spirituals. While interviewing elderly African Americans, the interviewers also received a great deal of information on slavery. Based on these interviews, the white officials who led this project ordered other states to document slaves' experiences. Eventually, the WPA amassed more than two thousand former slaves' stories in transcribed interviews. In the 1970s, George Rawick compiled the forty-one volume collection *American Slave: A Composite Autobiography* and made these sources broadly available to scholars and others. Just as the Southern Historical Society created its archive for the Lost Cause, these recordings became the archive of the Union Cause.[18]

The availability of historical records from the past mattered, but the present shaped the war's historical memory, including the civil rights movement. Ironically, these civil rights struggles, even black victories, advanced the Lost Cause; white Southerners embraced the Confederacy and its symbols in a backlash against school integration and the civil rights movement. During the 1950s and 1960s, the Confederate battle flag reemerged with its design prominently displayed on Southern state flags. John M. Coski chronicled *The Confederate Battle Flag: America's Most Embattled Emblem* (2005) and its history from the end of the Civil War through recent controversies about its placement in public spaces. According to Coski, "During the height of the civil rights movement in the 1950s and 1960s, [it] became the opposing symbol to the Stars and Stripes." While civil rights marchers carried American flags, "Segregationists often played into the protesters' strategy by taunting them with Confederate flags." Ironically, white Southerners who used the Confederate battle flag as a symbol of resistance to civil rights both re-enforced Confederate memory and revived the memory of the Union Cause. Connecting the Confederate flag to efforts to oppose civil rights reminded people of a failed nation that defended slavery. Even today, when the people attack the Confederate flag, they justify their action as much on its use as a symbol of resistance to civil rights as its status as a banner of a slave republic. Despite the controversies over this emblem, the fact that over one hundred and fifty years after the war ended, decades after the civil rights movement's major successes, this flag still flies demonstrated the surprising resilience of the Lost Cause in American memory.[19]

Fifty years ago, the battle between consensus history and civil rights politics came to a head at the centennial of the Civil War in the early 1960s. Much of the enthusiasm for this commemoration emanated from Cold War fears and the centennial's perceived ability to enhance American nationalism. Two factors worked against this "consensus history" of the Civil War, one racial and the other sectional.

Racially African Americans' agitation and actions together with their white allies allowed the civil rights movement to emerge from its status as a fringe movement to a political force in American society. In response, white Southerners embraced their Confederate identity to oppose the civil rights movement as demonstrated by their renewed allegiance to the Confederate flag. Likely there were many Americans in both sections who would have liked a commemoration that highlighted reunion and reconciliation, but current events made sectional harmony difficult to achieve. Robert J. Cook examined what he termed the *Troubled Commemoration: The American Civil*

War Centennial, 1961–1965 (2007) and explained why the centennial failed. Initially, it looked promising; the government created a commission as early as 1957 to organize a national commemoration chaired by Major General Ulysses S. Grant III, a retired army officer and grandson of the Civil War hero. The plan called for what Cook labeled a "Cold War pageant" and "a weapon of the cultural cold war—a popular heritage bonanza that would reinforce government calls for civic activism and vigilance by educating Americans about the brave deeds and deeply held values of their nineteenth-century precursors." This effort proved successful, and individual states, even in the former Confederacy, created commissions. Some white Southerners believed that this presented an opportunity to re-embrace their Confederate identity as part of their rejection of federal actions, as limited as these might have been, to expand civil rights.[20]

The commission's efforts began to unravel when South Carolinians invited the national Civil War Centennial Commission (CWCC) to hold its annual meeting during the Fort Sumter attack commemoration by the South Carolina state commission. While no African Americans participated in the national commission, there were black state commissioners, including the prominent historian John Hope Franklin. The New Jersey Commission included an African American woman, and this group decided to attend the South Carolina event; however, the hotel that planned to host the commissioners refused to house her because of her race. In response, Northern officials threatened to boycott the meeting. According to Cook, "Governor Otto Kerner of Illinois said simply, 'We cannot ignore the fundamental precept of equality for all people and still represent Illinois, the state of Abraham Lincoln.'" President Kennedy announced that federal funds could not be used to host an event at a segregated facility. Eventually, the meeting took place at the integrated Charleston Naval Base. Concurrently, Southern states formed their own "Confederate States Centennial Conference." In the aftermath of Charleston, a battle between liberals and conservatives on the commission led to the resignation of its leadership, including General Grant. In his place, Kennedy appointed Allan Nevins chair of the commission. Controversy continued with Nevins at the helm; not surprisingly, these new difficulties involved the commemoration of the Emancipation Proclamation. White Southerners and African Americans understood that this commemoration might be used to advance civil rights. Ultimately, white Northerners and white Southerners made sure that African American attempts to shape the message of the emancipation commemoration failed.[21]

African Americans and their allies were not silent during the centennial, however. In fact, many protested the centennial because its themes spoke more to the Cold War and not to the civil rights movement or even the Civil War. According to David W. Blight in *American Oracle: The Civil War in the Civil Rights Era* (2011), African American journalists deplored the centennial; "the black press, as well as many African American intellectuals, had been brutally critical of the centennial and its purpose from its beginning." One journalist protested the event and "accused the 'ex-Confederacy' of 'still attempting to win the peace' by 'bringing the Lost Cause before the nation'" One contemporary historian rejected this centennial in an address on "Negro History Week" protesting "that the South had 'captured' the CWCC." As a result, "the Civil War we hear about today is a fight of brave brother against brave brother, with both separately but equally righteous in their causes. There was an underlying issue in the war—slavery. The leaders of the Confederacy were fighting to perpetuate a slaveholding, slave breeding, slave driving society, based on the shameful belief that one man could own another." None of this message became part of the official centennial proceedings or was emphasized at its commemorations. The Lost Cause as historical memory was down, but not out. Memory changed slowly.[22]

Despite many obstacles, an African American, Martin Luther King, made the most enduring statement on the Union Cause during this era. Blight reminded Americans of the lesser-known opening of Martin Luther King's "I Have a Dream Speech" delivered from the steps of the Lincoln Memorial in 1963. The "I have a dream metaphor" resonates even today, but so might King's opening lines that resonated in Civil War memory. "Five score years ago, a great American, in whose symbolic shadow we stand today, signed the Emancipation Proclamation. This momentous decree came as a great beacon of light of hope to millions of Negro slaves who had been seared in the flames of withering injustice. It came as a joyous daybreak to end the long night of their captivity." While King remembered the past, he understood the necessity of emphasizing the present. "But one hundred years later, the Negro still is not free. One hundred years later, the life of the Negro is still sadly crippled by the manacles of segregation and the chains of discrimination." In the present, political and civil rights shared equal importance with the economic and social status of black Americans. "One hundred years later, the Negro lives on an island of poverty in the midst of a vast ocean of material prosperity. One hundred years later, the Negro is still languishing in the corners of American society and finds himself an exile in his own land." The Civil Rights and Voting Rights acts addressed some, but not all, of these problems: a failure that explains why Americans still fight the Civil War in historical memory.[23]

Robert Penn Warren produced what was likely the most elegant expression of white Civil War memory in *Legacy of the Civil War: Meditation on the Centennial* (1961). "The Civil War is our only 'felt' history—history lived in the national imagination. That is not to say that the War is always, and by all men, felt in the same way. Quite the contrary. But this fact is an index to the very complexity, depth, and fundamental significance of the event. It is an overwhelming and vital image of human, and national, experience." Warren, a white Southerner, placed both Union and slavery at the centerpiece of understanding the war, though he qualified his view by recognizing that others might not agree. "However we may assess the importance of slavery in the tissue of 'causes' of the Civil War—in relation to secession, the mounting Southern debt to the North, economic rivalry, Southern fear of encirclement, Northern ambitions, and cultural collisions—slavery looms up mountainously and cannot be talked away." While he acknowledged slavery as the war's cause, Warren nevertheless repeated a notion strong in Lost Cause circles: that of white Southerners' relief when slavery ended. "Many a Southerner, in one part of the soul at least, must have felt much as did the planter's wife who referred to the War as the time Mr. Lincoln set her free." Little evidence existed of the Southern Civil War generation's praise for emancipation and gratitude toward Lincoln. Like so many other white Southerners of his day, Warren was not partial to abolitionists. "Who can deny that, or deny that often they labored nobly? But who can fail to be disturbed and chastened by the picture of the joyful mustering of the darker forces of our nature in that just cause?" Slaves might not be disturbed by any force, dark or light, that ended slavery. Oddly, this notion of the abolitionists being both right and wrong resonated in the twenty-first century, long after one would have considered it out of fashion, a remnant of a long-gone era.[24]

Warren did not directly discuss memory, though he characterized it when he described the war's legacy. According to Warren, the South got the "Great Alibi" that "turns defeat into victory, defects into virtues." Warren claimed that "the most painful and costly consequences of the Great Alibi are found, of course, in connection with race." He made a direct connection to the present when he cited current events such as school integration and asked, "Does the man who, in the relative safety of mob anonymity, stands howling vituperation at a little Negro girl being conducted into a school building, feel himself at one with those gaunt, barefoot, whiskery scarecrows who fought it out, breast to breast, to the death, at the Bloody Angle at Spotsylvania, in May 1964?" Warren connected the past and the present, invoking the greatest icon of the Lost Cause. "Can the man howling in the mob imagine General R. E. Lee, CSA, shaking hands with Orval Faubus, Governor of Arkansas?" Similarly, Warren identified Northerners' "psychological heritage," for our purposes memory, as the "Treasury of Virtue" that is not "as comic or vicious as the Great Alibi, but it is equally unlovely. It may even be, in the end, equally corrosive of national, and personal, integrity." Warren believed that "the Northerner, with his Treasury of Virtue, feels redeemed by history . . . for all sins past, present, and future, freely given by the hand of history." Ironically, he rooted his notion of redemption in Northern memory. "The Northerner . . . being human, tends to rewrite history to suit his own deep needs," not something that seemed true in twentieth-century Civil War memory. Warren identified many elements of the Union Cause, including saving the Union and freeing the slaves as part of the virtuous cause. In contrast, he cited the racism of Northerners at the beginning of the war, the limited nature of the Emancipation

Proclamation, the failure of the Fourteenth and Fifteenth Amendments, and the corruption and excesses of the Gilded Age as tarnishing Northern morality. Warren demonstrated that even when an individual understood slavery's fundamental importance to Civil War memory, supported integration, or rejected yelling at little girls integrating schools, the Union Cause still came up short because of the reunited nation's failures.[25]

Part of the disconnect between evolving Civil War interpretations regarding how most Americans remembered the war can be explained by the critical role played by school texts; a middle-aged American's Civil War memory frequently reflected the textbooks written decades before, a vestige of high school or college history classes. As a result, the Lost Cause prospered long after scholars questioned it. Examining various editions of *The American Pageant* (1956–2015), a popular high school text, demonstrated how long it takes for newer interpretations to shape textbooks. Slavery and the coming of the Civil War received the same treatment in the first (1956), second (1961), and the third editions (1966); in fact, the author Thomas Bailey, distinguished diplomatic historian, used the same words on the same pages in the 1956 and 1961 editions. The civil rights movement's initial successes had not affected this study. While Bailey maintained that "the black curse of Negro Slavery could not be successfully white-washed, however, much Southerners might idealize the singing, dancing, and banjo strumming of the colored 'Old Folks at Home'"; he also presented Southerners' view of slavery's benefits without any critical analysis. In this retelling, "uprooted Africans, despite the harshness of their lot, often gave signs of contentment and even happiness." Despite this rather rosy portrait of slavery, Bailey accepted that "floggings were common." He blunted any indignation that this might provoke by arguing that "savage beatings were normally not administered without some provocation," but he failed to explain what these men and women might have done to deserve such treatment. His views of slavery shaped his Civil War memory. When Bailey described abolitionism, he characterized those that demanded immediate emancipation as "Garrisonian Hotheads" who "hastened freeing the slave by a number of years. But . . . at the price of a civil conflict which tore apart the social and economic fabric of the South." He emphasized the costs of the war—"a million whites . . . killed or disabled before some four million slaves could be freed"— suggesting that this was a bad bargain. This interpretation reflected the view of the Civil War when the author joined the Stanford faculty in the 1930s. In this case, a historian writing a textbook at the Civil War's centennial summarized the war based on views formed thirty years earlier for students who might remember the war in this way for another thirty years.[26]

Ironically, the passage of the Civil Rights Act and improving race relations did not create any momentum for the Union Cause, partly because as racial attitudes changed so too did American attitudes toward war. During the 1960s, America went to war itself with over a number of issues, including civil rights at home and an overseas war in Vietnam. The same year the Voting Rights Act passed, large numbers of ground troops deployed to defend South Vietnam from the communist North. Three years later, in late January 1968, a communist offensive during Tet—Vietnamese New Year—convinced many Americans that the United States faced imminent defeat. In April of that year, Martin Luther King's assassination ignited American cities. In June 1968, Robert F. Kennedy, John F. Kennedy's brother and a Democratic candidate for the presidency, succumbed to wounds suffered at the hands of an assassin. In August, protesters demonstrated, and police rioted at the Democratic Party Convention in Chicago making a shambles of the nominating process. In addition to these single events, young Americans created what they considered a counterculture that protested many different aspects of society, militarism, racism, sexism, and traditional values. The women's movement also emerged as part of this upheaval. The sum of all these events affected Civil War memory.[27]

Despite all of the momentum on the left, the Republicans led by Richard Nixon won the presidency in November 1968, partly as a reaction against the counterculture and violent disorder. Though Nixon promised peace with honor, he delivered neither. The United States and the North Vietnamese came to terms and ended their war, which allowed the United States to leave and the communists to rest their military. Two years later, South Vietnam fell to the North Vietnamese army and their southern communist allies. Between the election of Nixon in 1968 and the fall of South Vietnam in 1975 events conspired to sour Americans on the nation and its war. American soldiers overseas murdered villagers in My Lai; National Guardsmen murdered students at Kent State. Meanwhile, leaked Pentagon Papers revealed the deception associated with all of these murders and all of these war deaths. The era ended when Nixon resigned in the wake of the Watergate cover-up of the dirty tricks engineered by his reelection committee. Though most white Americans rejected the notion of African American inferiority, they also questioned American wars and the nation that fought them. As a result, the Union Cause did not benefit from changing racial views during the immediate aftermath of the Vietnam War.[28]

In 1979, four years after the fall of Saigon, Bailey, and his coauthor, David M. Kennedy, completed the sixth edition of *The American Pageant* (1979) and revamped the treatment of slavery. Slaves seemed less content, though Bailey and Kennedy still believed that slaves' provocations prompted savage beatings. The authors included an illustration documenting the horror of the international slave trade, and an illustration of a family sold on the auction block, reminding the reader of the horrors of the domestic slave trade. While Bailey and Kennedy condemned some of the worst features of slavery, they still divided abolitionists into reasonable gradualists and militant immediatists, though now they recognized the role of African American abolitionists in this struggle. Despite their post–civil rights sensibilities, the same language involving the cost of white lives to free black Americans remained unchanged from earlier editions. In the aftermath of Vietnam, discontent with war overcame changed racial views, and the Civil War seemed unnecessary, and the Union Cause questionable.[29]

Despite the persistence of elements of the Lost Cause, scholars began to look more closely at Civil War memory; Vietnam made Americans more cynical and more aware of how they might be manipulated. In 1973, Rollin G. Osterweis published *The Myth of the Lost Cause, 1865–1900*. Two years later, John Simpson described Southern Civil War memory as "The Cult of the Lost Cause." These scholars began the golden age of Lost Cause scholarship discussed in Chapter 1.[30]

It might have been skepticism about military leadership in the face of military defeat that led to a new focus on the common soldier. Decades earlier, Bell I. Wiley pioneered common soldier studies with his groundbreaking examination of *The Life of Johnny Reb: The Common Soldier of the Confederacy* (1943) and *The Life of Billy Yank: The Common Soldier of the Union* (1952). Wiley focused first on Confederate soldiers because his family had supported the South. In fact, when he examined U.S. soldiers, he "was fearful that my long attachment to Johnny Reb would prevent my treating his foe with the sympathy he deserved and fair historical treatment required." It would be hard to imagine scholars today suggesting that they would be challenged to treat Union soldiers fairly because they were more attached to their Southern counterparts. When Wiley wrote his book, the Lost Cause dominance in the American mind made this statement acceptable. Wiley's books compared the same aspects of Union and Confederate soldiers' daily lives, including what they wore and ate, and how they played and prayed. He did not devote space to soldiers' motivations, a subject that dominated scholarly debates in recent decades. When Wiley found differences between Union and Confederate soldiers, these often reflected Lost Cause ideas; for example, Union Soldiers "were not as deeply concerned with the war as Johnny Reb" because "the war was incidental to Northern life, while to southerners it was of transcendent importance." Echoing Lost Cause notions of the martial qualities of each side, Wiley suggested that "Johnny Rebs seem to have taken more readily to soldiering" partly because of the "strength in Southern society of the martial spirit," while Union soldiers demonstrated more "machinelike efficiency." African American soldiers received little attention. When Wiley discussed their performance, he quoted a Union officer who believed that with "long and careful discipline" a good black regiment was as good as a poor white one. The fact that Wiley, a student of Ulrich B. Phillips, even acknowledged black regiments represented a radical revision to Americans' memory of the common soldier.[31]

What was remarkable about this aspect of Civil War memory was how long it took for another historian to follow up on Wiley's works that appeared in 1943 and 1952, respectively. It was not until the 1980s that scholars re-examined the common soldier.

Partly, this might have been due to the notion that people thought that Wiley had said all that could be said. More likely, the Vietnam War affected Civil War studies; Americans revisited the Civil War after they achieved some distance for this divisive conflict. When scholars returned to this subject, cynicism about military leadership prompted interest in these neglected common soldiers. Moreover, Vietnam expanded the nature of these studies to include soldier motivation, because many believed that soldiers in Vietnam consisted of unmotivated American draftees. Gerald F. Linderman's *Embattled Courage: The Experience of Combat in the American Civil War* (1987) reflected post-Vietnam sensibilities and presumed a fundamental alienation between soldiers and the homefront based on the experience of combat. Union and Confederate soldiers abandoned their prewar ideals; civilians did not. Linderman viewed the generation of 1860 through the experience of the generation of 1960 and assumed that Civil War soldiers lost their ideological commitment to their cause.[32]

Not everyone agreed with Linderman, partly because the legacy of Vietnam influenced his views. Earl Hess disagreed and believed that soldiers' motivations reflected antebellum values and ideology including those in the title of his book—*Liberty, Virtue and Progress* (1997). Soldiers' values and ideology allowed them to persevere through the harsh reality of Civil War military service, a subject he developed in *The Union Soldier in Battle: Enduring the Ordeal of Combat* (1997). Hess focused on Union soldiers alone; no historian compared soldiers from both sides until James M. McPherson published *For Cause and Comrades: Why Americans Fought in the Civil War* (1997). The first part of the book title answers the second. Both sides fought for their comrades; each side fought for a cause. The notion that Confederate soldiers fought for a cause had always been part of Civil War memory. This evolution in common soldiers' studies began a longer-term effort to identify a distinct Union Cause that these men remembered.[33]

Studying the common soldier also made a difference in the purely military history aspect of the war. To many Americans, Civil War history meant specifically military history, particularly the importance of generals and other leaders. Contemporary battlefield studies include the story of common soldiers; among the many studies that used this new perspective were Joseph T. Glatthaar's *The March to the Sea and Beyond: Sherman's Troops in the Savannah and Carolinas Campaign* (1985); John J. Hennessy's *Return to Bull Run: The Campaign and Battle of Second Manassas* (1993), Stephen W. Sears's *To the Gates of Richmond: The Peninsula Campaign* (1992) and *Landscape Turned Red: The Battle of Antietam* (1983); Harry W. Pfanz's *Gettysburg: The Second Day* (1987) and many others. No military history book written since the 1980s could neglect common soldiers' perspectives.[34]

Most of the books cited in the previous paragraph examined eastern battles as opposed to those in the West, another bias encouraged by advocates of Confederate historical memory. In this sense of the word, the West included operations in and around the Mississippi River and its tributaries, later a region identified as the Midwest. Eastern generals became heroes of the Lost Cause partly because leading advocates of the Lost Cause were Virginians like Jubal Early. It is also true that eastern Confederate generals won more victories than their western counterparts. Ironically, even advocates of the Union Cause tended to favor eastern battles, though these engagements did not represent the Union army at its finest. As a result of neglecting the West, Grant's great victories never received the attention they deserved, explaining why Grant earned less recognition as a general than Lee as described in Chapter 2.

Thomas L. Connelly revitalized interest in the western theater by writing two studies on the most important army in the West, the Army of Tennessee. Connelly also studied Robert E. Lee's place in Civil War Memory. While Connelly's research agenda might seem to be disjointed, he identified a relationship between disinterest in the western theater and devotion to Lee. In the first volume of his study of the Army of Tennessee 1861–1862 published in 1967, he linked the neglect of the western theater with the deification of Lee. Connelly's best-known and most controversial work on Lee examined the "Marble Man" created by Lost Cause advocates, the perfect Christian, the perfect general, the perfect man. Connelly rejected this portrayal and emphasized Lee's human frailties and described him as "a troubled man, convinced that he had failed as a prewar career officer, parent, and moral individual." In addition to affecting Lee in memory, Connelly's work opened the door for more scholarly study of the West; the Battle of Shiloh, the war's bloodiest two days, is among the most significant omissions addressed in the books published in the1970s. When the western campaigns received some of the same attention the east received, the Union Cause benefited because of the Union army's military success in this theater and Confederate failures. Decades later, Alan T. Nolan in *Lee Considered: General Robert E. Lee and Civil War History* (1991) produced a comprehensive attack on Lee in memory and deconstructs what he termed the "mythic" Lee. Completed one year after the one-hundred and twenty-fifth anniversary of the war's end, Nolan assessed Lee's stance on slavery, his military decision-making, his postwar life, among other things, and decided that the Lee of memory was not the Lee of history—a Marble Man no more. Nothing embodies the power of the Lost Cause in Civil War memory more than the unquestioned acceptance of Lee as an American hero for more than a century after his efforts to destroy the Union, to ensure the survival of a slave republic, failed.[35]

While neglecting the western theater served the Lost Cause, a more important omission existed in the systematic neglect of African American soldiers. Black Americans wrote about their service: Du Bois's first section of *Black Reconstruction* and the prominent black historian Benjamin Quarles's *The Negro in the Civil War* (1953) and *Lincoln and the Negro* (1962). Unfortunately, only when white historians wrote about black service did it become a part of mainstream memory. Dudley T. Cornish's *The Sable Arm: Negro Troops in the Union Army, 1861–1865* (1956) represented the first comprehensive study of black soldiers' Civil War service written by a white historian. Like all Civil War memory, this study reflected a present interest in black military service. Cornish cited recent history "the Korean war" and the "final achievement of integration, and an end to segregated service in the several branches of the armed forces of the United States" as one reason that his study mattered. Cornish, a World War II veteran, discussed African American soldiers' actions on the battlefield and their struggles against discrimination. Other studies followed but a significant gap exists between this study and the next comprehensive examination of black soldiers. Forty years elapsed before Noah Trudeau fully documented their service, in *Like Men of War: Black Troops in the Civil War 1862–1865* (1998). Historians wrote studies of black soldiers: in fact, there were a number of excellent, more specialized, studies published in the 1990s; Joseph T. Glatthaar's *Forged in Battle: The Civil War Alliance of Black Soldiers and White Officers* (1990) is recognized as the pioneering study on black troops in this era. Glatthaar examined the relationship between soldiers and their leaders and concluded that though white officers maintained their prejudices they generally enjoyed good relations with their African American subordinates. Other scholars studied African Americans in the navy, black Louisianans, individual regiments and their battles. The 1990s produced enormously important works on black soldiers in the Civil War, but only after decades of scholarly neglect.[36]

Ironically this interest had little to do with written works, but emerged from the contemporary dominance of films as an art form. The success of the movie *Glory*— the story of one black regiment, the Fifty-Fourth Massachusetts, and its ill-fated charge on Fort Wagner, South Carolina—finally shifted attention to black soldiers and their legacy. The movie's genesis owed much to the fact that the Fifty-Fourth and its commander Robert Gould Shaw received extensive treatment from several sources. Peter Burchard wrote about the Fifty-Fourth in *One Gallant Rush: Robert Gould Shaw and His Brave Black Regiment* (1965). Shaw, who died at Wagner, left behind his letters; another white officer who survived wrote a regimental history of this unit, a documentary trail unusual for a black regiment. The people of Massachusetts built a monument to this unit in Boston, another rarity for a black regiment. All of these factors made the Fifty-Fourth the best-known African American regiment, sometimes the only known black regiment. Despite the success of this Oscar-winning movie, it has been more than two decades since moviemakers made black soldiers central to a Civil War movie's plot line suggesting that, at least in movies, it remained a white war.[37]

Despite amnesia about African American soldiers, the military experience of African Americans survived as the best documented aspect of the black Civil War experience. A concerted effort by a group of scholars at the University of Maryland recovered other aspects of this story. The Freedmen and Southern Society Project began in 1976 with a goal of finding and making accessible primary source documentation on emancipation and black military service. The critical word was accessible. Many of these sources were available at the National Archives in Washington, D.C. By transcribing and editing the 50,000 selected documents the Freedmen and Southern Society Project ensured that they were used by scholars. If there was a pattern in memory, archives and document collections mattered. The availability of the Southern Historical Society, the *Official Records of the War of the Rebellion*, and slave narratives of the Works Progress Administration all shaped Civil War memory. Cataloguing the memory of wartime emancipation and the black Civil War experience relied on the invaluable work of the Freedmen and Southern Society Project and its dedicated staff.[38]

Civil War memory neglected not only black Americans, but American women of all colors as well. This omission proved particularly ironic because Confederate women led the way in articulating and advocating the Lost Cause. Only when women and their lives became part of a larger historical narrative did women in the Civil War receive much attention. The women's movement of the 1960s prompted an interest in Civil War era women in two ways. First, as the status of women advanced in the present, people noticed women in the past. Second, as women advanced in the professions, they became historians and studied women. As early as 1959, Agatha Young documented *The Women in the Crisis: Women of the North in the Civil War* (1959). Seven years later, Mary Elizabeth Massey's *Bonnet Brigades* (1966) examined women in both sections. Despite the authors' different concentrations, both argued that the war expanded women's roles in society and wartime conditions allowed them to undertake tasks that they had not done or been allowed to do before the war, not a surprising finding during an era in which women struggled to redefine their roles outside the household. The most influential study surveyed Southern women who as a group had always received the lion's share of attention in Civil War memory. Anne Firor Scott in *The Southern Lady: From Pedestal to Politics* (1970) found that the war allowed women to enter both the workplace and eventually, as the decades passed, politics, through their participation in Progressive Era reform movements. Scott asserted that she studied "ladies" suggesting that during this first phase of Civil War women's history, most studies focused on upper and middle-class white women.[39]

In the next phase, scholars examined the effect of class and race on women's Civil War experience. George Rable in *Civil Wars: Women and the Crisis of Southern Nationalism* (1989) assessed how different classes of white Confederate women responded to the Civil War. He asserted that the war challenged some of their traditional roles; for example, when poor women petitioned the government for relief, they acted outside the home. After the war, traditional ideas of white Southern women's place reasserted itself, partly because women accepted their domestic roles. In contrast, Victoria Bynum's examination of what she termed "unruly women" in *Unruly Women: The Politics of Social and Sexual Control in the Old South* (1992) focused on those through whom "we can better grasp the impact of race and class on Southern women's behavior." Not surprisingly, Bynum viewed these women's action as part of a rejection of male rule and the dominant patriarchy. Race and the role of black women represented the last frontier in Civil War studies; Jacqueline Jones examined their Civil War experience as part of a broader study of black working women entitled *Labor of Love, Labor of Sorrow: Black Women, Work, and the Family, from Slavery to the Present* (1985).[40]

The last and most recent development in Civil War studies has been the realization that women's experience in the war included gender, evolving ideas of what men and women thought a woman or a man could or should do or be. One of the pioneering books in this field, LeeAnn Whites's *The Civil War as a Crisis in Gender, Augusta, Georgia, 1860–1890* (1995) examined one city, Augusta, Georgia, through the war and its aftermath. The crisis of gender she identified affected both men and women. Men had always defined themselves as men based on their relationships with their subordinates including women, children, and slaves. The end of slavery challenged this notion of dominance in one way, while hardships at home both during and after the war pushed women outside of the home and their domestic sphere. When the war was over, part of their commemorative efforts focused on reconstructing men's gender identity. Drew Gilpin Faust's *Mothers of Invention: Women of the Slaveholding South in the American Civil War* (1996) depicted "the half of the Confederacy's master class that was female." The war forced these women to engage "in a process of negotiation about what womanhood would come to mean in circumstances of a dramatic upheaval." Faust contended that these women turned against the war because of the Confederate government's policies, including conscription, suggesting that these women were not the Lost Cause stalwarts portrayed in Civil War memory. Faust identified the effect of her present and past when she explained that "the experiences of my own youth have not permitted me to forget how the disruptions of prevailing public values can create the opportunity for new choices within the seemingly most private aspects of individual lives." Gender studies reflected women's realization that despite changes in society that allowed women to become, among other things, historians, ideas about what women should be limited women.[41]

The diversity of women's experience in the war, divided as they were by section, race, and gender, meant that one of the most significant contributions to gender study was a collection of essays, *Divided Houses: Gender and the Civil War* (1992) edited by Catherine Clinton and Nina Silber. Among the topics it highlighted masculinity, what society expected of men and what they expected of themselves, including the complex intersection of race and gender as highlighted by the disparate views of black and white men. Gender analysis represented a critical way that Civil War memory studies became more complex because how people described their experiences, how they remembered, has always been filtered through the language of gender. As much attention as has been given to this issue, more should be done on memory and masculinity.[42]

The last decade of the 1990s included a return to documenting what women had done in the war as opposed to gendered analysis; however, this story included the battlefield and military camps. Awareness of modern women soldiers prompted a reassessment of the Civil War. Women integrated into the armed services in the 1970s; however, progress accepting women as equals took time. During the First Gulf War, in 1991, women served in large numbers on the battlefield. Women died, were taken as prisoners, and played other prominent roles in this conflict. In its aftermath, women flew in combat and served on warships. As a result of how women performed in recent operations, virtually all combat roles have been opened to women. In the studies produced in the decade after these changes, scholars and others explored the lives of women who served as spies, soldiers, nurses, and camp followers. Despite the availability of a collection of letters written by Sarah Wakeman, a soldier in the 153rd New York, it would have been hard to imagine Americans remembering the hundreds of women who served as soldiers in the Civil War if women's roles in the present had not changed. Now that gay men and women can serve openly in the military, more might be done on this issue, but only if the evidence documenting these soldiers' lives existed. Memory relied on someone leaving their memories behind to find, people like Sarah Wakeman; this type of evidence might not exist for gay Civil War soldiers.[43]

Historians and others debated the type of wars these men and women fought. Scholars examined the Civil War and compared it to "Total Wars," such as World War II. Total War has many definitions but at its basic levels, it was the total mobilization of society, to totally destroy enemy society, with little distinction between soldiers and civilians. Scholars began to make this comparison immediately after World War II; not surprisingly, Sherman's march came under greater scrutiny. In an article on "General William T. Sherman and Total War," John Bennett Walters argued as early as 1948 that the U.S. government recognized the laws of war and the distinction between civilians and soldiers, but that Sherman did not and was "the first of the modern generals to revert to the idea of the use of military force against the civilian population of the enemy." This interpretation was not merely military, but reflected Lost Cause advocates' indictment of Sherman's campaign. Walters described Sherman's actions as "wanton destruction and the outrages and indignities" that "created wounds which would remain sensitive for generations to come." After the Vietnam War, a war that no one would describe as total, James Reston Jr., author and journalist, made a more direct connection between the present and the past in his study *Sherman's March and Vietnam* (1984) in which his efforts to retrace Sherman's march were not about the nineteenth century but about the twentieth. According to Reston, "Sherman's soldiers and Westmoreland's [U.S. Commander in Vietnam] soldiers have important things in common." In the decades after Vietnam, historians turned away from a sole focus on Total War, without forgetting that the Civil War was terrible. Charles Royster termed the Civil War a "destructive war" in *The Destructive War: William Tecumseh Sherman, Stonewall Jackson and the Americans* (1991). Mark Grimsley argued in *The Hard Hand of War: Union Military Policy toward Southern Civilians, 1861–1865* (1995) that Union military policy evolved as the war dragged on and the Union Army treated civilians more harshly. It might have been the chronological distance from American involvement in a Total War like World War II, coupled with an understanding that even in wars not defined as "Total," such as Vietnam, civilians suffered that explained Royster and Grimsley's interpretations.[44]

If the end of the twentieth century marked the end of American war, then Civil War memory in the twenty-first century might have been different. Instead, the United States fought and continued to fight a series of wars in the aftermath of the September 11, 2001, attacks. David W. Blight's *Race and Reunion: The Civil War in American Memory* (2001) made one of the most important statements about Civil War memory within months of these watershed events. It won just about every award given to a Civil War book and constituted the penultimate statement on Civil War memory at the end of the twentieth century. On one level, this book assessed historical memory at the end of the nineteenth century, and on the other, it was a statement on historical memory at the end of the twentieth. Blight identified the link between race and reunion discussed in Chapter 3. In his view, Americans forgot slavery and race in the Civil War and that amnesia allowed them to embrace reunion and the Lost Cause. According to Blight, memory mattered to civil rights at the turn of the nineteenth century to the twentieth; African Americans loss in the battle for Civil War memory "was one part of the disaster that beset African Americans in the emerging age of Jim Crow." Specifically, defeat in the battle of memory and the victory of the Lost Cause allowed Southerners to codify white supremacy with Jim Crow and disenfranchisement laws with no interference from Northerners. Blight presents an extremely well-researched, well-written, and reasoned argument; however, I believe that Civil War memory reflected Northerners' and Southerners' racial attitudes in their end of the (nineteenth) century present. The same views prompted both Northerners' acquiescence to white Southerners' actions and shaped their Civil War memory. Through much of the century, race had little effect on Civil War memory because racial attitudes did not change. Instead, the evolution of Civil War memory reflected anxieties about the state of the union and attitudes towards the nation's wars. Once racial attitudes changed, Civil War memory changed; however, issues related to the nation and the wars it fights shaped Civil War memory even after the successes of the civil rights movement.[45]

The timing of Blight's work proved fortuitous. The election of the first black president eight years later fulfilled some of the Union Cause's promise; however, this election spurred discontent with both race and reunion, particularly because this election coincided with financial woes not seen since the Great Depression. Meanwhile, the many wars on terror prompted others to question war itself. As always, these factors shaped American Civil War memory at its one-hundred and fiftieth anniversary. Before any examination of the sesquicentennial, it is important to see how the Civil War played out in public memory, as found in monuments and at battlefields, and popular culture, such as in the movies and television programs. The question must be asked: did the Civil War in movies matter more than the Civil War in books when Americans remembered their greatest conflict?

FIVE

LANDSCAPE TURNED
WHITE: THE CIVIL WAR
IN PUBLIC MEMORY

The day a community unveiled a Civil War monument was an important memory milestone. In one particular memorial, soldiers and a sailor were prominently featured recognizing their Civil War service; behind the sculpture, a wall listed the men who served and died in the Civil War. In many ways, this monument represented a typical example of Civil War memorialization found in cities and towns across America. The memory it serves is unique. Dedicated in 1998, the African American Civil War Memorial in Washington, D.C., recognized the almost two hundred thousand black soldiers and sailors who served in the Union army and the navy. The nation's belated recognition of these men, almost at the war's sesquicentennial, told you a great deal about Civil War memory, in this case, the public memory of the war.[1]

The ongoing debate about the place of the Confederacy in public spaces after the Charleston shooting relates to broader memory trends discussed in earlier chapters including the contested nature of Civil War memory. John Bodnar in *Remaking America: Public Memory, Commemoration, and Patriotism in the Twentieth Century* (1992) provided a theoretical framework to explain how this affected Civil War memory. He observed that "public memory emerges from the intersection of official and vernacular cultural expressions." His description of vernacular memory seemed particularly applicable to the Civil War generation's activities that featured grassroots actions by disparate groups, in this case, Union and Confederate supporters.

African American Civil War Memorial, Washington D.C. (Carol M. Highsmith's America, Library of Congress, Prints and Photographs Division)

While he addressed larger issues of commemoration, he also discussed the particular experiences of the Civil War generation. "People who experienced the [Civil] [W]ar instituted a broad range of commemorative activities that viewed the wartime experience of ordinary people—the soldiers and those that grieved for them and supported them—in terms of a 'cult of sacrifice.'" Using Confederate supporters as his example, he analyzed how the vernacular Lost Cause evolved into a more official memory in Southern states due to proponents of the New South. "A rising class of southern industrialists who were anxious to resume activity with the North . . . de-emphasized commemorative activities centered on grief and sorrow for the dead and defeat itself and fostered a memory designed to speed the process of reunification." Much of the current protest against Lost Cause artifacts reflects their official status in Southern states and local jurisdictions. Thomas J. Brown appropriately assessed public memory at the state level in *Civil War Canon: Sites of Confederate Memory in South Carolina* because much of the contention over Civil War memory is at the state and local levels. Little has been written about sites of Civil War memory in Union states because Northern leaders embraced a noncontroversial, reconiliationist, Civil War memory. Bodnar attributed the origin of official memory directly to this type of attitude. "Cultural leaders and authorities at all level of society [who] . . . share a common interest in social unity, the continuity of existing institutions, and loyalty to the status quo" advocated "interpretations of the past and present reality that reduce the power of competing interests that threaten the attainment of their goals."[2]

At the federal level, efforts to create an official memory focused on national battlefields and these efforts succeeded for a time, but these were also subject to the same forces shaping broader Civil War memory, for example, changing racial attitudes. Civil War memory remained contested among various adherents of disparate vernacular memory(s) and against the official memory as espoused by both former Confederate states and the federal government. The removal of flags in South Carolina and other states reflected changes in official memory; the backlash against these actions demonstrates the power of the Lost Cause in vernacular memory. As a result, the debate over the Civil War in public memory will not soon be settled.

The battle over memory in the twenty-first century focused on monuments, partly because statuary represented the most ubiquitous marker of a Civil War public memory site. The most prominent memory issue related to these artifacts should be no surprise; it is the place of African Americans in memorials. Kirk Savage's *Standing Soldiers, Kneeling Slaves: Race, War, and Monument in Nineteenth-Century America* (1997) examined public monuments and how the "history of slavery and its violent end was told in the public space—specifically in the sculptural monuments that increasingly came to dominate public space in nineteenth-century America." Savage found neither African Americans nor emancipation central to this Civil War memorialization. Instead, he identified the common white soldier as their most prominent motif. According to Savage, "A whole new type of public monument emerged dedicated for the first time not to the illustrious hero but to the ordinary white man, the generic citizen soldier who had fought in the war on both sides." Instead of the common black soldier, Lincoln became the surrogate for memories of emancipation as demonstrated by the 1876 Emancipation Memorial. In this tableau, slaves received their freedom on their knees from Lincoln, as opposed to standing as soldiers. While Savage classified the predominant motifs in Civil War memorialization, Northern communities dispatched mostly white soldiers to war and their monuments reflected this fact. Moreover, their memorials followed a standard pattern, because they were

Courthouse and Confederate monument, Laurens, South Carolina. (Library of Congress)

Union Soldiers and Sailors Monument, Indianapolis, Indiana. (Library of Congress)

Union Soldiers and Sailors Memorial Arch, Brooklyn, New York. (Library of Congress)

mass-produced. According to an art historian, Cynthia Mills, in her introduction to *Monuments to the Lost Cause: Women, Art, and the Landscapes of Southern Memory* (2003), "The bulk of Confederate monuments were modest affairs, often purchased . . . directly from a commercial monument-making company." In fact, northerners and southerners "sometimes even commissioned [Statuary] from the same sculptors or firms, [only] distinguished by the uniform and hat." Were these monuments a function of a conscious decision for these communities, or a reflection of what was available and affordable? Artists sculpted individual statues for the elite; the generic, mass-produced, white common-soldier statue met the needs of hundreds of grieving communities.[3]

In contrast, African American soldiers were sometimes, albeit rarely, memorialized. Boston Common hosted the best-known commemoration, a bronze relief sculpture memorializing Robert Gould Shaw and his regiment—the Fifty-Fourth Massachusetts Infantry. Martin H. Blatt, Thomas J. Brown, and Donald Yacovone edited a collection of essays entitled *Hope and Glory: Essays on the Legacy of the Fifty-Fourth Massachusetts Regiment* (2001) that included chapters on this monument. While this monument honored the commander and his men, Shaw's image on horseback constituted the center of the sculpture suggesting to some that this is more of a memorial to a white commander and not his black soldiers. David Blight gave the artist, Augustus Saint-Gaudens, more credit because he described it as a "masterpiece, with its images of twenty-three black U.S. soldiers, their individuality and collective purpose captured almost miraculously in that relief." Looking at all Civil War memorials, only a handful featured black soldiers, including Civil War memorials in Brooklyn, New York, and Cleveland, Ohio. Later, the African American community built its own memorials to black military service in Norfolk, Virginia, and Frankfort, Kentucky.[4]

Not surprisingly, white soldiers' statues dominated the Southern landscape. As discussed in earlier chapters, white women sponsored many of these monuments to Confederate soldiers and their service. Cynthia Mills and Pamela H. Simpson edited a collection that examined women's efforts and the various stages of Southern Civil War monuments. According to Mills, "In the years immediately after the war . . . the cemetery was the focus of memorialization. With little money available, remembrance often took a modest, local form such as small shafts or obelisks in graveyards" as part of postwar "commemorative efforts [that] centered on the respectful burial of the dead and the creation of mourning rituals." As described in earlier chapters, Ladies Memorial Associations provided the initial impetus for Confederate monuments to memorialize the Confederate dead and the missing. Later, the UDC took charge and "the emphasis moved from mourning the dead to promoting the positive values of the Civil War effort." In this new stage, statues honored leading Confederate figures, for example, Robert E. Lee on Monument Avenue in Richmond dedicated in 1890; other Confederate leaders subsequently joined Lee. These women did not merely commemorate the Confederacy in its former capital; instead, they sponsored memorials in cities and town across the South. In the twentieth century, the commemorative focus changed. In 1918, the UDC erected the "Monument to Confederate Women" in Baltimore, an effort to shape the landscape in a Union state. Demonstrating the centrality of the faithful slave to the Lost Cause narrative, the UDC planned monuments to faithful slaves, particularly the figure of the "black mammy"—the slave who cared for her master's children. The UDC led the effort to place a memorial to the Confederate dead at Arlington National Cemetery in 1914; this sculpture included two African Americans, one a black mammy and the other a faithful slave who followed his master to war. The mammy stereotype represented one of the most powerful legacies of slavery. At the same time that Americans constructed this statue, they ate Aunt Jemima pancakes that consciously sold themselves as the product of a slave mammy. Maurice M. Manning's *Slave in a Box: The Strange Career of Aunt Jemima* (1998) captured the enduring nature of this iconography.[5]

Like much of Civil War memory, in the decades after the civil rights movement, rejecting the Lost Cause included challenging its monuments. In Richmond, Virginia officials added African American tennis player Arthur Ashe to Monument Avenue's

Confederate Memorial, Baltimore, Maryland, a Union slave state. (Library of Congress)

President Wilson looks on as the commander in chief of the United Confederate Veterans, Bennett H. Young, speaks at the dedication of the Confederate monument at Arlington National Cemetery in 1914. (Library of Congress)

Lost Cause landscape; recently in New Orleans, officials decided to remove Confederate icons like Robert E. Lee. Monuments remained a central locus of Civil War memory battles because when Southern states situated memorials on public land, they represented an "official" memory. When enough state or local residents rejected that memory, and its place in public spaces, removal seemed inevitable. Removing these symbols did not end the debate because of vernacular memory's power; just as African Americans and others in the Southern states had retained their allegiance to the federal cause, others accepted the tenets of the Lost Cause suggesting that the war over Civil War memory would not soon end.[6]

Civil War monuments may be divisive because they usually memorialized the dead of one side, battlefields less so because they might be used to commemorate both sides' wartime actions. Ironically, these places where Americans killed each other facilitated a reconciliationist narrative. If a national, official memory of the Civil War emerged in the twentieth century, it was on the battlefield parks controlled by the federal government. Not surprisingly, the memory favored sectional reconciliation, particularly at the expense of remembering slavery and African Americans. The most famous preserved battlefields featured white soldiers in battles with one another, such as Gettysburg, Antietam, and Shiloh. In contrast, other than Petersburg, most battlefields that commemorated black soldiers' wartime action were either lost or maintained by Southern states. As a result, the best-known Civil War sites of memory favored a white reconciliationist theme.

Despite how useful it might have been to save these landscapes of common sacrifice, preserving battlefields occurred only decades after the war's end. Perhaps time needed to pass before these sites of mourning would become sites of memory. Moreover, people lived on or near Civil War battlefields, partly because armies needed roads in order to move men and supplies, as they traveled toward places of strategic importance featuring roads and railroad terminals common to urban areas. Converting these areas to peaceful and profitable purposes might have been percived as more useful than retaining them as battlefields. To protect commemorative landscapes required a conscious effort to set aside this land and additional resources to transform these properties. The major battlefields that exist today were a product of efforts to preserve these spaces. Timothy B. Smith identified what he considered *The Golden Age of Battlefield Preservation: The Decade of the 1890s and the Establishment of America's First Five Military Parks* (2008). Smith recognized different phases of what he terms "generations of conservation." Initially a local issue, battlefield preservation affected a few sites; veterans and local citizens would mark specific areas, but not an entire battlefield. The second was the "golden age," and this took place in the 1890s when the largest battlefields were saved during the 1890s, including Gettysburg, Shiloh, Chickamauga, Chattanooga, and Antietam. While veterans led these efforts, they needed nonveterans' support, including politicians of both sections, to obtain the resources they required to purchase and maintain this land. Because of the need to receive support from northerners and southerners, commemorative landscapes maintained a reconciliationist memory of the war, an interpretation that shapes these parks even today. One question must be addressed: could Shiloh, Chickamauga, and Chattanooga battlefields in Southern states have been preserved without emphasizing reconciliation on these landscapes? Had veterans accepted a reconciliationist memory only to ensure that they could save places critical to their individual and collective memory?[7]

After the golden age ended, and during the next phase of battlefield development in the late 1920s and 1930s, fewer Civil War veterans survived; those who remained had less political influence. With fewer available resources and less willingness to allocate these to battlefields, smaller battlefield parks were created. Smith described these as "smaller, less monumented, and highly urbanized parks such as Fredericksburg and Spotsylvania, Kennesaw Mountain, Petersburg, Stones River, and Fort Donelson." By the last phase, in more recent decades, significant sections of battlefields were preserved; however, the Civil War Preservation Trust and private organizations led efforts to save battlefield acreage.[8]

One battlefield park was unique; Chickamauga functioned as both a relic of a Civil War battle and the training ground for modern soldiers. Bradley S. Keefer's *Conflicting Memories on the "River of Death": The Chickamauga Battlefield and the Spanish-American War, 1863–1933* (2013) chronicled this unique history—the battle, the creation of the park, and its subsequent use as a military camp, particularly in the Spanish-American War. While this development seemed similar to other battlefield preservation efforts, this park was unusual in that officials designated it as available for contemporary military training. When the United States declared war on Spain three years after the park was dedicated, volunteer soldiers trained at the facility. While most of these men never saw combat, hundreds died from diseases, such as typhoid fever. According to Keefer, the contrasting memories of Civil War and Spanish-American War veterans who had occupied this field represented a "story of what happens when one group of soldiers disagrees with another on the meaning and importance of the same piece of sacred ground." Given their different individual memories of their experiences, it would have been surprising if Civil War and Spanish-American War veterans interpreted this sacred space in the same way.[9]

Unlike Chicamaugua that has one significant study, Gettysburg generated enough scholary interest to use it as a case study in public memory. Edward Tabor Linenthal included Gettysburg in his examination of famous American battlefields in *Sacred Ground: Americans and Their Battlefields* (1993). Linenthal assessed this battlefield based on the paradigm of veneration, defilement, and redefinition that he identified in his broader study. He suggested that veneration at Gettysburg was about reconciliation. "In reunions, patriotic rhetoric on numerous ceremonial occasions,

and monument building, many Northerners—and many Southerners, as well—
came to celebrate Gettysburg as an 'American' victory. Because it was believed that
the bravery and heroism shown by the contending Union and Confederate forces
revealed a uniquely American form of commitment to a heartfelt principle." Despite
the emphasis on unity, controversies related to concerns about defilement emerged
when southerners wanted to memorialize their actions and Unionists questioned their
presence on this battlefield. Finally, in more modern times, at the one hundred and
twenty-fifth anniversary of the battle, the National Park Service (NPS) attempted to
emphasize the battle and its aftermath as demonstrating the importance of peace, by
commemorations at the Eternal Light Peace Memorial. Defilement at Gettysburg
reflected an ongoing struggle between vernacular and official memory.[10]

Carol Reardon's *Pickett's Charge in History and Memory* (1997) demonstrated how
this struggle played out among members of the Civil War generation. She documented
what happened at the battle and compared her findings to how it was remembered,
particularly as part of Gettysburg preservation efforts. Reardon highlighted aspects
of the charge's memory that were often forgotten, including disagreements among
Confederate supporters and survivors. In this instance, the book scrutinized the role
of North Carolinians in the charge. In what Reardon called the "Richmond version
of Pickett's Charge," Virginians persevered and moved forward, while North Carolinians retreated in the face of the enemy. Much of the difficulty between Virginians
and North Carolinian's memory played out over battlefield monuments and their
placement. Reardon identified Unionists refusal to honor Pickett's men, be they Virginians or North Carolinians. Unionists were prescient in their concern over efforts
to memorialize Southern soldiers on the Gettysburg battlefield; the charge became
the single most important aspect of the battle: much more crucial than Union efforts
to repel an invasion by Confederate forces.[11]

Jim Weeks in *Gettysburg: Memory, Market, and an American Shrine* (2003)
assessed not so much what veterans of the battle remembered, but how people
made money out of that memory. Weeks began with his family's childhood visits
to Gettysburg, including its tourist attractions, an essential part of his story. He
maintained that it was not only battlefield preservation that explained Gettysburg's
popularity; instead "the making of Gettysburg transpired as the nation underwent
a dramatic change in an industrializing America. Within little over three decades
after the battle, the United States became the world's greatest industrial power
and soon turned the corner from a producer to consumer nation." These trends
had a dual effect on Gettysburg. On one hand people wanted more "sacred space
to escape" commercialization; on the other hand, the nature of American society
made Gettysburg less sacred and more commercial. It might be valuable to look at
tourism and Civil War memory. Was Gettysburg a shrine to all Americans of all
sections due to the desire to attract tourists of all sections?[12]

As Gettysburg became commercial, various government entities worked to create the battle's official memory. Jennifer M. Murray, in *On a Great Battlefield: The Making, Management, and Memory of Gettysburg National Military Park, 1933–2012* (2014), traced the modern evolution of this landscape. Initially, battlefield management resided with the Gettysburg Battlefield Monument Association chartered by the state of Pennsylvania; later during the 1890s, the U.S. War Department took control and transferred operations in 1933 to the NPS. Regardless of who controlled the field, the consistent theme was reconciliation and reunion. Murray argued that Gettysburg and other preserved battlefields "became physical symbols to a reconciled nation." Murray singled out the reunions in 1913, described as a Peace Jubilee, and 1938, highlighted by the dedication of the Eternal Light Peace Memorial, for identification as critical milestones in the reconciliation process. As the NPS started to make its mark on the battlefield when it gained control over the field in 1933, none of this changed; in fact, the message of reconciliation became more central to the battlefield narrative. The NPS acquired the Gettysburg Cyclorama in 1942: the "360-degree painting depicting Pickett's Charge . . . [that] heralded the valor and courage of the Confederate assaulting forces." The battlefield's landscape centered on the cyclorama and "subsequent management decisions [were] driven by the prominence of the painting included the location of the agency's visitors center, the development of a tour route, and the introduction of various interpretive programs and mediums." As a result, "at the site of a key Union victory and the war's only notable battle in a northern state, visitors experienced a decidedly Confederate interpretation of the battle." Not surprisingly, the civil rights movement affected Gettysburg; President Lyndon Baines Johnson made a speech at the centennial of the battle in support of civil rights; however, during the same period, new Confederate monuments were welcomed to the park, and speeches at these occasions featured Lost Cause rhetoric. One speech could not change the park's overall message because it was embedded in the very landscape of remembrance.[13]

Officials at the NPS headquarters in Washington, D.C., shaped the memory of the Civil War at Gettysburg and other battlefield parks. In the last decade, the NPS engendered a number of controversies over the Gettysburg battlefield. First, the NPS partnered with a private, nonprofit entity to build a new visitor center and museum. Second, the battlefield and its landscape dramatically changed when the federal officials implemented efforts to return the field to its original, 1863, condition. As Murray explained, "While Civil War scholars largely applauded the Park Service's intention to create a historically accurate landscape, now popularly referred to as reclaiming the battlefield's 'historic integrity,' others decried the agency intention to 'rape' the battlefield they knew." Perhaps even more problematic for some, the NPS replaced many Lost Cause interpretations of this battle with a "more inclusive story-line that included exhibits on secession, slavery, and Reconstruction" that "challenged an entrenched reconciliationist narrative and underscored the pervasiveness of the Lost Cause mentality lingering in the twenty-first century." Changes in the official memory of Gettysburg and the broader Civil War that reflected the Union Cause would always be resisted because many Americans embraced the vernacular Lost Cause.[14]

Thomas A. Desjardin, in *These Honored Dead: How the Story of Gettysburg Shaped American Memory* (2004), suggested that battlefield preservation was critical to creating generations of historians, and this represented another distinct type of individual memory that shaped historical memory. Desjardin, like Weeks, reflected on his personal experiences as a child visiting with his family and as an adult working on the battlefield. After studying this battlefield, he concluded that "the truth about Gettysburg is buried beneath layer upon layer of flawed human memory and our attempts to fashion our past into something that makes our present a little easier to live in." He cited President Jimmy Carter, Egyptian president Anwar El Sadat, and Israeli prime minister Menachem Begin's 1970s visit to the battlefield as they struggled to hash out a peace accord as an example of its different meanings. According to Desjardin, Carter intended to show the cost of war and the promise of peace; the United States had overcome its bloody sectional struggle and reunited. Sadat, the soldier, was familiar with the battle and studied it closely as a military expert. Menachem Begin recited the Gettysburg Address from memory. Like everyone who comes to Gettysburg, as children or as adults, they found the meaning they were looking for; individual memory and interactions with battlefields and other public spaces represented another layer of Civil War memory that shapes historical memory.[15]

The NPS maintained more than battlefields; it also interpreted other historical sites. Paul A. Shackel in *Memory in Black and White: Race, Commemoration, and the Post-bellum Landscape* (2003) assessed its Civil War–related sites. As part of this study, Shackel assessed the portrayal of African Americans at NPS facilities. It was only in 1970 that the Park Service began to designate places significant to African American history as landmarks: prior to change, they were not considered of historical interest. After examining cases studies, including the Shaw Memorial, and Harpers Ferry—the site of John Brown's aborted slave uprising—Shackel concluded that in the contest "over how the Civil War should be remembered . . . African Americans invariably lost out to more powerful [white] interest groups," including many of those previously examined in this study. Shackel identified the reason the NPS embraced black history. In the aftermath of the civil rights movement, black Americans "gained a more powerful voice in the social and political memory of our nation." While recognizing African Americans in the Civil War's official memory represented a long overdue effort to correct the historical record, to what extent could the government referee between disparate vernacular Civil War memories? Could the government formulate a broadly accepted official memory that addressed the concerns of Americans who remember the Civil War in different ways?[16]

If battlefield studies have demonstrated anything, they have shown that the individual memories of a battlefield visit could shape how a person remembered the Civil War; however, the status of battlefields that featured black soldiers made attempts to create a more inclusive Civil War memory problematic. Some battlefield spaces were lost; Fort Wagner, the most famous disappeared, reclaimed by the sea. Others have been preserved by individual states, including Fort Pillow, Port Hudson, and Olustee. While these sites exemplified laudable efforts to preserve the legacy of the Civil War, most of these states had been part of the Confederacy and preserved these battlefields as Confederate battle sites.[17]

A visit to the Olustee battlefield in Florida demonstrated the challenges in using this space to create a more inclusive memory. The website for this state-operated facility explained that "this park commemorates the site of Florida's largest Civil War battle, which took place February 20, 1864. More than 10,000 cavalry, infantry and artillery troops fought a five-hour battle in a pine forest near Olustee. Three U.S. Colored Troops took part in the battle, including the now famous 54th Massachusetts." The battlefield visitors' center recognized black soldiers and their role in the battle. There are limits to this inclusivity. All of the monuments on the battlefield commemorate the service of Confederate soldiers. The UDC erected these memorials. Union soldiers and regiments at Olustee, either black or white, their lives and deaths, remain uncommemorated. A large cross in the local cemetery next to the battlefield represents the sole memorial to Union soldiers in this battle; it has been rumored that hundreds of missing U.S. soldiers, including African Americans, rest unmarked in this cemetery. A state report on the battlefield park in 2008 suggested that while the "mass grave of Union dead has not been definitively located [and] pinpointing the feature would not change the interpretive focus of the park, [though] it would answer one of the nagging questions about the battle and its aftermath." Currently, Confederate heritage organizations oppose a Union monument on this field, another battle in the ongoing struggle over Civil Memory in public spaces.[18]

Monuments have been built, battlefields preserved or not, but today there is a living reminder of the war; tens of thousands of contemporary Americans, uniformed and equipped like Civil War soldiers, reenact some aspect of the war, often at or near battlefields. Despite their desire to re-create the Civil War, they could not do so; no one is killed or even wounded at their gatherings. People reenact other wars, World War II, the Napoleonic Wars, and many other conflicts. Tony Horwitz in his examination of Civil War memory at the end of the twentieth century in *Confederates in the Attic: Dispatches from the Unfinished Civil War* (1998) chronicled this phenomenon.

According to Horwitz, more reenactors re-created the lives of Confederate soldiers. Confederate reenactors do not necessarily support the Lost Cause; however, it signified something about Civil War memory that the Confederacy had more men in uniform than the Union at the end of the twentieth century. In addition to reenactors, Horwitz found a number of people who were ideologically hardcore and advocated the Lost Cause version of history. Given the enduring power of the Lost Cause, the question becomes: were Confederates ever really in the attic?[19]

Reenactors connected the public and popular memory of the Civil War; they have been described as both. While they supplemented the portrayal of the war in public spaces, reenactors worked with filmmakers to re-create battles that shaped the war's popular memory. While historians cited in this chapter described personal visits to battlefields as critical to their Civil War memory, movies and other types of popular memory have exercised more impact on more people and, therefore, this phenomenon deserves its own examination. Until recently, few Americans knew about North Carolina's Fort Fisher, its importance in the Civil War, and the participation of black troops in this crucial Union victory. The movie *Lincoln* (2012) highlighted this critical battle—one of the largest land-sea battles in U.S. history; two black soldiers who were on their way to Fort Fisher spoke with Lincoln at the beginning of the movie. One scene, believed to be fictitious, in one movie, informed more Americans about this key final battle than the state historic site in North Carolina dedicated to its memory. Understanding the complex ways popular memory shaped memory is the subject of the next chapter.[20]

SIX

ROMANCE OR REUNION: THE CIVIL WAR IN POPULAR MEMORY

While the first monument to black troops honored the Fifty-Fourth Massachusetts Infantry in 1897, it took another ninety-two years until an Oscar-winning film chronicled the recruitment, training, and initial battles of this regiment—*Glory* (1989). Though not as commercially successful as other Civil War films, for example, *Gone with the Wind* (1939), this movie rejuvenated one of the most critical but lost elements of the Union Cause suggesting the importance of popular culture, including novels, movies, and television, to understanding Civil War memory.[1]

Most Americans have seen some aspect of the Civil War portrayed in popular culture. In fact, for many Americans, this constituted the single way they "remember" the Civil War. Despite the popularity of popular culture, it represents a more challenging way of understanding memory because it is difficult to delineate if it's about popularity or memory. When David O. Selznick produced *Gone with the Wind*, he wanted to make money. As a result of his efforts, he created the most effective twentieth-century messenger for Confederate memory. Did people embrace *Gone with the Wind* because it reflected a particular Civil War memory or because it was a masterfully done romantic melodrama that starred two of the most popular stars of their era? Nina Silber's study *The Romance of Reunion* (1993) examined how romance promoted reunion in the nineteenth century; however, was it the attraction of romance that makes something popular as opposed to the desirability of reunion?

Regardless of why people went to the movie, they viewed *Gone with the Wind* as a history lesson; for many Americans, the movie became their Civil War memory. Perhaps it said more about what was forgotten. If Americans truly understood and valued the Union Cause, *Gone with the Wind* would not have been as successful.[2]

In popular memory, like all memory, the present mattered as much, if not more, than the past. The very same factors that shaped other aspects of Civil War memory, including changing racial attitudes, affected popular memory. While a great deal has been written about the Civil War in popular memory, sectional bloodletting proved to be not very popular; only a handful of novels about the war became best sellers. Moreover, when the Civil War generation wrote about their experiences, their efforts seemed to have been disdained by literary scholars. The nature of their complaints often told you more about these scholars' view of their contemporary lives than Civil War literature. Best sellers or not, more Americans of successor generations experienced the Civil War through movies than books, though Hollywood produced fewer Civil War–themed movies than other action genres. Instead, Westerns dominated moviemaking in the twentieth century; Americans could enjoy the legends of the old West, without remembering the sectional divisions of the Civil War. Despite the paucity of Civil War movies, films had a disproportionate impact on memory. Movies like *Birth of a Nation* (1915) and *Gone with the Wind* (1939) defined the Civil War for many Americans. Similarly, once television emerged as the everyday conduit of popular culture, the few Civil War–themed television programs had an outsized influence on memory. Perhaps the most popular documentary ever filmed for television, *The Civil War* (1990) by Ken Burns, prompted an entire new generation of Americans to remember this conflict. Despite these few outliers, makers of popular culture hesitated to use the Civil War because of the divisive nature of its memory. When they did use the Civil War as a backdrop, its most romantic elements seemed the most successful and this might explain the triumph of the Lost Cause in popular memory.

While memory often reflected broad currents in society, individuals wrote books, made movies, and produced television programs. Jim Cullen focused on the role of these individuals using a case study approach in *The Civil War in Popular Culture: A Reusable Past* (1995). He assessed Carl Sandburg's *Lincoln* biographies that reassured Depression-era Americans concerned about the expanding powers of the federal government. During World War II, *Lincoln: The War Years* reminded Americans that they had been tested by war and emerged victorious. Cullen, like so many others, examined the movie *Glory* (1989), but not as a response to civil rights but to the Vietnam War. In his view, the filmmaker needed to depict a war that allowed its participants a share of glory. While Cullen correctly emphasized the role of individuals as producers of memory, these men and women's work reflected broader trends both in memory and in society; otherwise their products would not have been popular. Americans needed Lincoln in the Depression, and post-Vietnam era Americans wanted heroes.[3]

The great novels of the Civil War exemplified the relationship between the present and popular memory. Surprisingly, there had not been many truly popular Civil War novels. One would have expected the great defining moment in American history to produce more popular literature. Cullen identified the notion that authors wrote novels because of something in their present; however, their popularity, the response they evoked in American society, indicated something about the broader society's memory. The best-selling Civil War novel of all-time, or just about any type of novel, was *Gone with the Wind* (1936) by Margaret Mitchell. This paean to the Lost Cause featured faithful slaves and fair-minded slave owners who were part of an idyllic Southern-lifestyle that was gone with the wind after the war. Cullen assessed Mitchell's work and concluded that it reflected her anxiety about the "New Women" of the early twentieth-century discussed in chapter three. Mitchell came of age in Atlanta, the city that most represented the promise of the New South. Ironically, Mitchell portrayed Scarlett O'Hara, the heroine, as more willful and less self-sacrificing than the Lost Cause's idealized Confederate woman. Despite her obvious imperfections, the story of a spoiled Southern belle who overcame tremendous adversity in the Civil War and Reconstruction resonated with Americans weary from the prolonged economic depression. Moreover, this runaway best seller might tell you more about the popularity of romance than Civil War memory; however, Americans who read the book believed they "learned" about the Civil War.[4]

Removing romance from the analysis might demonstrate this relationship between popular memory and present concerns. Two great Civil War novels written eighty years apart contained no romance, nor even a single female character—*The Red Badge of Courage* by Stephen Crane published in 1895 and *The Killer Angels* by Michael Sharra issued in 1974. Crane was born after the war and had no memory of it. Despite his lack of combat experience, critics and readers embraced Crane's story of a young Union soldier who overcame his fear and became a hero. Literary merits might explain some of its success; however, like the novel *Gone with the Wind,* it appeared during a severe depression: in an era when industrialization, class strife, and gendered anxieties made Americans yearn for a simpler, more heroic time. These same types of gendered anxieties led to American involvement in Cuba and the Spanish-American War, which Crane covered as a journalist. Given the nature of historical memory, it is not surprising that only the next generation, those who knew the Civil War "second hand," could write a popular fictional book.[5]

In the aftermath of another war, the Vietnam War, Michael Shaara completed *The Killer Angels* (1974)—the classic novel depicting the Battle of Gettysburg. Shaara's study displayed a fascinating mix of Civil War memory themes. Confederate supporters would applaud his portrayal of their army, but perhaps not his view of Lee as a flawed general. In Shaara's novel General Longstreet, scapegoat of the Lost Cause, tried to stop Lee from making critical tactical errors that led to Confederate defeat.

The Union Cause also received its due. Joshua Lawrence Chamberlain, the commander of a Maine regiment, held the Union's flank against a Confederate attack; Winfield Scott Hancock halted Pickett's charge in the center. Both men fought for Union and black freedom though the author suggested that Confederates might not be fighting for slavery. The friendship between Hancock and a Confederate general supported the notion of a brothers' war that facilitated reunion based on shared heroism. When the novel debuted, it sold poorly, even after it received the Pulitzer Prize; America in the immediate aftermath of Vietnam had little room for heroes. Only as the years passed and Vietnam faded into memory did it sell, supporting the link between the present and popular memory.[6]

Both Crane and Shaara's works have been recognized for their literary merit; however, scholars neglected other Civil War literature because they believed the genre lacked literary merit. The first major study occurred at the centennial of the Civil War, Edmund Wilson's *Patriotic Gore: Studies in the Literature of the American Civil War* (1962). It was not the war's hundredth anniversary, nor the civil rights movement, but his view of war in general that prompted this pioneering study. "Having myself lived through a couple of world wars and having read a certain amount of history, I am no longer disposed to take very seriously the profession of 'war aims' that nations make." His hospital service in World War I might have shaped Wilson's views. Similarly, while he raged against conventional wars, atomic weapons and their potential to destroy mankind prompted his assessment of Civil War literature. On the surface, this seemed irrelevant to the Civil War memory; however, Wilson made the connection between 1962 and 1862. "We have seen, in our most recent wars, how a divided and arguing public opinion may be converted overnight into a national near-unanimity, an obedient flood of energy which will carry the young to destruction and overpower any effort to stem it." He then explained how he would assess the Civil War looking for the same response. "It will be seen in the pages that follow how automatically, on both sides of the contest, as soon as it had come to war, a Southerner like Lee who had opposed secession and did not approve of slavery was ready to fight to the death for both" reflecting the 1960s' view of Lee. Similarly, he wondered "how a Northerner like Sherman who knew the South, who had always got on well with the Southerners and who did not much object to slavery, became more and more ferocious to devour the South." The civil rights movement might have been changing racial views; however, Wilson seemed relatively unaffected. On one hand, he acknowledged, "the Negroes are rebelling against the whites, who are afraid of them, as they have always been"; on the other hand, "white southerners themselves are rebelling against the federal government, which they have never forgiven for laying waste their country, for reducing them to abject defeat and for needling and meddling of the Reconstruction." Wilson claimed that "it is possible to sympathize with both Negroes and white," though he did recognize that whites have been more violent. Modern war and contemporary concerns about nuclear annihilation prompted the first attempt to discuss the idea of Civil War literature.[7]

A decade later, Daniel Aaron in *The Unwritten War: American Writers and the Civil War* (1973) attempted to explain why, in his view, the Civil War created no literary masterpiece. His answer said something more important about Civil War memory than about the war's literary value. According to Aaron, literature suffered because veterans were reticent and could not convey the "real" war including its horrors. Aaron cited "spiritual censorship," or accepted discourse, that did not permit a writer to speak of certain experiences. "Disease, drunkenness, obscenity, blasphemy, criminality could only be alluded to if mentioned at all." Those who did not serve, he labeled these men "malingerers," included some of the greatest literary figures of the era; Mark Twain and Henry James Jr., who belonged to the Civil War generation, had not experienced it. Moreover, the writers who had experienced the war considered the genre's conventions and took into account the "predominantly female readership" and excluded many of the war's realities. He posited that class constraints affected the men who did serve, what he considered "gentlemen of peace and war." One exception to this rule existed: Ambrose Bierce, whose short story "Incident at Owl Creek Bridge" centered on a man executed for his role as a guerrilla fighter. Aaron cited a "general rule" that might explain the Civil War generation's failure. "National convulsions do not provide the best conditions for artistic creativeness."[8]

Still looking for a masterpiece, Aaron believed white Southerners were more capable of writing it because "a story of exploded expectation and of military and social disaster lends itself to literary treatments more readily than the vulgarity of victory." This idea explained the success of the Lost Cause in literature. He then proceeded to describe a person that might have written this unwritten masterpiece; he wanted a person who had fought in the war but separate from "southern preconceptions of caste and race and culture." No one of the Confederate generation could meet this condition. The only author Aaron believed could do it was William Faulkner; however, he violated a key criterion—someone who lived through the war. Like so many memory issues, Aaron tied the failure to write the great novel of the war to a refusal to address race. "The 'emotional resistance' blurring literary insight, I suspect, has been race. Without the long presence of chattel slavery, Americans would not have allowed the usual animosities springing from cultural differences to boil up into mutual hatreds." Americans could not come to terms with race and could not come to terms with the Civil War.[9]

Both Wilson and Aaron concerned themselves with high culture; only later did authors address popular culture. It took a very long time for a major study on Civil War literature in popular culture to appear. Alice Fahs's *The Imagined Civil War: Popular Literature of the North and South 1861–1865* (2001) rejected Aaron's claim. "Far from being an 'unwritten war,' the Civil War catalyzed an outpouring of war-related literature that has rarely been examined; war poetry, sentimental war stories, sensational war novels, war humor, war juveniles, war songs . . . that has often been designated, and then dismissed, as popular."[10]

While much of Fahs's research focused on the war, she also analyzed Civil War memory. Fahs assessed war juveniles, or children's books, and the differences between those written during the war and those written decades later in an essay "Remembering the Civil War in Children's Literature of the 1880s and 1890s" (2004). Oliver Optic (William Taylor Adams) wrote a series of wartime children's books about two brothers: one who served in the Union army and the other in the Union navy. Later, Optic published another series entitled "The Blue and the Gray Series"; these books included Confederate boys as heroes. Part of this emphasis on reconciliation was the desire to sell books to Southerners; however, Civil War memory, even in children's books, was about the present. According to Fahs, Optic's postwar series wanted children to remember a war in which "Northern and Southern soldiers had fought heroically for their separate causes . . . and [that] such heroism was more important than sectional differences. On the grounds of white heroism, a new version of nationalism could take shape." Overall, the memory that Optic and other children's writers enshrined in this era was a "war [that] had been—and should remain in memory—a white, masculinist experience in American life." Children's literature about the Civil War promoted both nationalism for all children and masculinity for boys and helped assuage late nineteenth-century anxieties discussed in Chapter 3.[11]

In the conclusion of *Imagined War*, Fahs assessed adult literature including Stephen Crane and other "writers in the 1890s, as they returned to the war to find within it the underpinnings of a robust new masculine identity, one that often abandoned earlier attributes of manhood such as self-restraint and 'civilized cultivation' in favor of 'unrestrained nature' and 'athletic virility.'" Fahs contented that this went beyond the late nineteenth century; "it was in the twentieth century that such masculinization achieved not just ascendancy but also an astonishing longevity." Gendered anxieties related to men and boys might explain the persistence of the Lost Cause in popular memory.[12]

The most popular novel of the Civil War has little to do with men and masculinity. A women, Margaret Mitchell, wrote *Gone with the Wind*. Scholars may have neglected Civil War literature because so much of it was written by women, mostly Confederate and Southern women. Sarah E. Gardner identified their prominent role in articulating the Lost Cause in *Blood and Irony: Southern White Women's Narratives of the Civil War, 1861–1937*. Just as the Ladies Memorial Associations and the United Daughters of the Confederacy framed the contours of Southern Civil War memory through commemorative activities, women writers, "participants in [a] paper battle" for memory, created and popularized the Lost Cause narrative for the broader American public.[13]

One of the most popular aspects of nineteenth-century Civil War memory was drawn, not written. Mark E. Neely Jr., Harold Holzer, and Gabor S. Boritt pioneered the study of *The Confederate Image: Prints of the Lost Cause* (1987), among the examples they used the famous Lost Cause portrait, *The Burial of Latané* (1864). In this painting, which was later a popular print, women on the home front buried a Confederate captain. In addition to loyal women, the print included faithful slaves who assisted at the burial and joined in the bereavement. Neely and Holzer analyzed the art created during and immediately after the war to "revive and sustain Confederate identity after the collapse of the Confederacy, providing a visual accompaniment to the embracing and enduring myth of the Lost Cause." Half of this book examined postwar art demonstrating its popularity. Similarly, Holzer and Neely looked at the art of the Union Cause in *The Union Image: Popular Prints of the Civil War North* (2000); in contrast, artists drew the vast majority of these works during the war and much less afterward. The same factors that made the Lost Cause more memorable than the Union Cause affected the popularity of Union themes after the war.[14]

If federal supporters had created art to commemorate their cause, it might not have sold well in the twentieth century; the strength of the Lost Cause persisted in images as in everything else. Gary W. Gallagher in *Causes Won, Lost, and Forgotten: How Hollywood and Popular Art Shape What We Know about the Civil War* (2008) assessed Civil War art in the second half of the twentieth century. He did not survey museums. Instead, he examined advertisements for popular art in Civil War magazines starting in the 1960s and ending in 2005. Gallagher considered Robert E. Lee, Stonewall Jackson, and Confederate forces as representative of the Lost Cause; among those he believed evocative of the Union Cause were Grant, Lincoln, and images of Unions soldiers. Gallagher calculated that the Lost Cause was 2.5 times more likely to be commemorated in these images; Lee and Jackson being number one and two in popularity. In contrast, when Grant appeared, he was usually with Lee at Appomattox. Gallagher also found that the Confederate battle flag played a much more prominent role in the twentieth and twenty-first centuries than it did in the nineteenth. He attributed this evolution to Confederate supporters' angry response to removing it from public spaces. Similarly, modern prints revealed a more intense religiosity; images of Jackson praying were popular reflecting a resurgence of evangelical faith in recent decades. More recently, the North prints experienced an increase in popularity. The hero of *The Killer Angels* and the movie *Gettysburg* (1993), Joshua Lawrence Chamberlain, emerged as the new star of the Civil War art demonstrating the interaction of different types of popular culture. Despite the rise of Chamberlain, based on Gallagher's survey, the Lost Cause won the battle of Civil War memory in art.[15]

The popularity of Chamberlain, a former Bowdoin College professor-turned regimental commander, demonstrated the power of movies. Jenny Barrett, a scholar of film and popular culture studies, in *Shooting the Civil War: Cinema, History and American National Identity* (2009) identified "the one abiding source of knowledge about the Civil War, however, is not the historical textbook, nor even the novel, but the cinema." She cited an estimated seven hundred movies and documentaries to support this claim. Despite the significant number of movies she identified, Barret believed that "there is no such thing as 'the Civil War film.'" Instead, Civil War movies might be family melodramas, Westerns, or combat films and followed the conventions of these genres. While she rejected the idea of a Civil War movie, she analyzed common elements in these films that buttressed American national identity. She identified a theme widely espoused in many Civil War Westerns—"All threats are overcome by unity," a common notion in Civil War combat films— "Being prepared to die for what is right." The message was clear. All challenges facing the United States could be overcome by national reunion based on the notion that Southerners fought and died for what they believed right. Accepting these ideas reinforced a shared national identity, remembering the Union Cause, sectional disunity, and a war against slavery, challenged American nationalism.[16]

Civil War films might not be a distinct genre because filmmakers made fewer films on the American sectional conflict than other more popular genres. Lawrence A. Kreiser Jr. and Randal Allred in their introduction to *The Civil War in Popular Culture: Memory and Meaning* (2014) discussed the millions of hits the term "Civil War" gets when typed into an Internet search engine, more than double any other war of its era. Despite this interest, moviemakers produced only a few hundred Civil War movies; the vast majority of these productions completed during the silent era. A 1964 analysis of Civil War movies was telling; John Kuiper identified 495 Civil War films, 359 released between 1910 and 1919. During the 1920s, 1930s, and 1950s, moviemakers produced about thirty films in each decade. While Kuiper made this assessment by decade, he noted that during World War I and World War II, Civil War moviemaking declined; in 1917, there were 18 films, in 1919, 3. Hollywood released no Civil War films in 1943 and 1945 with only 10 Civil War movies produced in the decade of the 1940s. Real wars made the reel Civil War less popular. In contrast, one study documented over 5,000 Westerns. As Richard Aquila in *The Sagebrush Trail: Western Movies and Twentieth-Century America* (2015) argued, Westerns "reflected and reinforced American beliefs in democracy, freedom, self-reliance, morality, nationalism, and heroism." For Americans, regardless of their Civil War memory, Westerns "offered powerful images of a mythic west, providing exhilarating tales, positive memories, and an unambiguous national identity." In contrast, Civil War movies evoke a time when American nationality was almost destroyed.[17]

Kuiper's qualitative assessment supported other findings related to Civil War memory; romance was the most prevalent theme in these movies. The romantic

Civil War had no room for race; only 9 percent of the characters in these films were African Americans. Kuiper maintained that filmmakers ignored black audiences and neglected African American characters; however, Americans remembered an all-white war and diversity would challenge that memory. Moreover, he found that "in their totality theatrical films of the Civil War . . . tended to favor the South," something that could be said for American Civil War memory.[18]

Decades after this study, scholars analyzed these films in relationship to Civil War memory. Bruce Chadwick in *Reel Civil War: Mythmaking in American Film* (2001) examined the silent era, the second decade of the twentieth century, and how it promoted the Lost Cause and "a moonlight-and-magnolias saga that featured trees dripping with Spanish Moss, gentlemen drinking mint juleps on the veranda, women prettifying themselves for the ball and countless soldiers becoming instant heroes." It was the "distortions presented in the . . . silent films on the war . . . [that] came to be accepted as fact by filmmakers" that partly explain why it took decades to challenge Lost Cause memory in popular culture. Among the themes identified by Chadwick, the South was an underdog that was not fighting for slavery; it was supported by faithful slaves, and the nation reunited because Southern women married Northern men. The reason for the dominance of the Lost Cause in this era, and why it remained unchallenged, is complex. Chadwick suggested two interrelated ideas. First, the Lost Cause dominated the Civil War memory of most Americans in both sections based on "information from school texts, newspapers, magazines, history books, novels, Broadway plays, songs and poems . . . [in original] and then movies," and second, and not surprisingly, the needs of each successive present in the following decades; "the myth of the hard-fighting Yankees and Confederates defending the America they believed to be theirs served as inspiration for Americans preparing to go into battle in the Spanish-American War, World War I, World War II, Korea, and Vietnam." Movies seemed little different than broader memory, the only question this suggested: did films represent filmmakers' memory or their understanding of American memory and what appeals to the broader public?[19]

In the decade studied by Chadwick, Hollywood released the first great Civil War movie, *Birth of a Nation* (1915). Chadwick examined this movie, as does everyone else who studied Civil War movies, because it was one of the two most popular Civil War movies ever made, with *Gone with the Wind* (1939) being the other. It did not merely present the Lost Cause version of Civil War memory; it presented a decidedly negative view of black Americans during Reconstruction. In one scene an African American soldier's attempt at rape is foiled only when the white women jumps from a cliff. The heroes in the story were the Ku Klux Klan who killed the rapist. Well after Reconstruction ended, white Southerners lynched black Americans accused of rape and other crimes. Was *Birth of a Nation* about justifying terrorizing African American in 1865 or in 1915?[20]

Recently, a scholar identified the enormous controversy about how this movie portrayed the Civil War and its aftermath. In 1915, the newly formed National Association for the Advancement of Colored People (NAACP) protested the portrayals in this movie. Dick Lehr in *The Birth of a Nation: How a Legendary Filmmaker and a Crusading Editor Reignited America's Civil War* (2014) described Boston-based African American leader William Monroe Trotter's "efforts to halt the spread of the movie that was at once a masterpiece in filmmaking technique and a virulent brand of hate speech." While this study focused on one black American's efforts, whites also rejected *Birth of a Nation* because of how it portrayed the Union Cause. In Kansas, the Grand Army of the Republic led the effort to ban the film and protested it elsewhere, supporting the notion that the Civil War generation contested Civil War memory into the twentieth century.[21]

Birth of a Nation might have been the first great Civil War movie, but there have been many others. Brian Steel Wills, in *Gone with the Glory: The Civil War in Cinema* (2007), examined Civil War movies from the silent era until today according to how these movies portrayed specific themes, such as the "Personal War" and how this conflict was "intensely personal for the individual who found themselves engulfed in it." While the effect of war on the individual was a universal theme found in many movies across the decades, Wills also noted how certain themes reflected contemporary concerns. Movies produced in the late 1960s, such as *Journey to Shiloh* (1968) in which naïve Texans traveled a long way to die in Tennessee, mirrored American angst about the Vietnam War. Similarly, Wills examined Civil War prisoners of war (POWs). If there was any Civil War memory that obsessed the Civil War generation it was treatment of POWs. Wills found that "until 1993, Civil War cinema largely ignored the plight of prisoners of war." Remembering POWs reflected post–Vietnam War sensibilities, a war in which Americans anger over the fate of prisoners and the missing veterans reflected a broader rejection of the government's treatment of veterans.[22]

Gary W. Gallagher's *Causes Won, Lost, and Forgotten* (2008) represented a more systematic examination of Civil War movies and memory. Gallagher documented what he considered the four "interpretative traditions created by participants in the conflict" that mirrored the collective memory of the Civil War generation. He identified four major streams of Civil War memory and how and when they seemed to dominate in films. Gallagher examined "the Lost Cause tradition," just as described in Chapter 1. He identified two distinct elements of Unionist Civil War memory based on how the Civil War had been portrayed in film—the Union Cause and the Emancipation Cause. The Union Cause "framed the war as preeminently an effort to maintain a viable republic in the face of secessionist actions." In contrast, the "Emancipation Cause tradition interpreted the war as a struggle to liberate 4 million slaves." Finally, what he considered, the Reconciliation Cause emphasized the "*American* virtues both sides manifested during the war, to exalt the restored nation that emerged from the conflict, and to mute the role of African Americans." Gallagher believed that these traditions could find common ground, the most recognizable connection linked the Lost Cause and the Reconciliation Cause. Supporters of Reconciliation accepted Lost Cause ideas, particularly when an appreciation of Southern military prowess promoted nationalism. In contrast, the Union Cause did not serve reconciliation very well because it reminded Americans that Confederate military prowess almost destroyed the Union. In contrast, David W. Blight in *Race and Reunion: The Civil War in American Memory* (2001) identified three major memory categories including the "reconiliationist," the "white supremacist," and the "emancipationist" vision of Civil War memory. Blight's categorizations reflected Americans' difficulty remembering a distinct Union cause.[23]

Gallagher found that the Union Cause appeared forgotten on the movie screen. Assessing films starting with the *Birth of the Nation* until the most recent releases, Gallagher supported broader findings on how Americans remembered the Civil War. According to Gallagher, "The Lost Cause narrative flourished for nearly half a century before losing ground, and eventually supremacy to the Emancipation and Reconciliation Causes." Critical to this success, *Birth of a Nation* and *Gone with the Wind* "exposed generations of Americans to strongly positive depictions of the Confederacy and the slave-holding South, as well as to hostile treatments of Reconstruction." After *Gone with the Wind*, many subsequent Civil War movies reflected the Lost Cause or a reconiliationist view. It took twenty-six years for the first major motion picture to depart from mainstream memory. First, the film *Shenandoah* (1965) was antiwar; the Virginia family at the center of this film wanted nothing to do with fighting. Second, their rejection of the war originated in the Confederacy's goal of defending slavery. Though it did very well at the box office, this movie seemed out of step with 1960s popular Civil War memory. Similarly, while Americans fought in Vietnam when it was released, they had not yet begun to question the war in any significant numbers. Jimmy Stewart, one of the most popular actors of this era, starred in this movie and that may explain the movie's success. *Shenandoah* demonstrated the dangers of assuming that a historical movie did well only because it reflected how Americans remembered the events being chronicled. Twenty-four years would pass before a Civil War movie challenged the Civil War master narrative. It was not until 1989 and the release of *Glory* that the Emancipation Cause emerged. Gallagher concluded that despite recognition of emancipation as the Union Cause, the war for the Union itself remained forgotten by modern filmmakers.[24]

Today, emancipation embodies the war's preeminent accomplishment; the Union Cause lost the battle for celluloid memory. Gallagher attributed this to filmmakers' antimilitarism. "Hollywood's recent Civil War films fail almost completely to convey any sense of what the Union Cause meant to millions of northern citizens.

More than that, they often cast the [Civil War] United States Army, a military force that saved the Republic and destroyed slavery, in a decidedly negative, post-Vietnam light." Only emancipation made the war worthwhile to many modern Americans moviemakers, an ironic evolution in how Americans remembered the Civil War.[25]

While there have been many Civil War films, there have not been as many television programs that portrayed this conflict. Limited budgets prohibited television producers from re-creating an expensive, historical experience. One short-lived syndicated television program, *The Gray Ghost* (1957–1958) chronicled the fictional adventures of a real Confederate guerilla in Northern Virginia—John Mosby. Its brief tenure might have been due to network concerns about a program that depicted a Confederate cavalryman who regularly outwitted Union soldiers. Moreover, this program debuted just as the fight for school desegregation was under way at the state and local levels. As a result of this unease, the network syndicated the program to CBS stations; only a Boston station refused to air the program. The program remained popular when televised by local stations, demonstrating the power of Lost Cause memory in the early years of the civil rights movement. Eventually, the network's failure to make new episodes led to its cancellation.[26]

Partly as a result of such fears, less controversial Westerns became the favored historical genre for much of the television's first decades. The sheer volume of Westerns produced meant sets and costumes were available. Sometimes a television program about the West featured a Civil War veteran, such as Johnny Yuma (*The Rebel*, 1959–1961); their character's Civil War experiences occupying one part of the character's backstory. While the Civil War had not been the subject of many weekly television

Colonel John Singleton Mosby, portrayed in the *Gray Ghost* television program, reunion of his command, on courthouse steps, Warrenton, Virginia, date unknown. (Library of Congress)

programs, there had certainly been some special television events about the Civil War, including two miniseries, *North and South* (1985, 1986) and *The Blue and Gray* (1982). Each series featured one Union and one Confederate family related by blood or marriage to one another emphasizing divided families as the war's greatest tragedy. Each series focused on distinct economic classes; the *North and South* featured elites and *The Blue and the Gray* portrayed the middle class. In *North and South*, the Southern family owned a plantation and slaves; the Northern family owned a factory operated by free labor. The slave-owning family usually treated their slaves well, and the factory owner sometimes treated his workers poorly. One member of the Northern family, an unsympathetic character, supported radical abolitionism. *The Blue and the Gray* had no slave owners and no abolitionists; neither side seemed ideologically committed to the conflict. The main protagonist is John, son of the Southern family. While he opposed slavery, his position as an illustrator for *Harpers Weekly* made him a self-professed neutral. In the end, the Southern family, including John, reunited to defend the farm against the rampaging Union army bent on destroying it. Both series indicated the war was about slavery; however, both remembered a war between white families and not a struggle for black freedom.[27]

Both miniseries premiered after the greatest TV historical series in both popularity and importance—*Roots* (1977). This twelve-hour miniseries based on Alex Haley's best-selling account of his family went all the way back to Africa to his purported ancestor—the kidnapped and enslaved Kunta Kinte. While only one section covered the Civil War, this series was about slavery and all of its horrors, emancipation and all its promise, even if these hopes were not fully realized. Nothing in this series supported Lost Cause ideas of faithful and happy slaves; instead, African Americans were brutalized, beaten, raped, and separated from their families. Since the time of this production, many scholars and others questioned the accuracy of Haley's story. True or false, at least 130 million Americans watched parts of this series—the most effective attack on the memory of slavery as a benevolent institution in popular memory.[28]

Ken Burns's series *The Civil War* (1990) related more directly to Civil War memory. A public broadcasting documentary and not a drama, it still managed ratings on par with the most successful entertainment programming on commercial stations. Burn used still photos, a haunting soundtrack, actors reading primary source documents, and a charismatic panel of experts to tell his story. It is difficult to say how many people have seen this documentary because it aired many times, including recently for the sesquicentennial.[29]

If anything best captured and shaped Civil War memory in the twentieth century's last decade, it was this series. Americans embraced the Union Cause, Emancipation, Reconciliation, and the Lost Cause all at the same time. Barbara Jean Fields, an African American historian, made sure the Union, Emancipationist, and race received their due. Burns recognized postwar reunion; he ended the series with a picture of the blue and gray veterans clasping hands at Gettysburg. The Lost Cause while down was not out. One of the experts, Shelby Foote emphasized critical aspects of Lost Cause memory including attributing Confederate defeat to overwhelming numbers. His soft Southern accent and grandfatherly appearance re-enforced the effectiveness of his presentation. Foote's interpretation formed in the 1950s when he wrote a multivolume history of the Civil War. Decades later, Foote's prominent role meant that his understanding, a product of an earlier era, received a broad hearing including stories about Nathan Bedford Forrest's military prowess. Forrest, a controversial figure, a slave trader before the war, had been accused of murdering surrendering black soldiers during the war and founding the Ku Klux Klan in its aftermath. Overall, *The Civil War* reflected broader Civil War memory trends at the end of this century. The Union cause, at least emancipation, had finally made a mark in American memory. Despite understanding the war was about slavery and race, Americans wanted reunion too, even if it meant that white Union soldiers reached out to white Confederate soldiers on the war's deadliest battlefield.[30]

Recently, in the aftermath of the Charleston shooting, officials removed Nathan Bedford Forrest's statue from a public park suggesting that the twenty-first century represents a new era in Civil War memory. Before the terrible events of June 2015, no one would have anticipated such a successful challenge to the Lost Cause in public spaces. Explaining the resiliency of the Lost Cause and the discovery of the Union Cause requires a close examination of twenty-first century Civil War memory.[31]

SEVEN

❧◦❧

THE REPUBLIC OF SUFFERING: CIVIL WAR MEMORY AT THE BEGINNING OF THE TWENTY-FIRST CENTURY

Ironically, before that terrible June night in Charleston, through much of the sesquicentennial, the battle over Civil War memory settled into an uneasy truce; in fact, certain factors, including the new wars of the twentieth century and social media, gave renewed life to old ideas: first, a new type of revisionism, a neo-revisionism that is both similar and different to the type that occurred between World Wars I and II. Similar, in that the long wars of the early twenty-first century and the war on terror prompted a renewed focus on death and suffering in the Civil War. Different, in that racial attitudes had changed so drastically that scholars excluded certain aspects of the original "revision," including rejecting emancipation. Surprisingly, despite the change in racial views, the Lost Cause showed a remarkable degree of resilience, particularly in an era when the Union Cause emerged as a subject of scholarly interest. Partly, this was due to the emergence of a national conservative movement that challenged the consensus on federal government's role in American life. While this conservatism is a nationwide movement, it emerged strongest among white Southerners who now dominate the Republican Party. The election of the first black president, Barack H. Obama, a victory of the political equality espoused by the Union Cause, created a racial backlash that shaped Civil War memory. One hundred and fifty years after the war's end the same contemporary issues affect Civil War memory—race and reunion, war and peace, union and nation.

This chapter chronicles the state of Civil War memory at the end of the ses-quicentennial, more than one hundred and fifty years after the surrender at Appo-mattox. Initially, memory work appeared to be still in the hands of academics and scholars who continued to expand just who should be remembered and how; how-ever, they also enlarged memory to include the war's catastrophic consequences. Drew Gilpin Faust's *Republic of Suffering: Death and the American Civil War* (2008) epitomized this trend. Scholars documented the effect of the war on slaves, veterans, women, prisoners of war, and Native Americans; all demonstrated that the United States during the war was truly a republic of suffering. Like the generation of 1865, whose suffering inspired these studies, the generation of 2015 became advocates for the war's disparate collective memories. The Union Cause's hold on the academy remained as strong as the Lost Cause had been in the past. Outside the ivory tower, the Lost Cause made a strong comeback. Partly it might have been about the unset-tled present, wars on terror at home and overseas, economic inequality in a globalized economy, the strains of race and nation in Bush, Obama, and now Trump's America. At the same time, it might have been about social media and the end of informa-tion gatekeepers. Civil War memory issues that seemed to reach a level of consensus at the end of the twentieth century, such as black Civil War soldiers and Lincoln's presidency, once again were contested but this time often in cyberspace—the new frontier of Civil War memory.[1]

The wars of the twenty-first century prompted some of the type of antiwar senti-ment that caused some revisionist twentieth-century scholars to highlight the war's human cost. Faust's magisterial study encapsulated this memory shift. According to Faust, it was death as much as any other factor that "created a veritable 'republic of suffering'" during and after the war. She assessed the long-term consequences of the Civil War in the United States and how "death created the modern American union—not just by ensuring national survival, but by shaping enduring national structure and commitments" including national cemeteries and widows' pensions. Despite her focus on the war's long-term consequences, much of her book concentrated on the very real "the work" of death—killing, burying, mourning, and accounting for the dead. According to Faust, "The work of death was Civil War America's most fundamental and most demanding undertaking." Accounting was critical to death in the Civil War because it was poorly executed. Many bodies were never identified, and relatives remained uncertain of their loved ones' fate.[2]

As a result of inadequate recordkeeping, no one knows how many Americans died in the war. Recently, two scholars presented different views on this casualty count. J. David Hacker in "A Census-Based Count of the Civil War Dead" (2011) in *Civil War History* analyzed census data from before and after the war and argued that about 750,000 fewer Americans were alive in 1870 than there should have been given an analysis of expected peacetime death rates. In contrast, Nicholas Marshall expressed his opinion on this recount in the title of his article in *The Journal of the Civil War Era*: "The Great Exaggeration: Death and the Civil War" (2014). Marshall placed these casualties in the context of demographics before and after the war. People died at an early age in the middle of the nineteenth century even during peacetime. It said something profound about Civil War memory and Civil War reality that it required the passage of one hundred and fifty years for scholars to place death as central to the meaning of the Civil War—exaggerated or not.[3]

Focusing on death might be a product of current wars. Past wars experienced higher death rates; however, today Americans seem more casualty averse. In a review article, "Revisionism Reinvented?: The Antiwar Turn in Civil War Scholarship" (2013), Yael A. Sternhell identified an "antiwar turn in Civil War scholarship." She reviewed studies that suggested the reinvigoration of the needless war strain in Civil War memory. David Goldfield in *America Aflame: How the Civil War Created a Nation* (2011) cited Avery O. Craven's influence on his work; however, he also believed that earlier generations missed evangelical Christians' role in the war's outbreak. What he said about the reason the war came reflects a complaint some people might make today. "Evangelicals never comprised a majority of the population, but their organization, wealth, use of technology and the media, and access to politicians, especially in the Republican Party, enabled them to infiltrate and influence the political process." Harry S. Stout in *Upon the Altar of the Nation: A Moral History of the Civil War* (2006) also blamed clergy and other religious figures but not for starting the war. Instead, he made a clear distinction between initiating a just war against slavery, and the way the war was conducted. He objected to clergy becoming "cheerleaders of the war's conduct" when military and political officials fought a Total War that targeted civilian populations. As a result of their support, religious men and women "sacralized" patriotism to the point where it was equal to or better than any religion.[4]

Religious men and women may have been wrong, but their actions were prompted by the need to deal with the war's massive death toll. Despite the lethality of Civil War combat, not everyone who died did so in battle; in fact, disease proved much more deadly. The grim demographics of death had been known, but not emphasized, partly because people did not want to remember that most soldiers did not die a glorious death in battle, but instead, a less romantic death, sickened in a hospital bed. This amnesia might explain why it took a long time for someone to write a comprehensive medical history of the Civil War. Margaret Humphreys in *Marrow of Tragedy: The Health Crisis of the American Civil War* (2013) described this conflict as "the greatest health disaster that this country has ever experienced, killing more than a million Americans and leaving others invalided or grieving." In her memory, "the war, for those who fought it, was less about heroism and more about the daily grind of disease, hunger, death, and disability." If any memory was lost, it was these types of medical issues. Humphreys also focused on gender issues including the central role played by women who healed the sick and treated the injured. Jane E. Schultz in *Women at the Front: Hospital Workers in Civil War America* (2004) assessed the role of women health-care workers. She did not focus solely on nurses who were usually elite or middle-class women. Most of the women who did hospital work were from the lower classes and included former slaves because most of the work that needed to be done was "domestic drudgery." These women "built fires to cook soup, washed patients' faces, irrigated noxious wounds, cleaned effluvia from the floors, changed bedding and scrubbed undergarments."[5]

Formerly enslaved women who performed these tasks were likely sickened by the disease endemic to wartime. Civil War memory neglected disease among soldiers, though people remembered it had occurred. Until Jim Downs documented black women and men's illnesses in *Sick from Freedom: African-American Illness and Suffering during the Civil War and Reconstruction* (2012), enslaved men and women had not been included in the war's toll. Not only did these men and women sicken and die like soldiers, Downs explains, but "disease and sickness had a more devastating and fatal effect on emancipated slaves than on soldiers." The next step in Civil War studies may be to remember the Civil War's long-term health consequences for all Americans, black and white, men and women, soldiers and civilians.[6]

Civil War scholars in the twenty-first century expanded the conventional narrative in other ways; Stephen Berry and his colleagues in an edited collection of essays entitled *Weirding the War: Stories from the Civil War's Ragged Edges* (2011) challenged the idea of a conventional Civil War memory. "Weirding" is, according to Berry, "the historians' equivalent of freakonomics (the use of economic theory to investigate atypical subjects in the hope of yielding fresh insights into typical social dynamics)." In a historical sense, Berry explained, it "is a way of alienating the past from its present purposes, releasing the past from its present work, and returning to the past a measure of its original 'foreignness.'" In this collection of essays, Amy Murrell Taylor examined African Americans who froze to death when expelled from Northern refugee camps, and Andrew L. Slap chronicled the story of African Americans who turned themselves out of camp and deserted the Union army. Most Americans remembered the honorable men in Civil War armies; these essays reminded us of the flexible nature of this notion. Kenneth W. Noe discussed the court-martial and acquittal of a Confederate officer who left his command in battle. Barton A. Myers explained how nineteenth-century men justified torturing women. While this type of suffering was rare, Joan E. Cashin analyzed a much more common misery—starvation. Diane Miller Sommerville discussed Confederate soldiers who had lost their minds, while LeeAnn Whites examined unconventional women who sacrificed for their cause—prostitutes during Missouri's guerrilla war. All weird the war, all make it much more dreadful than it had been portrayed by historians.[7]

LeeAnn Whites's women in their lives as prostitutes intersected with a guerilla war in Missouri. That subject has been one of the major beneficiaries in broadening the scope of Civil War studies. The first major study of guerilla warfare, what experts call insurgent warfare, appeared before the United States found itself embroiled in contingencies in the Middle East. Michael Fellman's *Inside War: The Guerilla Conflict in Missouri during the Civil War* (1989) examined the insurgency in this state as a way of establishing "the social and cultural meanings of such a war for ordinary Americans." He described the guerrilla war as a series of "cultural nightmares" that "blew off the cover of respectable society." While Fellman's study represented the pioneering work in this field, the twenty-first century treated the guerrilla war as less of an aberration and more central to the Civil War narrative. Daniel E. Sutherland's *A Savage Conflict: The Decisive Role of Guerrillas in the American Civil War* (2009) began by reflecting on guerilla war memory. "Most Americans think of the American Civil War as a clash of mighty armies. The so-called guerrillas of the war, we have been told, barely qualified as a 'sideshow.' They certainly did not influence how the war was fought or decide its outcome." Sutherland's title revealed his conclusions; he believed guerilla warfare was decisive because it set into motion changes "in Union military policy and strategy" that "produced a more brutal and destructive war that led to Confederate defeat." Sutherland's only recognition of the present was his reference to "the world's current—and understandable interest—in what had come to be known as *asymmetrical* or *compound* warfare." He acknowledged contemporary vernacular but only when he explained his decision to avoid current terminology. Despite eschewing modern terms, it would be inconceivable that this study would have been written unless military policy and strategy in guerrilla wars preoccupied twenty-first century Americans.[8]

In the wars of this century, controversy over the treatment of enemy combatants revived one of the most contentious issues for the Civil War generation—the treatment of prisoners of war. Unionists decried the treatment of their comrades at confederate prisons, such as Andersonville, which had the highest death toll of any prisons on either side. Confederates' supporters rejected responsibility for these conditions and cited the Union's superior resources as a factor that made the United States more culpable for poor conditions at their camps, including one in Elmyra, New York. Charles W. Sanders's *While in the Hand of the Enemy: Military Prisons of the Civil War* (2005) blamed both sides. "Although difficulties such as organizational incompetence, inexperience, and chronic shortages of essential resources certainly contributed to the horrors in the camps, these factors pale to insignificance when compared to the devastation wrought by Union and Confederate leaders who knew full well the horrific toll of misery and death their decisions and actions would exact in the camps." Benjamin G. Cloyd's *Haunted by Atrocity: Civil War Prisons in American Memory* (2010) scrutinized prisons as a way of examining Civil War memory itself. The author explains that he was not writing about Civil War prisons and what happened in this institution but how "each generation explored the prison controversy and shaped the interpretation of its history in response to their own contemporary political, social, cultural . . . needs."⁹

Using the memory of the best-known Civil War prison, Andersonville, demonstrated how Civil War memory evolved in response to contemporary needs. This prison experienced the highest death rate of all camps on either side. In the war's aftermath, the commandant's actions resulted in his execution. In the postwar decades, survivors refused to forget what happened there and created a body of work that made this prison central to the collective memory of Civil War POW experiences. As a result of their efforts, the government preserved the landscapes incarceration at the site of Andersonville prison, maintained as a National Historical Site and home to the National Prisoner of War Museum honoring prisoners from other wars. Probably, the most influential retelling of this prison's history was a 1955 Pulitzer Prize–winning novel by McKinley Kantor. The villains were Confederate officials, including the Swiss-born commandant Henry Wirz whose Germanic origins made it easier to suggest a connection with the Holocaust. In the 1990s this story was adapted for television. In 1959, Saul Levitt dramatized Wirz's trial into a play, *The Andersonville Trial,* which was adapted for television in the 1970s a version seen by many more people than the play. In this play, Wirz's defense that he was only obeying orders would have been a familiar one to individuals who had lived through World War II and the Nuremberg trials. Decades later, in a post-Vietnam America, William Marvel in *Andersonville: The Last Depot* (1994) appeared to blame Northern officials for demanding "absolute equality for all black prisoners" and accused Union veterans of exaggerating their experiences for political purposes after the war. Historians, novelists, playwrights all interpreted one of the most memorable experiences of the Civil War, the horrors of Andersonville, in light of their present.¹⁰

The men who survived these prisons and lived still suffered, as did so many others of their generation. Civil War studies became more about the Civil War era and aftermaths, particularly how wartime experience affected men and women including veterans and their families. The first book that broached the idea that veterans were about more than their organizations, such as the Grand Army of the Republic (GAR) and the United Confederate Veterans (UCV), was Eric T. Dean Jr.'s *Shook over Hell: Post-Traumatic Stress, Vietnam, and the Civil War* (1997). Dean compared Vietnam veterans and Civil War veterans and questioned the *sui generis* nature of Vietnam veterans' postwar experiences. After a careful examination of Civil War pension claims and the records of a nineteenth-century Indiana facility for the mentally ill, Dean argued that Civil War veterans "did not escape this misfortune, and that these men did indeed suffer from what we would today think of as PTSD." While Dean's efforts opened up an entire field of inquiry regarding Civil War veterans, his agenda was clear; this was about Vietnam veterans and their problems as is evident in the subtitle.¹¹

Recently, Craig A. Warren in *Scars to Prove It: The Civil War Soldier and American Fiction* (2009) examined seven novels that included the Civil War soldiers from 1895 to 2006. Among these novels were the well-known *The Red Badge of Courage* (1895) and *Gone with the Wind* (1937), and the lesser-known *None Shall Look Back* (1937) and *The Judas Field* (2006). Warren contended "that the relationship between veterans' narratives and Civil War fiction deserves careful study by anyone interested in the war and its literature." In his view the authors deserved credit for these novels, but also veterans; "the success and value of these works owe a great deal to the literary efforts of an earlier group of American writers—the soldiers who fought the Civil War and who later recorded in print their experiences and interpretations." Identifying the importance of veterans to literature proved critical; these men's contributions to collective memory became part of the way the war was remembered. John A. Casey Jr. in *New Men: Reconstructing the Image of the Veteran in Late-Nineteenth-Century Literature and Culture* (2015) asserted that the very idea of a veteran originated as a product of the Civil War. According to Casey, it was "no longer the marker of a temporary status, 'veteran' came to connote a new identity that was associated with a new state of consciousness. . . . Not simply one event in a man's life, military service in time of war became a defining experience." So the Civil War veteran, the postwar life of a former soldier, became an important idea in Civil War memory.[12]

If there were no more wars, the study of Civil War veterans might have atrophied in the twenty-first century; instead, new wars prompted a reexamination of the Civil War and its aftermath, including veterans' experience. Brian M. Jordan's study, *Marching Home: Union Veterans and Their Unending Civil War* (2014), invoked the experience of today's veterans to explain why troubled Civil War veterans were so long ignored. "Even today, as soldiers return home from new and more complex wars farther away and more difficult to imagine, we still have trouble seeing the pathos of American veteranhood." While his inspiration might partly be modern veterans, he was not comparing nineteenth and twenty-first-century veterans; instead, he examined Civil War veterans on their own terms. Jordan contended that because of the horrific nature of Civil War military service the Union veterans' Civil War never ended. The long march home that Jordan described was particularly difficult for those who were "hopelessly addicted to the laudanum they had first sampled in Civil War field hospitals. Especially for those sporting empty sleeves or staggering along with irksome and ill-fitting wooden legs, joblessness, vagrancy, and penury loomed. Vivid nightmares of the picket post and the prison pen mocked any proclamation of peace." Bringing his story back to the present, he described the "more than 26,000 veterans of the wars in Iraq and Afghanistan [that] dwell in homeless shelters; thousands suffering from posttraumatic stress and traumatic brain injuries [that] have yielded to drugs and alcohol . . . [while] bureaucratic delays have kept some veterans waiting impatiently for promised benefits."[13]

Similarly, James Marten in *Sing Not War: The Lives of Union and Confederate Veterans in Gilded Age America* (2011) examined marginalized veterans but in this case on both sides. Marten studied residents of soldiers' homes; these institutions served many purposes, including taking care of indigent and troubled veterans. Marten's study reflected his knowledge of contemporary veterans' issues. "Yet we do know that all veterans of major war—especially combat veterans—return to a different world than they left . . . haunted by the horrific images and dead friends, slowed at least temporarily by injuries or other weakening conditions, freed from routines and discipline that have become second nature. And of course, their friends and families and communities have changed, too." While both Northern and Southern veterans shared these problems, Marten maintained that Southerners had a more positive view of Confederate veterans than Northerners had of Union veterans, and this supported the Lost Cause narrative as discussed in Chapter 3.[14]

Confederate veterans had some of the same problems that Union veterans had according to Diane Miller Sommerville in "'Will They Ever Be Able to Forget?' Confederate Soldiers and Mental Illness in the Defeated South" (2011). Sommerville observed that "even a cursory view of sources shows what is certainly obvious to anyone with twenty-first-century sensibilities: that Confederate soldiers greatly suffered from the trauma of war." In fact, Sommerville contended "that Confederate veterans suffered even greater psychological damage than their Union counterparts." David Silkenat in his study *Moment of Despair: Suicide, Divorce, and Debt* in *Civil War Era North Carolina* (2011) discussed Confederate veterans' suicides, an urgent and increasingly relevant twenty-first-century issue for today's veterans. Jeffrey W. McClurken in *Taking Care of the Living: Reconstructing Confederate Families in Virginia* (2009) documented the challenges of rebuilding Southern families. Understanding veterans and their families represented another important gap in Civil War studies prompted by concerns about families dealing with modern wars.[15]

Similarly, a lack of federal aid made the lives of Confederate amputees more difficult. Brain Craig Miller's study *Empty Sleeves: Amputation in the Civil War South* (2015) examined Southern men who lost their limbs in the war. Complicating their postwar lives, amputees did not meet an essential criterion for Southerner's notions of manhood—being physically whole. Moreover, it would take decades, well after Northern veterans received pensions and prosthetic limbs, for these men to realize the assistance they needed from their states. Miller's work represented a first step in documenting the postwar effects of wartime medical trauma: another critical gap assessing the legacy of diseases such as diarrhea, which affected tens of thousands of former Civil War soldiers. Without a basic understanding of the Civil War's medical legacy, it will be impossible to assess the true cost of America's deadliest war.[16]

With all of the horrors identified in these studies, suffering that lasted decades after the war and the continuing misery of veterans and their families, it would seem likely that historians would completely turn away from the war. The broad acceptance of the Union Cause, specifically ending slavery, tempered the revival of antiwar revisionism; rejecting the war meant questioning the wisdom of emancipation. If controversy existed about the Union Cause, it revolved around the extent to which freeing slaves was emphasized over preserving the Union. Chandra Manning in *What This Cruel War Was Over: Soldiers, Slavery and the Civil War* (2007) emphasized Union soldiers' dedication to ending slavery. Gary W. Gallagher in *The Union War* (2011) disputed this notion and argued that Union soldiers and federal supporters fought for the preservation of the Union above all things. In his view, if anything had been discounted in assessments of the Union Cause it was devotion to union and nation. He attributed this deficiency to neglecting the importance of nation because modern scholars focused on race. Gallagher had in the previous decade assessed *The Confederate War: How Popular Will, Nationalism, and Military Strategy Could Not Stave Off Defeat* (1997), identifying the strength of Confederate nationalism, disputing the notion that the Confederacy failed because Southerners lost the will to fight.[17]

Historians challenged what they might consider the internal weakness of Civil War scholarship by expanding its borders beyond the United States and exploring the conflict as a transnational phenomenon. People had not forgotten the international dimension of the Civil War given the Confederacy's need for diplomatic recognition, and the Union's need to make sure that recognition never happened; people remembered the diplomatic history of the Civil War. Recently, this field of study expanded beyond the realm of diplomacy to analyze how the Civil War affected the world and conversely how the world affected the Civil War. This new focus could be directly traced to globalization and awareness of the interconnectivity of nations and the permeability of borders. Mark E. Neely Jr.'s *The Civil War and the Limits of Destruction* (2007) looked across the Rio Grande to the Mexican Civil War that occurred at the same time as the U.S.'s internecine struggle; he compared the level of violence in the U.S Civil War to the level of violence in the Mexican Civil War. In his view, there was no comparison. The Mexican government routinely executed large numbers of captured rebels; the United States did not because an idea existed in nineteenth-century minds that there were defined limits in war. Two different books by outstanding scholars examined Britain's role—Amanda Foreman's A *World on Fire: Britain's Crucial Role in the American Civil War* (2010) and R. J. M. Blackett's *Divided Hearts: Britain and the American Civil War* (2001)—demonstrating the interest in the Civil War as a transitional phenomenon.[18]

Don H. Doyle reframed the traditional diplomatic history approach to the Civil War and examined *The Cause of All Nations: An International History of the American Civil War* (2015). Informed by twenty-first century approaches to international issues, Doyle examined how the "Civil War can be understood as a contest of smart power," a modern term defined as "the adroit combination of *hard-power* coercion with *soft-power* appeals to basic values." While hard power seemed to be clear enough, soft power may be harder to understand. Doyle explained that soft power was used "to appeal to the fundamental values and interest of the foreign country, to demonstrate that the two countries in question share common aspirations." The South did much better wielding soft power in the beginning of the war, portraying secession as a matter of self-determination not slavery, and suggesting that some of the basic elements of the Lost Cause may have originated in the international campaign for diplomatic recognition. Andre M. Fleche's *The Revolution of 1861: The American Civil War in the Age of Nationalist Conflict* (2012) demonstrated the appeal of the confederacy's message in an era when nations, such as Hungary, Poland, and Ireland, struggled to achieve national self-determination. The North's ability to wield soft power against the South improved when the war was about freedom and the end of slavery after the Emancipation Proclamation. Ultimately, Doyle's conclusion invoked elements of the Union Cause that would be familiar to its earliest advocates. Some Europeans "were horrified to see government of the people seriously imperiled in the one place it had achieved its most enduring success. Abraham Lincoln was hardly boasting when he referred to America as the 'last best hope on earth.'" Internationalizing the Civil War did not change basic elements in American Civil War memory.[19]

Globalizing the war constituted only one element in broadening boundaries that had been clearly delineated between the sections; memory now included the border states and their own singular experiences as described in Aaron Astor's *Rebels on the Border: Civil War, Emancipation, and the Reconstruction of Kentucky and Missouri* (2012) and Christopher Phillips's *The Civil War in the Border South* (2013) and *The Rivers Ran Backward: The Civil War and the Remaking of the American Middle Border* (2016). Did the border include occupied areas? Citizens of a nation engaged in a battle for loyalty in occupied areas might be sensitized to the ephemeral nature of this fidelty. Judkin Browning in *Shifting Loyalties: The Union Occupation of Eastern North Carolina* found that white Southerner's loyalties shifted depending on circumstance. Not surprisingly, African Americans persevered in their Unionist allegiances.[20] Similarly the war's border moved westward to the Midwest and beyond. Adam Arenson's *The Great Heart of the Republic: St. Louis and the Cultural Civil War* (2011) described this city as the center of a "cultural civil war" between the North, South, and West over who would dominate the nation. Ari Kelman's *A Misplaced Massacre: Struggling over the Memory of Sand Creek* (2013) redefined the traditional idea of what constituted Civil War studies to include the wars against Native Americans in his examination of a massacre in Civil War Colorado and how it was remembered in the decades since the war.[21]

Other boundaries related to ethnicity had limited most Civil War studies to native-born Americans; the twenty-first century saw the maturity of immigrant Civil War studies. People remembered immigrants had fought as portrayed in Ella Lonn's

Foreigners in the Union Army and Navy that appeared in 1951. Calling Civil War soldiers 'foreigners' revealed a great deal about how Americans felt about immigrants in this era; even as soldiers, they were not Americans. William L. Burton's *Melting Pot Soldiers* (1998), which examined Union soldiers, reconsidered the same issues in 1998. Burton emphasized their American identity as a product of a "melting pot."[22]

In the twenty-first century, Americans, sensitized by diversity studies, took another look at immigration. Scholars studied immigrants in the Confederate army; the Lost Cause downplayed the role of immigrants who served their cause insisting that the Union singularly relied on foreign-born soldiers. David T. Gleeson in *The Green and the Gray: The Irish in the Confederate States of America* (2013) examined not only how they embraced their Confederate identity but also how they understood their Irish identity. The Irish in the Union were better known and have been the subject of numerous studies, including Susannah Ural's *The Harp and the Eagle: Irish-American Volunteers and the Union Army, 1861–1865* (2006). She theorized that while Irish men served in Northern armies for a number of reasons, there was a "common thread" in the way they characterized their support for the Union. "Irishmen routinely explained their actions in terms of the Irish and their American heritage, more often than not in that order." Similarly, Christian B. Keller's study of *Chancellorsville and the Germans: Nativism, Ethnicity, and Civil War Memory* (2007) demonstrated how the view of immigrants changed from emphasizing their American identity to appreciating ethnicity. Keller suggested that Germans' dissatisfaction with their treatment as Union soldiers prompted them to resist the melting pot and to cling more strongly to their ethnic identity.[23]

Awareness of the immigrant experience shaped Civil War memory, as did concern over environmental issues; it took a surprisingly long time to focus on how war shaped the environment and landscapes. According to Lisa M. Brady in *War upon the Land: Military Strategy and the Transformation of Southern Landscapes during the American Civil War* (2012), "The physical destruction of the war called into question some of the most fundamental assumptions Americans had been making about nature and its role in the nation's economic, political, and cultural development." While this destruction affected the war's military strategies, in the war's aftermath, Americans' view of nature changed "and helped shape a new American relationship with the natural world, in which conservation became a vaunted ideal." In a new take on expansion of the government, she cited the "increased federal power to decide what elements in the natural treasury would become permanent fixtures of the national landscape," such as national parks. Similarly, Megan Kate Nelson assessed the war's effect on landscape in her aptly titled *Ruin Nation: Destruction and the American Civil War* (2012). Nelson defined "'ruins' as a material whole that has violently broken into parts; enough of these parts must remain in situ, however, that the observer can recognize what they used to be." Ruins could be cities, homes, trees, and men. Was a nation that had witnessed buildings turn to rubble live on television on a warm September day finally able to see the Civil War's ruins?[24]

Meanwhile, soldiers had to deal with the ruin of their bodies caused by disease. Kathryn Shively Meier in *Nature's Civil War: Common Soldiers and the Environment in 1862 Virginia* (2013) considered two interrelated but generally separate ideas, the Civil War and its effect on the landscape and the Civil War and its effect on soldiers' health. Meier believed that soldiers understood, in ways that nineteenth-century medical professionals did not, the link between the two. Soldiers' self-care included measures to address environmental issues, like polluted water that caused illness. It would be difficult to imagine anyone writing about the Civil War before the early twenty-first century making this link; only in an era when Americans ate organic and gluten-free foods, while wearing sunscreen, would a scholar identify self-care in soldiers' letters.[25]

Environmental history might have been new, but gender studies were more familiar; however, interest in masculinity and how men and women believed a man should act represented a new focus for Civil War studies. Two contrasting studies illustrated this new approach: Lorien Foote's *The Gentlemen and the Roughs: Violence, Honor, and Manhood in the Union Army* (2010) and Stephen W. Berry's *All That Makes a Man: Love and Ambition in the Civil War South* (2003). Foote argued that there was no unity in the North, particularly across different social and economic classes, as to what constituted manhood. The contest over these ideas played out in army conflicts between officers and enlisted men viewed through the lens of military discipline. Berry focused less on men's relationship with men; instead, he emphasized their relationship with women: the romantic love they felt for their wives and girlfriends. He suggested that love and ambition were related to one another and that men were ambitious to demonstrate that they were worthy of love and needed women to validate their accomplishments. When Lost Cause advocates championed the notion that Southern men fought for their wives and girlfriends, there might be a gendered basis for this understanding of wartime actions.[26]

Similarly, the Lost Cause emphasized the religious aspect of Southerners' wartime experiences. Recently, major studies on Civil War religion filled a surprising gap in our understanding of this conflict. Among the most critical presents shaping this phenomenon originated in the resurgence of evangelical Christianity in the last few decades. Moreover, anyone studying soldiers' letters during the recent revival of interest in the common soldier discussed in Chapter 4 could not ignore the importance of religion in these men's lives and deaths. Two major studies assessed this phenomenon. Steven E. Woodworth's *While God Is Marching On: The Religious World of Civil War Soldiers* (2001) focused on common soldiers of both sides who shared a Protestant faith. Sean A. Scott examined Protestant religion on the home front in *A Visitation of God: Northern Civilians Interpret the Civil War* (2011) and

Unionists belief "that the Union was sacred and had to be preserved at all costs since God would achieve his divine purposes through it." Religion of the Union Cause represents a significant gap in Civil War memory studies. George C. Rable studied Catholics and Jews, black and white Americans, and soldiers and civilians alike in *God's Almost Chosen Peoples: A Religious History of the American Civil War* (2010). Looking at the complexity of section, race, gender, class, and religious denominations, these studies likely represented the first word and not the last word on the subject of religion in the Civil War. One avenue of investigation is, what about men and women who did not believe?[27]

Rable also authored one of the major battle studies of this period, *Fredericksburg! Fredericksburg!* (2002). If the present trends in Civil War memory have affected Civil War memory, it emerged in the area of purely military studies. Few academics wrote battlefield studies though these studies remained popular among the broader public and sold well: Allen C. Guelzo's *Gettysburg: The Last Invasion* (2013) was on the *New York Times* best-seller list. Earl Hess, who had written a number of well-received specialized military studies, including volumes on tactics and fortifications, and Gary Gallagher, who completed important memory studies, separately authored articles lamenting the status of military history in Civil War studies at almost the same time in 2014. While both men cited many of the studies discussed in this book and recognized their critical contribution to Civil War studies, they decried how few Civil War scholars studied and taught military history. Despite this concern, innovative approaches applied to battle and campaign studies suggested a way to revitalize the military history of the Civil War. Glenn David Brasher's *The Peninsula Campaign and the Necessity of Emancipation: African Americans and the Fight for Freedom* (2012) examined the interrelationship between the series of battles in 1862 Virginia and the acceptance of the Emancipation Proclamation. Mark M. Smith's *The Smell of Battle, the Taste of Siege: A Sensory History of the Civil War* (2015) applied the notion of sensory history—how battles sounded, smelled, and even tasted—to re-create the actual experience of Civil War battle. Given the nature of memory and sensory stimulus, the Civil War generation might have recalled intense sensory experiences better than they remembered the facts of the battle.[28]

While the smell of Civil War battle represents the leading edge of battlefield history, it took almost as long for anyone to examine the Civil War home front, the final frontier of Civil War studies. Some aspects of the war at home have been covered in studies of Southern and Northern women; however, there were others at home, children and men who never served. James Marten pioneered the study of young people in *The Children's Civil War* (1998). More recently, J. Matthew Gallman in *Defining Duty in the Civil War: Personal Choice, Popular Culture, and the Union Home Front* (2015) assessed how people who did not serve, including military-age men, defined their duty to the Union and the war effort. Only a society that fought two wars simultaneously overseas with only a small percentage of the population in military service would have even contemplated the notion of duty at home.[29]

At the sesquicentennial of the Civil War, we could no longer smell battles, but they remained with us in our memory. With no real personal memory, we viewed the war through a prism of the present. In this present, the United States voted a black man into office, President Barack H. Obama; some Americans rejected the legitimacy of his presidency. His term of office began right after the United States, and the world experienced an economic collapse. While these short-term challenges were daunting, they reflected a long-term reality; the United States operated within a globalized economy that has fostered stagnant wages for the middle class and increasing economic inequality. As Americans struggled at home, they also fought two long wars overseas. After experiencing the worst terrorist attack on U.S. soil that killed thousands of Americans, the federal government expanded its power to deal with potential threats. Many Americans vacillated between fear and uncertainty and still feel uneasy over this expansion. If that was not enough, cultural and social changes had challenged the nature of marriage—same-sex marriage, and ideas of gender— transgendered individuals. All of these developments created a political, social, and cultural backlash, which in turn affected Civil War memory.

One of the best signals to gauge Civil War memory had been shifts in the status of Lincoln and Lee. Doris Kearns Goodwin's best-selling book *Team of Rivals: The Political Genius of Abraham Lincoln* (2005) portrayed Lincoln as a loving father, and Union martyr. Steven Spielberg focused on parts of this study, specifically the passage of the Thirteenth Amendment, and made the movie *Lincoln* (2012). In addition to a brilliant screenplay, Daniel Day-Lewis sublime performance as Lincoln will shape the president's memory for decades. Other authors had written biographies extolling the virtues of the sixteenth president. In 1994, Merrill D. Peterson wrote a book on *Lincoln in American Memory* that identified all positive themes related to his memory including "Savior of the Union, Great Emancipator, Man of the People, the First American, and the Self-made Man." In contrast, twenty years later John McKee Barr felt compelled to examine *Loathing Lincoln: An American Tradition from the Civil War to the Present* (2014) by systematically identifying Lincoln hatred, partly inspired by the contemporary strength of the anti-Lincoln movement. To some extent, the enormously successful anti-Lincoln author, Thomas J. DiLorenzo, made other academics aware of this phenomenon; one of his book titles, *Lincoln Unmasked: What You're Not Supposed to Know about Dishonest Abe* (2006), captured his view of Lincoln. DiLorenzo asserted that the war had nothing to do with stopping slavery since Lincoln was a racist, but everything to do with the size of government, tariffs, and a centralized banking system. On the other side of the political spectrum, Lerone Bennett Jr.'s book *Forced into Glory: Abraham Lincoln's White Dream* (1999) maintained that Lincoln only signed the Emancipation Proclamation because events forced his hand. Lincoln's racism prompted him to work for colonization and the removal of African Americans from the United States, a type of ethnic cleansing. The other side's iconic leader, Robert E. Lee received a similar reappraisal. The most important twenty-first-century study of Lee, Elizabeth Brown Pryor's *Reading the Man: A Portrait of Robert E. Lee through His Private Letters* (2007) presented a more nuanced and complex portrait of the man: neither saint nor sinner, but a man of his times. It might be some time before this idea becomes more accepted because of Lee's broad acceptance as an American hero.[30]

Similarly, the memory of African American military service in the Civil War represented another status indicator in Civil War Memory. The memory of the African American soldiers who served the Union Cause was bolstered by William A Dobak's *Freedom by the Sword: The U.S. Colored Troops, 1862–1867* (2013) and Richard M. Reid's *Freedom for Themselves: North Carolina's Black Soldiers in the Civil War Era* (2008). One tragic aspect of their service highlighted in the last decade and one-half, the massacre of black troops by Confederate soldiers, received comprehensive treatment in several books. George S. Burkhardt wrote of *Confederate Rage, Yankee Wrath: No Quarter in the Civil War* (2007). Two books on the Fort Pillow massacre, the best known of these atrocities, were published in 2005. Kevin M. Levin chronicled the memory of another of these incidents in *Remembering the Battle of the Crater: War as Murder* (2012).[31]

Ironically, the memory of black military service has taken an unusual twist, the controversial discovery of what has been termed black Confederates, the tens of thousands of African Americans who supposedly served as rebel soldiers. The confusion over black military service was rooted, ironically, in slavery. African Americans did serve with the Confederate army, and thus they were literally servants, either body servants, cooks, or laborers; they were not regularly enlisted in the Confederate army. If they had been soldiers their service records would document their enlistment; almost 200,000 African Americans in the Union army and navy left this type of evidence. One type of servant emerged as particularly problematic, the body servant who cared for Confederate soldiers, particularly officers. In some instances, these men appeared very close to their owners, and risked their lives to help them. In addition, some states gave pensions to slaves who had served with the Confederate army; the laws that authorized these expenditures specified that these payments were for servants not soldiers. Kevin Levin, who examined the memory of the Crater, explained why "Black Confederates [came] Out of the Attic and Into the Mainstream" in the *Journal of the Civil War Era* (2014). Levin credited the success of the Union Cause and its emphasis on black military service with inspiring modern-day Confederate supporters, such as the Sons of Confederate Veterans (SCV), to research possible black Confederates. Bruce Levine examines this phenomenon in his essay "In Search of a Usable Past: Neo-Confederates and Black Confederates" (2006) and argued that modern Confederate supporters believed that "painting the Confederate Army as a sea of both black and white faces, it is hoped, will convey a different impression of the war's significance" and portray a cause that could not have been about slavery because it was served by African American soldiers."[32]

The role of black Confederates sparked a controversy in a Civil War venue discussed in earlier chapters—the school textbook. Carol Sheriff began her research on "Virginia's Embattled Textbooks: Lessons (Learned and Not) from the Centennial Era" (2012) when her daughter brought home her fourth-grade textbook. This text did not represent a Lost Cause version of the war; in fact, it covered slavery and emancipation as the cause and consequence of the war. Ironically, the author's view might have been too favorable to the federals since it overstated Unionist support for emancipation. According to Sheriff, the problematic passage "tells Children [that] 'Thousands of Southern blacks fought in the Confederate ranks, including two battalions under the command of Stonewall Jackson.'" No one anywhere had found evidence of these battalions. Sheriff speculated that this might have been a well-intentioned effort to demonstrate diversity and "agency" by African Americans portraying them as active participants in the war and not just as its victims. Based on this and other inaccuracies, Sheriff examined other Virginia texts and found most of them "pro-Confederate by design," though none of the older textbooks made the same statements about black Confederates supporting the notion that this was a new turn in Confederate Civil War memory.[33]

A somewhat different issue shaped Texas textbooks. In 2010, the state's educational officials approved guidelines based on the "Texas Essential Knowledge and Skills"; among the many changes, textbooks emphasized the Christian origin of the nation's founding. These new standards provided specific guidelines on the cause of the Civil War. "The Student is expected to explain reasons for the involvement of Texas in the Civil War such as states' rights, slavery, sectionalism, and tariffs." Placing states' rights first and slavery second effectively minimized its importance. The last "cause," tariffs, reflected another recent notion; the Civil War generation rarely complained about tariffs in their list of grievances against the Union. It might be that contemporary concerns about taxes made the idea of tariffs, taxes on imports, an acceptable reason for a Civil War. The first textbooks reflecting this guidance have been written and are in use in Texas schools. While it might seem that one state's texts did not matter, the size of the school book market in Texas meant that their standards had the potential to influence other states' textbooks. Southern textbooks more than any other type of book shaped Civil War memory.[34]

People read textbooks and sometimes forgot their lessons. The *New York Times'* regular column for the Civil War sesquicentennial, "Disunion," made up some of that gap by featuring columns written by Civil War scholars and experts. Moreover, textbooks often repeated older thinking; these brief articles reflected many of the academic

Civil War narratives described earlier in this chapter. Despite the value of this effort, the end of the sesquicentennial meant the end of this column. As a result, the war's aftermath, Reconstruction, critical to the status of race and reunion, remained forgotten. While Disunion was the voice of many, the *Atlantic* magazine provided a vehicle for an African American's views on a variety of Civil War issues. Ironically, Ta-Nehisi Coates's best-known contribution was an essay in the *Atlantic* Civil War commemorative issue (2012), "Why Do so Few Blacks Study the Civil War?" If African Americans do not study the war in the twenty-first century and beyond, the black experience may one day be lost, again.[35]

Given the number of people who watched movies, as opposed to those who read newspaper columns, film might better reflect popular Civil War memory. Twenty-first-century movies certainly demonstrated the same issues seen in the twentieth. Movies that reflected the Lost Cause view of the war do much better than what one would think at the sesquicentennial. *Gods and Generals* (2003) directed by Ronald F. Maxwell depicted Stonewall Jackson as a Christian martyr, fighting for his home, not slavery, under the direction of the other Lost Cause icon, Robert E. Lee. Jackson's African American cook played a prominent role suggesting that he too fought for his home. In other films, it was not the Confederate Cause, or the Union cause, which did well in this period, but the antiwar cause. In *Cold Mountain* (2004), Confederate women surrendered well before Appomattox rejecting the war because of the privations on the home front. Similarly, Martin Scorsese's *Gangs of New York* (2002) chronicled the story of the Union home front falling apart during the 1863 draft riots in New York. Southern dissent received major motion picture treatment; *The Free State of Jones* chronicled a section of Mississippi that seceded from secession because many of the residents—black and white—rejected Confederate rule.[36]

It became very hard to make a broader statement about what this said about Civil War memory; this was not the Hollywood of *Gone with the Wind* (1939) when a few major companies controlled the film industry; someone like Ronald F. Maxwell with enough financial resources could make a film like *Copperheads* (2013). In a nod to the revisionism, *Copperhead* featured a villainous abolitionist harassing a person accused for his antiwar views. Recently, a low budget film, *Field of Lost Shoes* (2014), highlighted a smaller battle that loomed large to Confederate supporters—the Battle of New Market and the story of the Virginia Military Institute cadets who won a critical Confederate battle in the Shenandoah Valley. Given the many outlets for movies, DVDs, computer-streaming sites like Netflix, and the fact that making movies could be done with less-expensive cameras and editing equipment, movies reflected a variety of Civil War memories. In terms of traditional box-office results and film awards, *Lincoln* (2012), the penultimate statement of the Union Cause in the movies, was by far the most successful Civil War movie of this era.[37]

Much of this study focused on books that have been published, movies that have been produced, and statues that have been commissioned; the twenty-first century and the advent of the Internet allows information to flow without institutional approvals. Many of the books discussed in this study had been peer reviewed by historians, a design for a statue was approved, and a producer made a movie if someone financed the effort. In contrast, anyone with minimal equipment could create a website and write a blog about the Civil War. Technical expertise is no longer a barrier; new software programs made it simple. A quick search using Google found "Weebly," which one reviewer praised as "easy to use." Focusing on the Civil War in school texts might be useless, because most contemporary students acquired their information from sources other than books. Instead, as the study of Civil War memory evolved with twenty-first century technology, the Internet might be the most important way of examining how Americans remembered the war. An obvious place to start might be a website called "Civil War Memory" hosted by Kevin M. Levin who wrote about the Crater and memory. Levin had been an active participant in the black Confederate debate and supported a Union Cause interpretation of the war. A reading of the comments on his blog entries revealed a strong resistance to this view. Supporters of what they termed Confederate Heritage operated their own websites; according to one South Carolina–based site their mission was "to engage in the preservation of Southern history and the protection of Confederate burial sites, battlefields, monuments, symbols and historic objects of the Confederate States of America." The Alabama-based Confederate Heritage Fund remembered the Civil War as "Lincoln's Tax War" solely fought to "collect a 40% import tax." The Union Cause also employed social media; the United States Colored Troops (USCT) Headstone project adopted Facebook as a forum for its efforts to locate and photograph the grave markers of USCT soldiers. While social media allowed non-academics to participate in debates about the Civil War, academics exploited new technologies to engage a broader audience. Brooks D. Simpson, a professor at Arizona State University, used his "Crossroads" blog to comment on Civil War issues including the Confederate flag. If anyone asks, where is the future of Civil War memory? The answer would be in cyberspace, the Internet, and social media.[38]

As we come to the end of this survey, the end of the second term of the first black president, the end of the Civil War sesquicentennial, it is clear that Civil War memory has little to do with the war; instead it is about now, whenever now is, reinterpreted by each generation to address their needs. Where it goes from here, what some have called post-Charleston, is difficult to say. However, as this book goes to press, officials in New Orleans removed the statute of Robert E. Lee from its prominent place in the public space, a victory for the Union cause. In contrast, the protests accompanying this removal suggest that the memory of the Civil War is still contested two year after that terrible night in Charleston. Although the future of Civil War memory is uncertain, based on how . . . Americans have remembered the Civil War, its memory will be about whatever present needs a past. The American Civil War is our great national myth, central to the American nation: what Americans think they are, or what they hope to be. Charles P. Roland called the Civil War, *The American Iliad* (1991), "the epic story of the American people." I would like to suggest that Civil War memory is the American *Odyssey*. Just as Ulysses spent decades trying to get home after the war, so have Americans spent decades trying to complete their own journey homeward from the Civil War, if only in memory.[39]

NOTES

INTRODUCTION

1. Cassie Cope and Andrew Shain, "Haley Calls for Confederate Flag Removal," *The State* (Columbia, S.C.), June 22, 2015, accessed January 11, 2017, http://www.thestate.com/news/politics-government/politics-columns-blogs/the-buzz/article25157617.html; Valerie Bauerlein, "Confederate Flag Removed from South Carolina State House," *Wall Street Journal*, July 20, 2015, accessed January 1, 2017, http://www.wsj.com/articles/confederate-flag-removed-from-south-carolina-statehouse-1436538782; "The Victims: 9 Were Slain at Charleston's Emanuel AME Church, *National Public Radio*, June 18, 2015, accessed January 1, 2017, http://www.npr.org/sections/thetwo-way/2015/06/18/415539516/the-victims-9-were-slain-at-charlestons-emanuel-ame-church; Jim Galloway, "A Monument to MLK Will Crown Stone Mountain," *Atlanta Journal and Constitution*, October 12, 2015, accessed January 17, 2017, http://politics.blog.ajc.com/2015/10/11/a-monument-to-mlk-will-crown-stone-mountain/; "Bowdoin to Discontinue Annual Academic Award in the Name of Jefferson Davis," *Bowdoin in the News*, October 21, 2015, accessed January 11, 2017, http://community.bowdoin.edu/news/2015/10/bowdoin-to-discontinue-annual-academic-award-in-the-name-of-jefferson-davis/.

2. William Faulkner, *Requiem for a Nun* (1951; repr., New York: Vintage, 2012), 73.

3. The study of memory, both collective and historical, is an interdisciplinary effort that has produced a rich body of work. The following are key works that shaped my understanding of this field. Maurice Halbwachs, *On Collective Memory*, ed. and trans. Lewis Coser (Chicago: University of Chicago Press, 1992); Pierre Nora, "Between Memory and History: *Les Lieux de*

Mémoire," Representations 26 (Spring 1989), 7–24; Jeffrey K. Olick, Vered Vinitzky-Seroussi, and Daniel Levy, eds., *The Collective Memory Reader* (New York: Oxford University Press, 2011). See the bibliographic essay for more on memory and history.

4. For the gender implications of amputation, see Brian Craig Miller, *Empty Sleeves: Amputation in the Civil War South* (Athens: University of Georgia Press, 2015).

5. John Bodnar, *Remaking America: Public Memory, Commemoration, and Patriotism in the Twentieth Century* (Princeton, NJ: Princeton University Press, 1992), 13.

6. Gary W. Gallagher, *Causes Won, Lost, and Forgotten: How Hollywood and Popular Art Shape What We Know about the Civil War* (Chapel Hill: University of North Carolina Press, 2008), 42, 43, 45–50, 69, 84, 85, 92, 95–96, 98, 117.

7. Robert Brent Toplin, ed., *Ken Burns's The Civil War: Historians Respond* (New York: Oxford University Press, 1996), xv, xvi; Barbara Liston, "Confederate Flag Supporters Rise Up to Defend Embattled Symbol," *Reuters*, July 12, 2015, accessed January 11, 2017, http://www.reuters.com/article/us-usa-confederate-ride-idUSKCN0PM11Q20150712.

CHAPTER ONE

1. Elizabeth R. Varon, *Appomattox: Victory, Defeat, and Freedom at the End of the Civil War* (New York: Oxford University Press, 2014), 69; Robert Penn Warren, *The Legacy of the Civil War: Meditations on the Centennial* (New York: Random House, 1961), 15; Edward A. Pollard, *The Lost Cause: A New Southern History of the War of the Confederates* (New York: E.B. Treat & Co., 1866).

2. For some key works outlining the Lost Cause see, Gary W. Gallagher and Alan T. Nolan, eds., *The Myth of the Lost Cause and Civil War History* (Bloomington: Indiana University Press, 2000); Rollin G. Osterweis, *The Myth of the Lost Cause, 1865–1900* (Hamden, CT: Archon Books, 1973); Gaines M. Foster, *Ghosts of the Confederacy: Defeat, the Lost Cause and the Emergence of the New South, 1865–1913* (New York: Oxford University Press, 1987); Thomas L. Connelly and Barbara L. Bellows, *God and General Longstreet: The Lost Cause and the Southern Mind* (Baton Rouge: Louisiana State University Press, 1982); William C. Davis, *The Cause Lost: Myths and Realities of the Confederacy* (Lawrence: University Press of Kansas, 1996).

3. Connelly and Bellows, *God and General Longstreet*, 2; Osterweis, *The Myth of the Lost Cause*, ix, x.

4. Charles Reagan Wilson, *Baptized in Blood: The Religion of the Lost Cause 1865–1920* (1980; repr., Athens: University of Georgia Press, 2009), x, 1, 2; W. Scott Poole, *Never Surrender: Confederate Memory and Conservatism in the South Carolina Upcountry* (Athens: University of Georgia Press, 2004), 3.

5. Foster, *Ghosts of the Confederacy*, 4, 5, 6.

6. John R. Neff, *Honoring the Civil War Dead: Commemoration and the Problem of Reconciliation* (Lawrence: University Press of Kansas, 2004), 2, 5.

7. Caroline E. Janney, *Burying the Dead but Not the Past: Ladies' Memorial Associations and the Lost Cause* (Chapel Hill: University of North Carolina Press, 2008).

8. Ibid., 2, 3, 6.

9. Ibid., 3.

10. LeeAnn Whites, *The Civil War as a Crisis in Gender: Augusta, Georgia, 1860–1890* (Athens: University of Georgia Press, 1995), 14.

11. Antoinette G. Van Zelm, "Virginia Women as Public Citizens: Emancipation Day Celebrations and Lost Cause Commemorations, 1863–1890," in *Negotiating Boundaries of Southern Womanhood: Dealing with Powers That Be*, ed. Janet L. Coryell et al. (Columbia: University of Missouri Press, 2000), 71, 72, 73.

12. Victoria E. Ott, "Love in Battle: The Meaning of Courtships in the Civil War and Lost Cause," in *Children and Youth during the Civil War Era*, ed. James Marten (New York: New York University Press, 2012), 126; Michele Gillespie, "Peddling the Lost Cause: A Southern White Woman at Work," in *The Struggle for Equality: Essays on Sectional Conflict, the Civil War, and the Long Reconstruction*, ed. Orville Vernon Burton, Jerald Podair, and Jennifer L. Weber (Charlottesville: University of Virginia Press, 2011), 219.

13. Gary W. Gallagher, *Lee and His Generals in War and Memory* (Baton Rouge: Louisiana State University Press, 1998), xii, 199, 200.

14. Gary W. Gallagher, "Jubal A. Early, the Lost Cause, and Civil War History: A Persistent Legacy," in *The Myth of the Lost Cause and Civil War History*, ed. Gary W. Gallagher and Alan T. Nolan (2000; repr., Bloomington: Indiana University Press, 2010), 43; William Garrett Piston, *Lee's Tarnished Lieutenant: James Longstreet and His Place in Southern History* (Athens: University of Georgia Press, 1987), x; Michael Shaara, *The Killer Angels: The Classic Novel of the Civil War* (1974; repr., New York: Ballantine Books, 1996).

15. Richard D. Starnes, "Forever Faithful: The Southern Historical Society and Confederate Historical Memory," *Southern Cultures* 2, no. 2 (Winter 1996): 178, 179.

16. James C. Cobb, "How Did Robert E. Lee Become an American Icon?" *Humanities* 32, no. 4 (July 2011): 30; Michael A. Ross, "The Commemoration of Robert E. Lee's Death and the Obstruction of Reconstruction New Orleans," *Civil War History* 51, no. 2 (June 2005): 136.

17. Thomas L. Connelly, *Army of the Heartland: The Army of Tennessee, 1861–1862* (Baton Rouge: Louisiana State University Press, 1967), x; Thomas L. Connelly, *Autumn of Glory: The Army of Tennessee, 1862–1865* (Baton Rouge: Louisiana State University Press, 1971); Thomas L. Connelly, *The Marble Man: Robert E. Lee and His Image in American Society* (Baton Rouge: Louisiana State University Press, 1977), xii.

18. Wallace Hettle, *Inventing Stonewall Jackson: A Civil War Hero in History and Memory* (Baton Rouge: Louisiana State University Press, 2011), 2, 28, 69.

19. Donald E. Collins, *The Death and Resurrection of Jefferson Davis* (Lanham, MD: Rowman & Littlefield, 2005), 156.

20. Carol Reardon, "William T. Sherman in Postwar Georgia's Collective Memory, 1864–1914," in *Wars within a War: Controversy and Conflict over the American Civil War*, ed. Gary W. Gallagher and Joan Waugh (Chapel Hill: University of North Carolina Press, 2009), 230.

21. Edward Caudill and Paul Ashdown, *Sherman's March in Myth and Memory* (Lanham, MD: Rowman & Littlefield Publishers, 2008), 3, 6, 67.

22. Anne Sarah Rubin, *Through the Heart of Dixie: Sherman's March and American Memory* (Chapel Hill: University of North Carolina Press, 2014), 1.

23. William A. Blair, *With Malice toward Some: Treason and Loyalty in the Civil War Era* (Chapel Hill: University of North Carolina Press, 2014), 1.

24. Alexander H. Stephens, *A Constitutional View of the Late War between the States: Its Causes, Character, Conduct, and Results, Presented in a Series of Colloquies at Liberty Hall,* 2 vols. (Philadelphia: National Publishing Company, 1868–1870), 1:10, 1:12, 1:43, 2:659, accessed January 14, 2017, https://archive.org/details/constitutionalvi00lcstep (vol. 1); and https://archive.org/details/constitutionalv1870step (vol. 2); Thomas E. Schott, *Alexander H. Stephens of Georgia: A Biography* (Baton Rouge: Louisiana State University Press, 1988).

25. Terry A. Barnhart, *Albert Taylor Bledsoe: Defender of the Old South and Architect of the Lost Cause* (Baton Rouge: Louisiana State University, 2011), 1, 5, 6.

26. Foster, *Ghosts,* 104–114, membership figures, 107.

27. Steven E. Sodergren, "'The Great Weight of Responsibility': The Struggle over History and Memory in *Confederate Veteran* Magazine," *Southern Cultures* 19, no. 3 (Fall 2013): 29, 31, 32, 41.

28. Seth Weitz, "Defending the Old South: The Myth of the Lost Cause and Political Immorality in Florida, 1865–1968," *The Historian* 71, no. 1 (Spring 2009): 80; W. Scott Poole, "Religion, Gender, and the Lost Cause in South Carolina's 1876 Governor's Race: 'Hampton or Hell!'" *Journal of Southern History* 68, no. 3 (August 2002): 576; Rod Andrew Jr., "'My Children on the Field': Wade Hampton, Biography, and the Roots of the Lost Cause," in *The Great Task Remaining before Us: Reconstruction as America's Continuing Civil War,* ed. Paul A. Cimbala and Randall M. Miller (New York: Fordham University Press, 2010), 140.

29. Charles F. Holden, "'Is Our Love for Hampton Foolishness?': South Carolina and the Lost Cause," in *The Myth of the Lost Cause and Civil War History,* ed. Gary W. Gallagher and Alan T. Nolan (2000; repr., Bloomington: Indiana University Press, 2010), 43, 67; Kevin M. Levin, "William Mahone, the Lost Cause, and Civil War History," *Virginia Magazine of History & Biography* 113, no. 4 (September 2005), 381, 407.

30. Glenn W. LaFantasie, *Gettysburg Requiem: The Life and Lost Causes of Confederate Colonel William C. Oates* (New York: Oxford University Press, 2006), xxiv, xxv.

31. Robert Emmett Curran, "The Irish and the Lost Cause: Two Voices," *U.S. Catholic Historian* 31, no. 1 (2013): 131, 132; David T. Gleeson, *The Green and the Gray: The Irish in the Confederate States of America* (University of North Carolina Press, 2013), 8, 9, 24.

32. John C. Inscoe, *Race, War, and Remembrance in the Appalachian South* (Lexington: University Press of Kentucky, 2008), 324; Matthew C. Hulbert, "Constructing Guerrilla Memory: John Newman Edwards and Missouri's Irregular Lost Cause," *Journal of the Civil War Era* 2, no. 1 (March 2012): 60, 64. See also, Matthew C. Hulbert, *The Ghosts of Guerilla Memory: How Civil War Bushwhackers Became Gunslingers in the American West* (Athens: University of Georgia Press, 2016).

CHAPTER TWO

1. For the Cause Victorious see, Neff, *Honoring the Civil War Dead.* For the Won Cause, see Barbara A. Gannon, *The Won Cause: Black and White Comradeship in the Grand Army of the Republic* (Chapel Hill: University of North Carolina Press, 2011). The Union Cause is

more common, see Caroline E. Janney, *Remembering the Civil War: Reunion and the Limits of Reconciliation* (Chapel Hill: University of North Carolina Press, 2013).

2. Neff, *Honoring,* 1, 7, and 137. In his study, he identified the Cause Victorious as "the central tenets of Northern mythology." For our purposes, it will be treated as an indicator of collective memory, see Neff, *Honoring,* 8.

3. Neff, *Honoring,* 9; Janney, *Remembering,* 5.

4. For two earlier studies of the GAR, see Mary R. Dearing, *Veterans in Politics: The Story of the GAR* (Baton Rouge: Louisiana State University Press, 1952); Stuart McConnell, *Glorious Contentment: The Grand Army of the Republic, 1865–1900* (Chapel Hill: University of North Carolina Press, 1992), 206.

5. Gannon, *Won Cause,* 5–7.

6. Ibid., 7, 8.

7. Robert Hunt, *The Good Men Who Won the War: Army of the Cumberland Veterans and Emancipation Memory* (Tuscaloosa: University of Alabama Press, 2010), 5. For the debate over Total War, see Robert A. Doughty, Ira D. Gruber, Roy K. Flint, Mark Grimsley, George C. Herring, Donald D. Horward, and John A. Lynn, *The American Civil War: The Emergence of Total Warfare* (Lexington, MA: D. C. Heath, 1996); Daniel E. Sutherland, *The Emergence of Total War* (Fort Worth, TX: Ryan Place Publishers, 1996); Mark E. Neely Jr., "Was the Civil War a Total War?" *Civil War History* 50, no. 4 (December 2004): 434–458; Charles Royster, *The Destructive War: William Tecumseh Sherman, Stonewall Jackson, and the Americans* (New York: Vintage, 1993); Mark Grimsley, *The Hard Hand of War: Union Military Policy toward Southern Civilians,* 1861–1865 (Cambridge: Cambridge University Press, 1995); Mark E. Neely Jr., *The Civil War and the Limits of Destruction* (Cambridge: Harvard University Press, 2007).

8. Paul H. Buck, *The Road to Reunion, 1865–1900* (Boston: Little, Brown and Company), 240; Janney, *Remembering,* 5–8.

9. Janney, *Remembering,* 7: M. Keith Harris, *Across the Bloody Chasm: The Culture of Commemoration among Civil War Veterans* (Baton Rouge: Louisiana State University Press, 2014), 2, 14.

10. Brian Matthew Jordan, "'Living Monuments': Union Veteran Amputees and the Embodied Memory of the Civil War," *Civil War History* 57, no. 2 (June 2011): 121, 122.

11. Frances M. Clarke, "Forgetting the Women: Debates over Female Patriotism in the Aftermath of America's Civil War," *Journal of Women's History* 23 no. 2 (Summer 2011), 64.

12. Janney, *Remembering,* 125–126; Gannon, *Won Cause,* 57–71.

13. "Address at the Grave of the Unknown Dead," Arlington, Virginia, May 30, 1871, Frederick Douglass Papers, Library of Congress, reel 14, quoted in David W. Blight, *Frederick Douglass' Civil War: Keeping Faith in Jubilee* (1989; repr., Baton Rouge: Louisiana State University Press, 1991), 222–223; David W. Blight, *Race and Reunion: The Civil War in American Memory* (Cambridge: Belknap Press of Harvard University Press, 2001), 2.

14. W. Fitzhugh Brundage, *The Southern Past: A Clash of Memory and Race* (Cambridge: Harvard University Press, 2005), 59–60.

15. William A. Blair, *Cities of the Dead: Contesting the Memory of the Civil War in the South, 1865–1914* (Chapel Hill: University of North Carolina Press, 2004), 12; Van Zelm, "Virginia Women as Public Citizens: Emancipation Day Celebrations and Lost Cause

Commemorations, 1863–1890," 73; Kathleen A. Clark, *Defining Moments: African American Commemoration and Political Culture in the South, 1863–1913* (Chapel Hill: University of North Carolina Press, 2005), 3.

16. Mitch Kachun, *Festivals of Freedom: Memory and Meaning in African-American Emancipation Celebrations, 1808–1915* (Amherst: University of Massachusetts Press, 2003), 150, 154; William Wells Brown, *The Negro in the American Rebellion: His Heroism and His Fidelity*, introduction by John David Smith (1867; repr., Athens: Ohio University Press, 2003).

17. Joseph T. Wilson, *The Black Phalanx: African-American Soldiers in the War of Independence, the War of 1812 and the Civil War* (1890; repr., New York: DaCapo, 1994), unpaged preface; George Washington Williams, *A History of the Negro Troops in the War of the Rebellion 1861–1865*, introduction by John David Smith (1888; repr., New York: Fordham University Press, 2012), xxxvii.

18. Thomas Wentworth Higginson, *Army Life in a Black Regiment and Other Writings* (1870; repr., New York: Penguin, 1997); Luis F. Emilio, *A Brave Black Regiment: The History of the Fifty-Fourth Regiment of Massachusetts Volunteer Infantry, 1863–1865* introduction by Gregory W. Urwin (1894; repr., Boston: DaCapo, 1995); Gannon, *Won Cause*, 58.

19. Joan Waugh, "Ulysses S. Grant, Historian," in *The Memory of the Civil War in American Culture*, ed. Alice Fahs and Joan Waugh (Chapel Hill: University of North Carolina Press, 2004), 22.

20. Waugh, "Grant, Historian," 23; Stephen Davis, "'A Matter of Sensational Interest': The *Century* 'Battles and Leaders' Series," *Civil War History* 27, no. 4 (December 1981): 338.

21. Waugh, "Grant, Historian," 6, 8. For Grant's view of war, see Ulysses S. Grant, *Personal Memoirs* (1885; repr., New York: Modern Library, 1999), 611.

22. Joan Waugh, *U. S. Grant: American Hero, American Myth* (Chapel Hill: University of North Carolina Press, 2009), 2, 3.

23. Merrill D. Peterson, *Lincoln in American Memory* (New York: Oxford University Press, 1994), 26, 27, 35.

24. Barry Schwartz, *Abraham Lincoln and the Forge of National Memory* (Chicago: University of Chicago Press, 2000), 23.

25. M. Keith Harris, "Slavery, Emancipation, and Veterans of the Union Cause: Commemorating Freedom in the Era of Reconciliation, 1885–1915," *Civil War History* 53, no.3 (September 2007): 270; Elizabeth R. Varon, *Appomattox: Victory, Defeat, and Freedom at the End of the Civil War* (Chapel Hill: University of North Carolina Press, 2014), 3.

26. Anne E. Marshall, *Creating a Confederate Kentucky: The Lost Cause and Civil War Memory in a Border State* (Chapel Hill: University of North Carolina Press, 2010), 1, 2, 4.

27. Ibid., 5, 6.

28. Tom Lee, "The Lost Cause That Wasn't: East Tennessee and the Myth of Unionist Appalachia" and Robert M. Sandow, "'Grudges and Loyalties Die Do Slowly': Contested Memories of the Civil War in Pennsylvania's Appalachia," in *Reconstructing Appalachia: The Civil War's Aftermath*, ed. Andrew L. Slap (Lexington: University Press of Kentucky, 2010): 306 and 269–292.

29. W. Scott Poole, "Memory and the Abolitionist Heritage: Thomas Wentworth Higginson and the Uncertain Meaning of the Civil War," *Civil War History* 51, no. 2 (June 2005): 202–203, 204.

30. John Stauffer, *The Black Hearts of Men: Radical Abolitionists and the Transformation of Race* (Cambridge: Harvard University Press, 2001), 282–283.

31. Christian B. Keller, *Chancellorsville and the Germans: Nativism, Ethnicity, and Civil War Memory* (New York: Fordham University Press, 2007), 82, 147

32. Edward J. Blum, *Reforging the White Republic: Race, Religion, and American Nationalism, 1865–1898* (Baton Rouge: Louisiana State University Press, 2005), 14.

33. Thomas J. Pressly, *Americans Interpret Their Civil War* (New York: The Free Press, 1962), 139, 141, 143.

CHAPTER THREE

1. Bruce Catton, *Reflections on the Civil War*, ed. John Leekley (New York: Promontory Press, 1981), 228. For a sampling of Catton's work, his *Army of the Potomac* trilogy, see *Mr. Lincoln's Army* (1951; Garden City, NY: Doubleday, 1951); *Glory Road* (Garden City: Doubleday, 1952); *A Stillness at Appomattox* (Garden City: Doubleday, 1953).

2. Blight, *Race and Reunion*.

3. Karen L. Cox, *Dixie's Daughters: The United Daughters of the Confederacy and the Preservation of Confederate Culture* (Gainesville: University Press of Florida, 2003).

4. Ibid., 3, 26.

5. Joseph Moreau, *Schoolbook Nation: Conflicts over American History Textbooks from the Civil War to the Present* (Ann Arbor: University of Michigan Press, 2003), 83.

6. James M. McPherson, "'Long-Legged Yankee Lies': The Southern Textbook Crusade," in *The Memory of the Civil War in American Culture*, ed. Alice Fahs and Joan Waugh (Chapel Hill: University of North Carolina Press, 2004), 68, 73.

7. Moreau, *Schoolbook Nation*, 89.

8. Paul M. Gaston, *The New South Creed: A Study in Southern Mythmaking* (1970; repr., Montgomery, AL: New South Books, 2002), 28; Foster, *Ghosts of the Confederacy*, 6.

9. Foster, *Ghosts of the Confederacy*, 7.

10. Nina Silber, *The Romance of Reunion: Northerners and the South, 1865–1900* (Chapel Hill: University of North Carolina Press, 1993), 5, 9, 10.

11. Ibid., 172–173.

12. Patrick J. Kelly, "The Election of 1896 and the Restructuring of Civil War Memory," in *The Memory of the Civil War in American Culture*, ed. Alice Fahs and Joan Waugh (Chapel Hill: University of North Carolina Press, 2004), 180, 181, 182.

13. G.J.A. O'Toole, *The Spanish War: An American Epic 1898* (New York: Norton, 1984); David F. Trask, *The War with Spain in 1898* (1981; repr., Lincoln: University of Nebraska Press [Bison], 1996); Ivan Musicant, *Empire by Default: The Spanish-American War and the Dawn of the American Century* (New York: Henry Holt and Co., 1998); Brian McAllister Linn, *The Philippine War, 1899–1902* (Lawrence: University Press of Kansas, 2000); David J. Silbey, *A War of Frontier and Empire: The Philippine American War, 1899–1902* (New York: Hill and Wang, 2007).

14. Gannon, *The Won Cause*, 174–176.

15. Nina Silber, "Emancipation without Slavery: Remembering the Union Victory," in *In the Cause of Liberty: How the Civil War Redefined American Ideals*, ed. William J. Cooper Jr. and John M. McCardell Jr. (Baton Rouge: Louisiana State University Press, 2009), 108.

16. Cecilia Elizabeth O'Leary, *To Die For: The Paradox of American Patriotism* (Princeton, NJ: Princeton University Press, 1999), 5, 6, 195. Francesca Morgan assessed black and white women's groups and the idea of "female nationalism." See, *Women and Patriotism in Jim Crow America* (Chapel Hill: University of North Carolina Press, 2005), 2.

17. Janney, *Remembering the Civil War*, 10.

18. Schwartz, *Abraham Lincoln and the Forge of National Memory*, 7, 24.

19. Barry Schwartz, *Abraham Lincoln in the Post-Heroic Era: History and Memory in Late Twentieth-Century America* (Chicago: University of Chicago Press, 2008), 15.

20. Nina Silber, "Abraham Lincoln and the Political Culture of New Deal America," *Journal of the Civil War Era* 5, no. 3 (September 2015): 348.

21. Gary W. Gallagher, "Shaping Public Memory of the Civil War: Robert E. Lee, Jubal A. Early, and 'Douglas Southall Freeman,'" in *The Memory of the Civil War in American Culture*, ed. Alice Fahs and Joan Waugh (Chapel Hill: University of North Carolina Press, 2004), 45–48; Douglas Southall Freeman, *Lee*, abr. ed., introduction by Richard Harwell (1934; repr., New York: Touchstone, 1991), 114; Connelly, *The Marble Man*.

22. Foster, *Ghosts of the Confederacy*, 178–180.

23. Thomas J. Pressly, *Americans Interpret Their Civil War*, 2nd ed. (New York: Free Press, 1962), 16–17, 146.

24. Ibid., 166, 170–171, 172, 176. Rhodes multivolume history is available at Hathi Trust Digital Library, accessed January 20, 2017, https://catalog.hathitrust.org/Record/000586114.

25. John David Smith, *An Old Creed for the New South: Proslavery Ideology and Historiography, 1865–1918* (1985; reprint with a new preface, Carbondale: Southern Illinois University Press, 2008), 105; James Ford Rhodes, *History of the United States from the Compromise of 1850 to the McKinley-Bryan Campaign of 1896*, vol. 7 (New York: The Macmillan Company, 1920), 355.

26. James Ford Rhodes, *History of the United States from the Compromise of 1850 to the Final Restoration of Home Rule at the South in 1877*, vol. 7 (New York: The Macmillan Company, 1920), 168, 290, 291.

27. John R. Lynch, "Some Historical Errors of James Ford Rhodes," *Journal of Negro History* 2, no. 4 (October 1917): 345, 355. For more on John R. Lynch see his autobiography, *Reminiscence of an Active Life: The Autobiography of John Roy Lynch*, ed. John Hope Franklin (1970, repr., Jackson: University Press of Mississippi, 2008) and for his historical assessment of Reconstruction, see John R. Lynch, *The Facts of Reconstruction* (New York: Neale Publishing, 1913), accessed January 20, 2017, https://archive.org/details/factsofreconstruc00lync. For more on Rhodes, see Robert Cruden, *James Ford Rhodes: The Man, the Historian, and His Work* (Cleveland, OH: Press of Western Reserve University, 1961).

28. Blight, *Race and Reunion*, 11; Woodrow Wilson, *Division and Reunion, 1829–1909* (1893: repr., New York: Longmans, Green, and Co., 1914), unpaged preface, 123, 125, 239, 356. The copy of Wilson's study cited here was owned by a student at the University of Illinois and may have been used as a textbook.

29. Hugh Tulloch, *The Debate on the American Civil War Era* (Manchester, UK: Manchester University Press, 1999), 21, 38; Edward Channing, *A Student's History of the United States* (New York: The Macmillan Company, 1902), accessed January 20, 2017, https://archive.org/details/astudentshistor05changoog, 482, 605.

30. Edward Channing, *A History of the United States: The War for Southern Independence, 1849–1865*, volume 6 (New York: Macmillan, 1925), 3, 18, 19, accessed January 20, 217, https://archive.org/details/historyofuniteds06chan.

31. Pressly, *Americans Interpret*, 230–232; Charles A. Beard, *An Economic Interpretation of the Constitution of the United States* (1913; repr., Mineola, NY: Dover, 2004).

32. Charles A. Beard and Mary R. Beard, *The Rise of American Civilization* (1927; repr., New York: Macmillan, 1961), 2, 53–54, 100.

33. Oliver Perry Chitwood, *A History of Colonial America* (1931; repr., New York: Harper, 1961), 351, 352, 355, quoted in Gary B. Nash, "American History Reconsidered: Asking New Question about the Past," in *Learning from the Past: What History Teaches Us about School Reform*, ed. Diane Ravitch and Maris A. Vinovkis (Baltimore: Johns Hopkins University Press, 1995), 136–137.

34. Ulrich B. Phillips, *American Negro Slavery: A Survey of the Supply, Employment and Control of Negro Labor as Determined by the Planation-Regime* (1918; repr., Baton Rouge: Louisiana State University Press, 1966), 306, 307, 343. For more on Phillips, see John David Smith, "Ulrich B. Phillips: Dunningite or Phillipsian Sui Generis," in *The Dunning School: Historians, Race, and the Meaning of Reconstruction*, ed. John David Smith and J. Vincent Lowery (Lexington: University Press of Kentucky, 2013), 133–156.

35. Eric Foner foreword to *The Dunning School: Historians, Race, and the Meaning of Reconstruction*, ed. John David Smith and J. Vincent Lowery (Lexington: University Press of Kentucky, 2013), ix–xii. Claude G. Bowers, *The Tragic Era: The Revolution after Lincoln* (Cambridge, MA: The Riverside Press, 1929); Paul H. Buck, *The Road to Reunion, 1865–1900* (Boston: Little, Brown and Company, 1937). For a Pulitzer Prize–winning repudiation of the Dunning School that believed the only problem with Reconstruction was that it ended, see Eric Foner, *Reconstruction: America's Unfinished Revolution* (New York: HarperCollins, 1988).

36. Pressly, *Americans Interpret*, 277, 278; Charles W. Ramsdell, "The Changing Interpretation of the Civil War," *Journal of Southern History* 3, no. 1 (February 1937): 11, 12, 13, 16, 27 and "The Natural Limits of Slavery Expansion," *Southwestern Historical Quarterly* 33, no. 2 (October 1929): 111.

37. Frank L. Owsley, "The Irrepressible Conflict," in Twelve Southerners, *I'll Take My Stand: The South and the Agrarian Tradition*, introduction by Susan V. Donaldson (1930; repr., Baton Rouge: Louisiana State University Press, 2006), 62, 71, 74, 77–78, 83.

38. J. G. Randall, "The Blundering Generation," *Mississippi Valley Historical Review* 27, no. 1 (June 1940): 3, 4, 7, 20.

39. Avery O. Craven, *The Repressible Conflict 1830–1861* (Baton Rouge: Louisiana State University Press, 1939), 5, 34, 37, 38, 42.

40. Avery O. Craven, *The Coming of the Civil War*, 2nd ed. rev. (1942; repr., Chicago: University of Chicago Press, 1971), 82–83.

CHAPTER FOUR

1. James M. McPherson, *Battle Cry of Freedom: The Civil War Era* (New York: Oxford University Press, 1988), x.

2. James M. McPherson, *The Negro's Civil War: How American Negroes Felt and Acted during the War for the Union* (New York: Pantheon Books, 1965). See also James M. McPherson, *The Struggle for Equality: Abolitionists and the Negro in the Civil War and Reconstruction* (Princeton, NJ: Princeton University Press, 1964).

3. For a brilliant survey of U.S. history during this period, see James T. Patterson, *Grand Expectations: The United States, 1945–1974* (New York: Oxford University Press, 1996); the notion of the "Good War" is discussed and disputed in Studs Terkel, *"The Good War": An Oral History of World War II* (New York: The New Press, 1984).

4. John Higham, "The Cult of the 'American Consensus: Homogenizing Our History,'" *Commentary* 27 (February 1959): 94.

5. Ibid., 94–95, 100.

6. Allan Nevins, *Ordeal of the Union* (New York: Scribner's, 1947–1971); James L. Crouthamel, "*Allan Nevins's Ordeal of the Union*: A Review Essay," *New York History* 54 no. 1 (January 1973): 59–66.

7. David M. Potter, *The Impending Crisis: 1848–1861*, completed and edited by Don E. Fehrenbacher (New York: Harper Torchbooks, 1976), 36, 49.

8. Jacqueline Anne Goggin, *Carter G. Woodson: A Life in Black History* (Baton Rouge: Louisiana State University Press, 1993); E. R. Thomas, review of *The Repressible Conflict, 1830–1861 by Avery Craven*, in *Journal of Negro History* 24, no. 3 (July 1939): 345–348.

9. W.E.B. Du Bois, *Black Reconstruction in America 1860–1880* (1935; repr., New York, Touchstone [Simon and Schuster] 1995), 1. It is extraordinary that *Black Reconstruction* was published by a mainstream publisher, Harcourt and Brace, and this may be due to Du Bois's position as a leading black scholar and interest in black issues prompted by the Harlem Renaissance. See Claire Parfait, "Rewriting History: The Publication of W.E.B. Du Bois's Black Reconstruction in America (1935)," *Book History* 12, no.1 (January 1, 2009), 266–294.

10. John David Skrentny, "The Effect of the Cold War on African-American Civil Rights: America and the World Audience 1945–1968," *Theory and Society* 27, no. 2 (April 1998): 237–285.

11. Patricia Sullivan, *Lift Every Voice: The NAACP and the Making of the Civil Rights Movement* (New York: New Press, 2009); Taylor Branch, *Parting the Waters: American in the King Years 1954–1963* (New York: Simon & Schuster, 1988).

12. John David Smith, *An Old Creed for the New South: Proslavery Ideology and Historiography, 1865–1918* (1985; repr., Carbondale: Southern Illinois University Press, 2008), 270–272; Richard Hofstadter, "U. B. Phillips and the Plantation Legend," *Journal of Negro History* 29, no. 2 (April 1944): 109–124; Herbert Aptheker, *American Negro Slave Revolts* (1943; repr., New York: International Publishers, 1974).

13. Kenneth M. Stampp, *And the War Came: The North and the Secession Crisis, 1860–1861* (1950; repr., Baton Rouge: Louisiana State University Press, 1970), ix, xi, xvii; Kenneth M. Stampp, *The Peculiar Institution: Slavery in the Ante-bellum South* (1956; repr., New York: Vintage, 1989), vii, viii.

14. Stampp, *And the War Came*, xiv, xvii.

15. Stanley M. Elkins, *Slavery: A Problem in American Institutional and Intellectual Life* (1959; repr., Chicago: University of Chicago Press, 1976). For a response to Elkins see Anne J. Lane, ed., *The Debate over Slavery: Stanley Elkins and His Critics* (Urbana: University of Illinois Press, 1971).

16. C. Vann Woodward, *The Burden of Southern History*, 3rd ed. (1960; repr., Baton Rouge: Louisiana State University Press, 2008), 8, 9, 12, 13.

17. Eugene D. Genovese, *Roll, Jordan, Roll: The World the Slaves Made* (New York: Random House, 1974); John W. Blassingame, *The Slave Community: Plantation Life in the Antebellum South* (New York: Oxford University Press 1972); Herbert G. Gutman, *The Black Family in Slavery and Freedom, 1750–1925* (New York: Vintage Books, 1977); Lawrence W. Levine, *Black Culture and Black Consciousness: Afro-American Folk Thought from Slavery to Freedom* (New York: Oxford University Press, 2007); Albert J. Raboteau, *Slave Religion: The "Invisible Institution" in the Antebellum South* (1978; repr., New York: Oxford University Press, 2004); Deborah Gray White, *Ar'n't I a Woman?: Female Slaves in the Plantation South* (1985; repr., New York: W.W. Norton, 1999). See also, John B. Boles, *Black Southerners, 1619–1869* (Lexington: University Press of Kentucky, 1984) and Willie Lee Rose, *Slavery and Freedom*, ed. William W. Freehling (New York: Oxford University Press, 1982).

18. George P. Rawick, *From Sundown to Sunup: The Making of the Black Community*, vol. 1 in *The American Slave: A Composite Autobiography*, 41 volumes (Westport, CT: Greenwood Publishing, 1972–1979).

19. John M. Coski, *The Confederate Battle Flag: America's Most Embattled Emblem* (Cambridge: Belknap Press of Harvard University Press, 2005), 138.

20. Robert J. Cook, *Troubled Commemoration: The American Civil War Centennial, 1961–1965* (Baton Rouge: Louisiana State University Press, 2007), 15. See also, Jon Wiener, "Civil War, Cold War, Civil Rights: The Civil War Centennial in Context, 1960–1965," in *The Memory of the Civil War in American Culture*, ed. Alice Fahs and Joan Waugh (Chapel Hill: University of North Carolina Press, 2004), 237–257.

21. Cook, *Troubled Commemoration*, 104.

22. David W. Blight, *American Oracle: The Civil War in the Civil Rights Era* (Cambridge: Belknap Press of Harvard University Press, 2011), 20, 21.

23. Ibid., 1, 2.

24. Robert Penn Warren, *The Legacy of the Civil War: Meditations on the Centennial* (New York: Random House, 1961), 4, 7, 8, 23.

25. Ibid., 55, 57, 59.

26. Thomas A. Bailey, *The American Pageant: A History of the Republic,* 1st ed. and 2nd ed. (Boston: D.C. Heath and Co., 1956, 1961), 364–368, 372; Thomas A. Bailey, *The American Pageant: A History of the Republic,* 3rd ed., vol. 1 (Boston: D.C. Heath and Company, 1966). See pages on "slavery" in index of each volume for pages and identical treatment.

27. A number of fine books have been written on the 1960s; here are two. David R. Farber, *The Age of Great Dreams: America in the 1960s* (New York: Hill & Wang, 1994) and Todd Gitlin, *The Sixties: Years of Hope, Days of Rage* (New York: Bantam Books, 1987).

28. Patterson, *Grand Expectations*, 442–447, 678–742.

29. Thomas A. Bailey and David M. Kennedy, *The American Pageant: A History of the Republic,* 6th ed., vol. 1 (Lexington, MA: D.C. Heath and Co., 1979), 334–342.

30. Rollin G. Osterweis, *The Myth of the Lost Cause, 1865–1900* (Hamden, CT: Archon Books, 1973); Foster, *Ghosts of the Confederacy*; Thomas Lawrence Connelly and Barbara L. Bellows, *God and General Longstreet: The Lost Cause and the Southern Mind* (Baton Rouge: Louisiana State University Press, 1982); John A. Simpson, "The Cult of the 'Lost Cause,'" *Tennessee Historical Quarterly* 34, no. 4 (Winter 1975): 350–361.

31. Bell Irvin Wiley, *The Common Soldier in the Civil War* (New York: Grosset and Dunlap, 1952), Book 1, 14–15, 315, 360–361. This volume is a reprint of Bell Irvin Wiley, *The Life of Johnny Reb: The Common Soldier of the Confederacy* (New York: Bobbs-Merrill, 1943) and *The Life of Billy Yank: The Common Soldier of the Union* (New York: Bobbs-Merrill, 1952).

32. Gerald F. Linderman, *Embattled Courage: The Experience of Combat in the American Civil War* (New York: Free Press, 1987).

33. The study of the Civil War common soldier represents a rich literature; I chose some of the more important works that seemed to reflect significant evolutions of this subfield. Earl J. Hess, *Liberty, Virtue, and Progress: Northerners and Their War for the Union* (New York: Fordham University Press, 1997); Earl J. Hess, *The Union Soldier in Battle: Enduring the Ordeal of Combat* (Lawrence: University Press of Kansas, 1997); and James M. McPherson, *For Cause and Comrades: Why Men Fought in the Civil War* (New York: Oxford University Press, 1997). Sailors have been neglected until recently; see Michael Bennett, *Union Jacks: Yankee Sailors in the Civil War* (Chapel Hill: University of North Carolina Press, 2004).

34. These represent only a sample of books that use common soldiers' accounts. Joseph T. Glatthaar, *The March to the Sea and Beyond: Sherman's Troops in the Savannah and Carolinas Campaign* (New York: New York University Press, 1985); John J. Hennessy, *Return to Bull Run: The Campaign and Battle of Second Manassas* (1993; repr., Norman: University of Oklahoma Press, 1999); Stephen W. Sears, *To the Gates of Richmond: The Peninsula Campaign* (New York: Ticknor & Fields, 1992) and *Landscape Turned Red: The Battle of Antietam* (New York: Mariner Books, 1983); Harry W. Pfanz, *Gettysburg: The Second Day* (Chapel Hill: University of North Carolina Press, 1987).

35. Thomas Lawrence Connelly, *Army of the Heartland: The Army of Tennessee, 1861–1862* (1967; repr., Baton Rouge: Louisiana State University Press, 2001); *Autumn of Glory: The Army of Tennessee, 1862–1865* (Baton Rouge: Louisiana State University Press, 1971); and *The Marble Man,* xii; Alan T. Nolan, *Lee Considered: General Robert E. Lee and Civil War History* (Chapel Hill: University of North Carolina Press, 1991), 3. For two studies on Shiloh that reflect the turn to the West, see Wiley Sword, *Shiloh: Bloody April* (New York: Morrow, 1974) and James L. McDonough, *Shiloh: In Hell before Night* (Knoxville: University of Tennessee Press, 1977). The western theater is still not as well documented as the eastern theater; much more remains to be examined. For an excellent summary of the western theater, see Earl J. Hess, *The Civil War in the West: Victory and Defeat from the Appalachians to the Mississippi* (Chapel Hill: University of North Carolina Press, 2012).

36. Du Bois, *Black Reconstruction*; Bell Irvin Wiley, *Southern Negroes 1861–1865* (New Haven, CT: Yale University Press, 1938); Benjamin Quarles, *The Negro in the Civil War* (1953; repr., Boston: Da Capo, 1989) and *Lincoln and the Negro* (1962; repr., New York: Da

Capo, 1991); Dudley T. Cornish, *The Sable Arm: Black Troops in the Union Army, 1861–1865* (1956; repr., Lawrence: University Press of Kansas, 1987) xiii; Joseph T. Glatthaar, *Forged in Battle: The Civil War Alliance of Black Soldiers and White Officers* (New York: Free Press, 1990); Noah Andre Trudeau, *Like Men of War: Black Troops in the Civil War*, 1862–1865 (Boston: Little, Brown, 1998); David L. Valuska, *The African American in the Union Navy, 1861–1865* (New York: Garland, 1993); James G. Hollandsworth Jr., *The Louisiana Native Guards: The Black Military Experience during the Civil War* (Baton Rouge: Louisiana State University Press, 1995); and Edward A. Miller Jr., *The Black Civil War Soldiers of Illinois; The Story of the Twenty-Ninth U.S. Colored Infantry* (Columbia: University of South Carolina Press, 1998).

37. Peter Burchard, *One Gallant Rush: Robert Gould Shaw and His Brave Black Regiment* (New York: St. Martin's Press, 1965); Luis F. Emilio, *A Brave Black Regiment: History of the Fifty-Fourth Regiment of Massachusetts Volunteer Infantry, 1863–*1865 (1894; repr., New York: Da Capo Press, 1995). See also Russell Duncan, *Where Death and Glory Meet: Colonel Robert Gould Shaw and the 54th Massachusetts Infantry* (Athens: University of Georgia Press, 1999); Martin H. Blatt, Thomas J. Brown, and Donald Yacovone, eds., *Hope and Glory: Essays on the Legacy of the 54th Massachusetts Regiment* (Amherst: University of Massachusetts Press, 2001).

38. These documents are published in Ira Berlin et al., *Freedom: A Documentary History of Emancipation*, series 1, vols. 1, 2, 3, series 2, one volume, series 3, volumes 1 and 2, publishers various, 1985–2013.

39. Agatha Young, *The Women in the Crisis: Women of the North in the Civil War* (New York: McDowell, Obolensky, 1959); Mary Elizabeth Massey, *Bonnet Brigades* (New York: Knopf, 1966); Anne Firor Scott, *The Southern Lady: From Pedestal to Politics, 1830–1930* (Chicago: University of Chicago Press, 1970).

40. George C. Rable, *Civil Wars: Women and the Crisis of Southern Nationalism* (Urbana: University of Illinois Press, 1989); Victoria E. Bynum, *Unruly Women: The Politics of Social and Sexual Control in the Old South* (Chapel Hill: University of North Carolina Press, 1992), 1; Jacqueline Jones, *Labor of Love, Labor of Sorrow, Black Women, Work, and the Family from Slavery to the Present* (New York: Basic Books, 1985).

41. LeeAnn Whites, *The Civil War as a Crisis in Gender: Augusta, Georgia, 1860–1890* (Athens: University of Georgia Press, 1995); Drew Gilpin Faust, *Mothers of Invention: Women of the Slaveholding South in the American Civil War* (Chapel Hill: University of North Carolina Press, 1996), xiii.

42. Catherine Clinton and Nina Silber, eds., *Divided Houses: Gender and the Civil War* (New York: Oxford University Press, 1992).

43. Elizabeth D. Leonard, *All the Daring of the Soldier: Women of the Civil War Armies* (New York: W.W. Norton, 1999); DeAnne Blanton and Lauren M. Cook, *They Fought Like Demons: Women Soldiers in the American Civil War* (Baton Rouge: Louisiana State University Press, 2002); Sarah Rosetta Wakeman, *An Uncommon Soldier: The Civil War Letters of Sarah Rosetta Wakeman, alias Pvt. Lyons Wakeman 153rd Regiment New York State Volunteers, 1862–1864*, ed. Lauren Cook Burgess (New York: Oxford University Press, 1996).

44. John Bennett Walters, "General William T. Sherman and Total War," *Journal of Southern History* 14, no. 4 (November 1948): 448, 480; James Reston Jr., *Sherman's March and Vietnam* (New York: MacMillan, 1984), 8; T. Harry Williams, *Lincoln and His Generals* (New York:

Knopf, 1952); Charles W. Royster, *The Destructive War: William Tecumseh Sherman, Stonewall Jackson, and the Americans* (New York: Knopf, 1991); Mark Grimsley, *The Hard Hand of War: Union Military Policy toward Southern Civilians, 1861–1865* (Cambridge: Cambridge University Press, 1995). For a history of the Total War argument and a critique, see Mark Neely Jr., "Was the Civil War a Total War?" *Civil War History* 37, no. 1 (March 1991): 5–28.

45. Blight, *Race and Reunion*, 198.

CHAPTER FIVE

1. United States, National Park Service, "African American Civil War Memorial Website: History and Culture," accessed January 22, 2017, http://www.nps.gov/afam/learn/historyculture/index.htm; Emma Login, "Contemporary War Memorials and the Urban Landscape: The Memorialization of Marginalized Groups in Washington D.C," in *Mapping Generations of Traumatic Memory in American Narratives,* ed. Dana Mihăilescu, Roxanna Oltean, and Mihaela Precup (Newcastle upon Tyne, UK: Cambridge Scholars Publishing, 2014), 212–213.

2. Bodnar, *Remaking America*, 13, 28, 31; Thomas J. Brown, *Civil War Canon: Sites of Confederate Memory in South Carolina* (Chapel Hill: University of North Carolina Press, 2015).

3. Kirk Savage, *Standing Soldiers, Kneeling Slaves: Race, War, and Monument in Nineteenth-Century America* (Princeton: Princeton University Press, 1997), 3, 19; Cynthia Mills and Pamela H. Simpson, eds., *Monuments to the Lost Cause: Women, Art, and the Landscapes of Southern Memory* (Knoxville: University of Tennessee Press, 2003), xix.

4. David W. Blight, "The Shaw Memorial in the Landscape of Civil War Memory," in *Hope and Glory: Essays on the Legacy of the Fifty-Fourth Massachusetts Regiment*, ed. Martin H. Blatt, Thomas J. Brown, and Donald Yacovone (Amherst: University of Massachusetts Press, 2001), 80; Rhonda L. Reymond, "Memorials, U.S.," in *American Civil War: The Definitive Encyclopedia and Document Collection*, ed. Spencer C. Tucker, 6 vols. (Santa Barbara, CA: ABC Clio, LLC, 2013), vol. 3: 1260.

5. Mills and Simpson, eds., *Monuments to the Lost Cause*, xvi, xviii, xxi, 149–163, 203–218; Maurice M. Manning, *Slave in a Box: The Strange Career of Aunt Jemima* (Charlottesville: University of Virginia Press, 1998).

6. Mills and Simpson, eds., *Monuments to the Lost Cause*, 241–248; Ben Brumfield and Ralph Ellis, "New Orleans Votes to Remove Confederate, Civil War Monuments," cnn.com, accessed January 22, 2017, http://www.cnn.com/2015/12/17/us/new-orleans-confederate-monuments-vote/

7. Timothy B. Smith, *The Golden Age of Battlefield Preservation: The Decade of the 1890s and the Establishment of America's First Five Military Parks* (Knoxville: University of Tennessee Press, 2008), 1, 220.

8. Ibid., 2.

9. Bradley S. Keefer, *Conflicting Memories on the "River of Death": The Chickamauga Battlefield and the Spanish-American War, 1863–1933* (Kent, OH: Kent State University Press, 2013), 1.

10. Edward Tabor Linenthal, *Sacred Ground: Americans and Their Battlefields* (Champaign: University of Illinois Press, 1993), 1, 89, 90.

11. Carol Reardon, *Pickett's Charge in History and Memory* (Chapel Hill: University of North Carolina Press, 1997), 70. For newspaper coverage, see Barbara A. Gannon, *The Won Cause: Black and White Comradeship in the Grand Army of the Republic* (Chapel Hill: University of North Carolina Press, 2011), 186–187.

12. Jim Weeks, *Gettysburg: Memory, Market, and an American Shrine* (Princeton, NJ: Princeton University Press, 2003), 7, 8.

13. Jennifer M. Murray, *On a Great Battlefield: The Making, Management, and Memory of Gettysburg National Military Park, 1933–2012* (Knoxville: University of Tennessee Press, 2014), 2, 14, 47.

14. Ibid., 1.

15. Thomas A. Desjardin, *These Honored Dead: How the Story of Gettysburg Shaped American Memory* (Cambridge, MA: Da Capo Press, 2004), xvi, 4–6.

16. Paul A. Shackel, *Memory in Black and White: Race, Commemoration, and the Post-Bellum Landscape* (Lanham, MD: Altamira Press, 2003), 1.

17. Michael Weeks, *The Complete Civil War Road Trip Guide: More Than 500 Sites from Gettysburg to Vicksburg* (New York: The Countryman Press, 2016), 59, 99, 253, 273.

18. "Welcome to Olustee Battlefield Historic State Park," Florida State Parks, accessed January 22, 2017, http://www.floridastateparks.org/olusteebattlefield/; State of Florida, Department of Environmental Protection, Division of Recreation and Parks, "Olustee Battlefield Historic State Park, Unit Management Plan," May 19, 2008, accessed January 22, 2017, http://www.dep.state.fl.us/parks/planning/parkplans/OlusteeBattlefieldHistoricStatePark.pdf, 1, 20; Lizette Alvarez, "Blue and Gray Still in Conflict at Battle Site," *New York Times*, January 16, 2014, accessed January 22, 2017, http://www.nytimes.com/2014/01/17/us/blue-and-gray-still-in-conflict-at-a-battle-site.html?_r=0

19. Tony Horwitz, *Confederates in the Attic: Dispatches from the Unfinished Civil War* (New York: Pantheon, 1998).

20. *Lincoln,* directed by Stephen Spielberg (Burbank: Touchstone Home Entertainment, 2013), DVD. For an examination of the two distinct battles at Fort Fisher that compose the Wilmington Campaign, see Chris E. Fonvielle Jr., *The Wilmington Campaign: Last Rays of Departing Hope* (Mechanicsburg, PA: Stackpole Books, 1997).

CHAPTER SIX

1. Martin H. Blatt, Thomas J. Brown, and Donald Yacovone, eds., *Hope and Glory: Essays on the Legacy of the Fifty-Fourth Massachusetts Regiment* (Amherst: University of Massachusetts Press, 2001), 1, 215–235.

2. Nina Silber, *The Romance of Reunion: Northerners and the South, 1865–1900* (Chapel Hill, NC: University of North Carolina Press, 1993). For new perspectives on *Gone with the Wind*, see James A. Crank, ed., *New Approaches to Gone with the Wind* (Baton Rouge: Louisiana State University Press, 2015).

3. Jim Cullen, *The Civil War in Popular Culture: A Reusable Past* (Washington, DC: Smithsonian Institution Press, 1995).

4. Ibid., 65–107.

5. Lee Clark Mitchell, ed., *New Essays on the Red Badge of Courage* (New York: Cambridge University Press, 1986), 3–7, 11, 77–78, 83, 88–91.

6. Michael Shaara, *The Killer Angels* (1974; repr., New York: Ballantine Books, 1996); Michael D. Sharp, ed., "Michael Shaara," *Popular Contemporary Writers*, vol. 9 (Tarrytown, NY: Marshall Cavendish, 2006), 1247–1262.

7. Edmund Wilson, *Patriotic Gore: Studies in the Literature of the American Civil War* (1962; repr., London: Hogarth Press, 1987), unpaged author biography, xxiii, xxxiii, xlii, xliv.

8. Daniel Aaron, *The Unwritten War: American Writers and the Civil War* (1973; repr,. Tuscaloosa: University of Alabama Press, 2003), xvii, xviii, 91–92, 149–163, 181–192.

9. Ibid., 227–228, xviii.

10. Alice Fahs, *The Imagined Civil War: Popular Literature of the North and South, 1861–1865* (Chapel Hill: University of North Carolina Press, 2001), 1.

11. Alice Fahs, "Remembering the Civil War in Children's Literature of the 1880s and 1890s," in *The Memory of the Civil War in American Culture*, ed. Alice Fahs and Joan Waugh (Chapel Hill: University of North Carolina Press, 2004), 79, 80, 86, 91.

12. Fahs, *Imagined Civil War*, 317–318.

13. Sarah E. Gardner, *Blood and Irony: Southern White Women's Narratives of the Civil War, 1861–1937* (Chapel Hill: University of North Carolina Press, 2004), 5.

14. Mark E. Neely, Jr., Harold Holzer, and Gabor S. Boritt, *The Confederate Image: Prints of the Lost Cause* (Chapel Hill: University of North Carolina Press, 1987); Mark E. Neely Jr. and Harold Holzer, *The Union Image: Popular Prints of the Civil War North* (Chapel Hill: University of North Carolina Press, 2000). For a history of the painting, *The Burial of Latané*, and an analysis of its meaning, see Drew Gilpin Faust, *Southern Stories: Slaveholders in Peace and War* (Columbia: University of Missouri Press, 1992), 148–159.

15. Gary W. Gallagher, *Causes Won, Lost, and Forgotten: How Hollywood and Popular Art Shape What We Know about the Civil War* (Chapel Hill: University of North Carolina Press, 2008), 136–207.

16. Jenny Barrett, *Shooting the Civil War: Cinema, History and American National Identity* (New York: I. B. Tauris, 2009), 3, 5, 188, 189.

17. Lawrence A. Kreiser Jr. and Randal Allred, *The Civil War in Popular Culture: Memory and Meaning* (Lexington: University Press of Kentucky, 2014), 1; John B. Kuiper, "Civil War Films: A Quantitative Description of a Genre," *Journal of the Society of Cinematologists* 4/5 (1964/1965): 82, 83; Michael R. Pitts, *Western Movies: A Guide to 5,105 Feature Films* (Jefferson, NC: McFarland, 2013); Richard Aquila, *The Sagebrush Trail: Western Movies and Twentieth-Century America* (Tucson: University of Arizona Press, 2015), 7.

18. Kuiper, "Civil War Films," 86, 87–88.

19. Bruce Chadwick, *The Reel Civil War: Mythmaking in American Film* (New York: Knopf, 2001), 6, 7, 9, 13.

20. Ibid., 3–4, 96–129. For a contemporary record on lynchings that document not only the number of extralegal killings but also the fact that only a small percentage, 21 percent, were for those accused of rape; many men and women were murdered for lesser alleged crimes, see Facts on File Inc., *The 1916 World Almanac and Books of Facts* (New York: Press Publishing Co., 1915), 275, accessed January 25, 2017, https://books.google.com/books?id=MWY3AA AAMAAJ&printsec=frontcover&source=gbs_ge_summary_r&cad=0#v=onepage&q&f=false.

21. Dick Lehr, *The Birth of a Nation: How a Legendary Filmmaker and a Crusading Editor Reignited America's Civil War* (New York: Public Affairs, 2014), xvi; "Kansas Bars 'Nation' Film," *The Moving Picture World*, February 12, 1916, 996; Leslie A. Schwalm, *Emancipations Diaspora: Race and Reconstruction in the Upper Midwest* (Chapel Hill: University of North Carolina Press, 2009), 239.

22. Brian Steel Wills, *Gone with the Glory: The History of the Civil War in Cinema* (Lanham, MD: Rowman and Littlefield, 2007), 4, 52, 101–106, 166.

23. Gallagher, *Causes, Won, Lost, and Forgotten*, 2; David W. Blight, *Race and Reunion; The Civil War in American Memory* (Cambridge: Belknap Press of Harvard University Press, 2001), 2.

24. Gallagher, *Causes Won, Lost, and Forgotten*, 42, 51–54.

25. Ibid., 92.

26. James A. Ramage, *Gray Ghost: The Life of Col. John Singleton Mosby* (1999; repr., Lexington: University Press of Kentucky, 2010), 342; Paul Ashdown and Edward Caudill, *The Mosby Myth: A Confederate Hero in Life and Legend* (New York: Scholarly Resources, 2002), 179–191.

27. David B. Sachsman, S. Kittrell Rushing, and Roy Morris Jr., eds., *Memory and Myth: The Civil War in Fiction and Film from Uncle Tom's Cabin to Cold Mountain* (West Lafayette, IN: Purdue University Press, 2007), 246; John M. Cassidy, *Civil War Cinema: A Pictorial History of Hollywood and the War between the States* (Missoula, MT: Pictorial Histories Publishing House, 1986), 149–169.

28. John De Vito and Frank Tropea, *Epic Television Miniseries: A Critical History* (Jefferson, NC: McFarland, 2010), 6, 31–40. A recent biography of Haley addressed the issue of *Root*'s accuracy in detail. See Robert J. Norrell, *Alex Haley: And the Books That Changed a Nation* (New York: St. Martin's Press, 2015), 175–202.

29. Robert Brent Toplin, ed., *Ken Burns's The Civil War: Historians Respond* (New York: Oxford University Press, 1997), xv, xvi, xx–xxi.

30. Ibid., xvi, 21, 28, 33–34, 44, 55, 110, 112.

31. Ryan Poe, "City Council Begins Process That Could Move Forrest Statue, Grave," *Commercial Appeal* (Memphis), July 7, 2015, accessed January 24, 2017, http://www .commercialappeal.com/news/government/city/city-council-begins-process-that-could-move-forrest-statue-grave-ep-1177334513-324362511.html.

CHAPTER SEVEN

1. Drew Gilpin Faust, *This Republic of Suffering: Death and the American Civil War* (New York: Knopf Doubleday Publishing Group, 2008).

2. Ibid., xiii, xiv, xviii. See also Drew Gilpin Faust, "'We Should Grow Too Fond of It': Why We Love the Civil War," *Civil War History* 50, no. 4 (December 2004): 368–383. Mark S. Schantz also studied mass killing in his study *Awaiting the Heavenly Country: The Civil War and American Culture of Death*. Instead of focusing on how the war transformed the United States, he emphasized how antebellum culture prepared Americans for the war. "Americans came to fight the Civil War in the midst of a wider cultural world that sent them messages about death that made it easier to kill and be killed," including the idea of heaven. Mark S. Schantz,

Awaiting the Heavenly Country: The Civil War and America's Culture of Death (Ithaca, NY: Cornell University Press, 2008), 2.

3. J. David Hacker, "A Census-Based Count of the Civil War Dead," *Civil War History* 57, no. 4 (December 2011): 307–348; Nicholas Marshall, "The Great Exaggeration: Death and the Civil War," *Journal of the Civil War Era* 4, no. 1 (March 2014): 3–27.

4. Yael A. Sternhell, "Revisionism Reinvented?: The Antiwar Turn in Civil War Scholarship," *Journal of the Civil War Era* 3, no. 2 (June 2013): 239–256; David Goldfield, *America Aflame: How the Civil War Created a Nation* (New York: Bloomsbury Publishing USA, 2011), 3; Harry S. Stout, *Upon the Altar of the Nation: A Moral History of the Civil War* (New York: Viking, 2006), xvii, xviii. For a wide-ranging and enormously impressive narrative on Southern History and memory, see David Goldfield, *Still Fighting the Civil War: The American South and Southern History* (Baton Rouge: Louisiana State University Press, 2002).

5. Margaret Humphreys, *Marrow of Tragedy: The Health Crisis of the American Civil War* (Baltimore: Johns Hopkins University Press, 2013), 1, 2; Jane E. Schultz, *Women at the Front: Hospital Workers in Civil War America* (Chapel Hill: University of North Carolina Press, 2004), 2. See also, Shauna Devine, *Learning from the Wounded: The Civil War and the Rise of American Medical Science* (Chapel Hill: University of North Carolina Press, 2014).

6. Jim Downs, *Sick from Freedom: African-American Illness and Suffering during the Civil War and Reconstruction* (Oxford: Oxford University Press, 2012), 4.

7. Stephen Berry, ed., *Weirding the War: Stories from the Civil War's Ragged Edges* (Athens: University of Georgia Press, 2011), 5.

8. Michael Fellman, *Inside War: The Guerilla Conflict in Missouri during the Civil War* (New York: Oxford University Press, 1989), xvi, xvii, xviii; Daniel E. Sutherland, *A Savage Conflict: The Decisive Role of Guerrillas in the American Civil War* (Chapel Hill: University of North Carolina Press, 2009), ix, x, xii. Civil War guerilla studies represent a vibrant subfield. See Barton A. Myers, *Executing Daniel Bright: Race, Loyalty, and Guerrilla Violence in a Coastal Carolina Community, 1861–1865* (Baton Rouge: Louisiana State University Press, 2011); Joseph M. Beilein Jr. and Matthew C. Hulbert, eds., *The Civil War Guerrilla: Unfolding the Black Flag in History, Memory, and Myth* (Lexington: University Press of Kentucky, 2015); Mark W. Geiger, *Financial Fraud and Guerrilla Violence in Missouri's Civil War, 1861–1865* (New Haven, CT: Yale University Press, 2010). For more on how guerilla warfare in the United States may have shaped the evolution of the international law on war, see John Fabian Witt, *Lincoln's Code: The Laws of War in American History* (New York: Free Press, 2012).

9. Benjamin G. Cloyd, *Haunted by Atrocity: Civil War Prisons in American Memory* (Baton Rouge: Louisiana State University Press, 2010), 3; Charles W. Saunders Jr., *While in the Hands of the Enemy: Military Prisons of the Civil War* (Baton Rouge: Louisiana State University Press, 2005), 2.

10. Cloyd, *Haunted*, 132–135, 140, 164; McKinley Kantor, *Andersonville* (1955; repr., New York: Penguin, 2015); Saul Levitt, *The Andersonville Trial* (1960; repr., New York: Dramatist Play Service, 1988); Hollywood Television Theater, *The Andersonville Trial*, directed by George C. Scott, written by Saul Levitt (Public Broadcasting System, May 17, 1970); William Marvel, *Andersonville: The Last Depot* (Chapel Hill: University of North Carolina Press, 1994), x–xi.

11. Eric T. Dean Jr., *Shook over Hell: Post-Traumatic Stress, Vietnam, and the Civil War* (Cambridge, MA: Harvard University Press, 1997), 26, 71. For a study on the homecoming of World War II veterans see, Thomas Childers, *Soldier from the War Returning: The Greatest Generation's Troubled Homecoming from World War II* (Boston: Houghton Mifflin Harcourt, 2009).

12. Craig A. Warren, *Scars to Prove It: The Civil War Soldier and American Fiction* (Kent, OH: Kent State University Press, 2009), 4, 8; John A. Casey Jr., *New Men: Reconstructing the Image of the Veteran in Late-Nineteenth-Century American Literature and Culture* (New York: Fordham University Press, 2015), 2.

13. Brian Matthew Jordan, *Marching Home: Union Veterans and Their Unending Civil War* (New York: Liveright, 2014), 4, 8.

14. James Marten, *Sing Not War: The Lives of Union and Confederate Veterans in Gilded Age America* (Chapel Hill: University of North Carolina Press, 2011), 11, 19, 20.

15. Diane Miller Sommerville, "Will They Ever Be Able to Forget?: Confederate Soldiers and Mental Illness in the Defeated South," in *Weirding the War: Stories from the Civil Wars Ragged Edges*, ed. Stephen Berry (Athens: University of Georgia Press, 2011), 322; David Silkenat, *Moments of Despair: Suicide, Divorce, and Debt in Civil War Era North Carolina* (Chapel Hill: University of North Carolina Press, 2011); Jeffrey W. McClurken, *Take Care of the Living: Reconstructing Confederate Veteran Families in Virginia* (Charlottesville: University of Virginia Press, 2009). See also Diane Miller Sommerville, "'A Burden too Heavy to Bear': War Trauma, Suicide, and Confederate Soldiers," *Civil War History* 59, no. 4 (December 2013): 453–491.

16. Brian Craig Miller, *Empty Sleeves: Amputation in the Civil War South* (Athens: University of Georgia Press, 2015), 1–16.

17. Chandra Manning, *What This Cruel War Was Over: Soldiers, Slavery and the Civil War* (New York: Knopf, 2007); Gary W. Gallagher, *The Union War* (Cambridge, MA: Harvard University Press, 2011) and *The Confederate War: How Popular Will, Nationalism, and Military Strategy Could Not Stave Off Defeat* (Cambridge, MA: Harvard University Press, 1997).

18. Mark E. Neely Jr., *The Civil War and the Limits of Destruction* (Cambridge, MA: Harvard University Press, 2007); Amanda Foreman, *A World on Fire: Britain's Crucial Role in the American Civil War* (New York: Random House, 2010); R. J. M. Blackett, *Divided Hearts: Britain and the American Civil War* (Baton Rouge: Louisiana State University Press, 2001).

19. Don H. Doyle, *The Cause of All Nations: An International History of the American Civil War* (New York: Basic books, 2015), 4, 10; Andre M. Fleche, *The Revolution of 1861: The American Civil War in the Age of Nationalist Conflict* (Chapel Hill: University of North Carolina Press, 2012).

20. Aaron Astor, Rebels on the Border: *Civil War, Emancipation, and the Reconstruction of Kentucky and Missouri* (Baton Rouge: Louisiana State University Press, 2012); ChristopherPhillips, *The Civil War in the Border South* (Santa Barbara, CA: Praeger, 2013); Christopher Phillips, *The Rivers Ran Backward: The Civil War and the Remaking of the American Middle Border* (New York: Oxford University Press: 2016); Stephen V. Ash, *When the Yankees Came: Conflict and Chaos in the Occupied South, 1861–1865* (Chapel Hill: University of North

Carolina Press, 1999); Judkin Browning, *Shifting Loyalties: The Union Occupation of Eastern North Carolina* (Chapel Hill: University of North Carolina Press, 2011).

21. Adam Arenson, *The Great Heart of the Republic: St. Louis and the Cultural Civil War* (Cambridge, MA: Harvard University Press, 2011), 2; Ari Kelman, *A Misplaced Massacre: Struggling over the Memory of Sand Creek* (Cambridge, MA: Harvard University Press, 2013).

22. Ella Lonn, *Foreigners in the Union Army and Navy* (1951; repr., New York: Greenwood Press, 1969); William L. Burton, *Melting Pot Soldiers: The Union's Ethnic Regiments* (New York: Fordham University Press, 1998).

23. David T. Gleeson, *The Green and the Gray: The Irish in the Confederate States of America* (Chapel Hill: University of North Carolina Press, 2013), 6; Susannah J. Ural, *The Harp and the Eagle: Irish-American Volunteers and the Union Army, 1861–1865* (New York: New York University Press, 2006), 3; Christian B. Keller, *Chancellorsville and the Germans: Nativism, Ethnicity, and Civil War Memory* (New York: Fordham University Press, 2007). See also Susannah J. Ural, ed., *Civil War Citizens: Race, Ethnicity, and Identity in America's Bloodiest Conflict* (New York: New York University Press, 2010).

24. Lisa M. Brady, *War upon the Land: Military Strategy and the Transformation of Southern Landscapes during the American Civil War* (Athens: University of Georgia Press, 2012), 2, 5; Megan Kate Nelson, *Ruin Nation: Destruction and the American Civil War* (Athens: University of Georgia Press, 2012), 2.

25. Kathryn Shively Meier, *Nature's Civil War: Common Soldiers and the Environment in 1862 Virginia* (Chapel Hill: University of North Carolina Press, 2013).

26. Lorien Foote, *The Gentlemen and the Roughs: Violence, Honor, and Manhood in the Union Army* (New York: New York University Press, 2010); Stephen W. Berry II, *All That Makes a Man: Love and Ambition in the Civil War South* (New York: Oxford University Press, 2003).

27. Steven E. Woodworth, *While God Is Marching on: The Religious World of Civil War Soldiers* (Lawrence: University Press of Kansas, 2001); Sean A. Scott, *A Visitation of God: Northern Civilians Interpret the Civil War* (New York: Oxford University Press, 2011), 4; George C. Rable, *God's Almost Chosen Peoples: A Religious History of the American Civil War* (Chapel Hill: University of North Carolina Press, 2010).

28. George C. Rable, *Fredericksburg! Fredericksburg!* (Chapel Hill: University of North Carolina Press, 2002); Allen C. Guelzo, *Gettysburg: The Last Invasion* (New York: Knopf, 2013); Earl J. Hess, "'Where Do We Stand?': A Critical Assessment of Civil War Studies in the Sesquicentennial Era," *Civil War History* 60, no. 4 (December 2014); 371–403: Gary W. Gallagher and Kathryn Shively Meier, "Coming to Terms with Civil War Military History," *Journal of the Civil War Era* 4, No. 4 (December 2014), 487–508; Glenn David Brasher, *The Peninsula Campaign and the Necessity of Emancipation: African Americans and the Fight for Freedom* (Chapel Hill: University of North Carolina Press, 2012); Mark M. Smith, *The Smell of Battle, the Taste of Siege: A Sensory History of the Civil War* (New York: Oxford University Press, 2015).

29. James Marten, *The Children's Civil War* (Chapel Hill: University of North Carolina Press, 1998) and *Children for the Union: The War Spirit on the Northern Home Front* (Chicago: Ivan R. Dee, 2004); J. Matthew Gallman, *Defining Duty in the Civil War: Personal Choice,*

Popular Culture, and the Union Home Front (Chapel Hill: University of North Carolina Press, 2015). For more on the home front, see J. Matthew Gallman, *Mastering Wartime: A Social History of Philadelphia during the Civil War* (New York: Cambridge University Press, 1990) and *The North Fights the Civil War: The Home Front* (Chicago: Ivan R. Dee, 1994).

30. Doris Kearns Goodwin, *Team of Rivals: The Political Genius of Abraham Lincoln* (New York: Simon and Schuster, 2005); Merrill D. Peterson, *Lincoln in American Memory* (New York: Oxford University Press, 1994), 27; John McKee Barr, *Loathing Lincoln: An American Tradition from the Civil War to the Present* (Baton Rouge: Louisiana State University Press, 2014); Thomas DiLorenzo, *Lincoln Unmasked: What You're Not Supposed to Know about Dishonest Abe* (New York: Three Rivers Press, 2006); Lerone Bennett Jr., *Forced into Glory: Abraham Lincoln's White Dream* (Chicago: Johnson Publishing Company, 1999); Elizabeth Brown Pryor, *Reading the Man: A Portrait of Robert E. Lee Through His Private Letters* (New York: Penguin, 2007). Among the many fine recent works on Lincoln that viewed him favorably, see James M. McPherson, *Tried by War: Abraham Lincoln as Commander in Chief* (New York: Penguin, 2008); Michael Burlingame, *Abraham Lincoln: A Life*, 2 vols. (Baltimore: Johns Hopkins University Press, 2008); Eric Foner, *The Fiery Trial: Abraham Lincoln and American Slavery* (New York: W.W. Norton, 2010).

31. William A. Dobak, *Freedom by the Sword: The U.S. Colored Troops, 1862–1867* (Washington, DC: Center for Military History US Army, 2011); Richard M. Reid, *Freedom for Themselves: North Carolina's Black Soldiers in the Civil War Era* (Chapel Hill: University of North Carolina Press, 2008); George S. Burkhardt, *Confederate Rage, Yankee Wrath: No Quarter in the Civil War* (Carbondale: Southern Illinois University Press, 2007); John Cimprich, *Fort Pillow, A Civil War Massacre, and Public Memory* (Baton Rouge: Louisiana State University Press, 2005); Andrew Ward, *River Run Red: The Fort Pillow Massacre in the American Civil War* (New York: Viking, 2006); Kevin M. Levin, *Remembering the Battle of the Crater: War as Murder* (Lexington: University Press of Kentucky, 2012). A recently completed examination of the three black regiments recruited from Massachusetts including the Fifty-Fourth and Fifty-Fifth Massachusetts Infantry, and the Fifth Massachusetts Cavalry has set a high bar for anyone studying these units, see Douglas R. Egerton, *Thunder at the Gates: The Black Civil War Regiments That Redeemed America* (Philadelphia: Basic Books, 2016).

32. Kevin M. Levin, "Black Confederates: Out of the Attic and into the Mainstream," *Journal of the Civil War Era* 4, no. 4 (December 2014): 627–635; Bruce Levine, "In Search of a Usable Past: Neo-Confederates and Black Confederates," in *Slavery and Public History: The Tough Stuff of American Memory*, ed. James Oliver Horton and Lois E. Horton (2006; repr., Chapel Hill: University of North Carolina Press, 2009), 190. For more on the failed effort to arm black confederates, see Bruce Levine, *Confederate Emancipation: Southern Plans to Free and Arm Slaves during the Civil War* (New York: Oxford University Press, 2006).

33. Carol Sheriff, "Virginia's Embattled Textbooks: Lessons (Learned and Not) from the Centennial Era," *Civil War History* 58, no.1 (March 2012), 41, 43, 55.

34. State of Texas, "Texas Essential Knowledge and Skills for Social Studies," Chapter 113. Subchapter B., Middle School, accessed January 11, 2017, http://ritter.tea.state.tx.us/rules/tac/chapter113/ch113b.html; Rick Jervis, "Controversial Textbooks Headed to Classrooms,"

USA Today, November 17, 2014, accessed January 11, 2017, http://www.usatoday.com/story/news/nation/2014/11/17/texas-textbook-inaccuracies/19175311/.

35. The Editors, "Disunion: The Final Q &A," *New York Times*, June 10, 2015, accessed January 11, 2017, http://opinionator.blogs.nytimes.com/2015/06/10/disunion-the-final-q-a/; Ta-Nehisi Coates, "Why Do So Few Blacks Study the Civil War," *The Atlantic,* accessed January 11, 2017, http://www.theatlantic.com/magazine/archive/2012/02/why-do-so-few-blacks-study-the-civil-war/308831/.

36. *Gods and Generals*, directed by Ronald F. Maxwell (2003; Burbank, CA: Warner Home Video, 2003), DVD; *Cold Mountain*, directed by Anthony Minghella (2003; Santa Monica, CA: Miramax Home Entertainment, 2004), DVD; *Gangs of New York*, directed by Martin Scorsese (2002; Miramax Home Entertainment, 2003), DVD; *Free State of Jones*, directed by Gary Ross, 2016, based on a book by Victoria E. Bynum, *The Free State of Jones, Mississippi Longest Civil War* (Chapel Hill: University of North Carolina Press, 2001).

37. *Copperhead*, directed by Ronald F. Maxwell (2013; Burbank, CA: Warner Home Video, 2014), DVD; *Field of Lost Shoes*, directed by Sean McNamara (2014; Santa Monica, CA: Arc Entertainment, 2014), DVD.

38. Steven Benjamins, "Weebly Review," SiteBuilderReport, accessed January11, 2017, http://www.sitebuilderreport.com/reviews/weebly/our-review; Kevin M. Levin, "Black Confederates," *Civil War Memory Blog*, accessed January 11, 2017, http://cwmemory.com/?s=black+confederates; "CHT-Confederate Heritage Trust, Inc.," accessed January 11, 2017, http://www.csatrust.org/, "Confederate Heritage Fund," accessed January 11, 2017, http://confederateheritage.org/; Facebook Page, "United States Colored Troops (USCT) Headstone Project," accessed January 11, 2017, https://www.facebook.com/UsctBuriedInVirginia; Brooks D. Simpson, "Crossroads: Where History, Scholarship, the Academic Life, and Other Stuff Meet," accessed January 11, 2017, https://cwcrossroads.wordpress.com/.

39. Janell Ross, "'They Were Not Patriots': New Orleans Removes Monument to Confederate Gen. Robert E. Lee," *Washington Post*, May 19, 2017, accessed May 20, 2017, www.washingtonpost.com/national/new-orleans-begins-removing-monument-to-confederate-gen-robert-e-lee/2017/05/19/c4ed94f6-364d-11e7-99b0-dd6e94e786e5_story.html?utm_term=.fb42aad12bf6; Charles P. Roland, *An American Iliad: The Story of the Civil War* (1991; repr., Lexington: University Press of Kentucky, 2004), xii; Homer, *The Odyssey*, translated by Robert Fagles (New York: Penguin, 1996).

BIBLIOGRAPHIC ESSAY

Scholars demonstrated little interest in either American memory or Civil War memory until recently. This delay may be due to the fact that scholars from other disciplines, such as sociology, pioneered memory studies. Difficult and discipline-specific jargon hampers interdisciplinary exchange even when the subjects, history and memory, appear so inherently linked. Moreover, most of these scholars were Europeans reacting to World War I, which prompted these men and women to examine memory. The Civil War generation, particularly former Confederates, would have understood why they did so. Like the Civil War, the Great War destroyed an entire generation and much of the continent's political and social order. Scholars interested in understanding memory as it relates to history begin with Maurice Halbwachs, a French sociologist who died in a concentration camp in the next great cataclysm—World War II. Before his death he articulated many of the concepts used in this study including collective memory, see Maurice Halbwachs, *On Collective Memory*, ed. and trans. by Lewis A. Coser (1992) for an introduction to his work.

Like all academic subjects other scholars have expanded on Halbwachs's ideas. For a single-volume reader that includes both classical and contemporary selections on collective memory, see Jeffrey K. Olick, Vered Vinitzky-Seroussi, and Daniel Levy, eds., *The Collective Memory Reader* (2011). For a concise explanation of how collective memory relates to historical studies, see Jeffrey K. Olick and Joyce Robbins, "Social Memory Studies: From 'Collective Memory' to the Historical Sociology of Mnemonic Practices," *Annual Review of Sociology* 24 (1998): 105–140.

Understanding Civil War memory requires an understanding of another concept introduced by Pierre Nora—"Sites of Memory" or *Les Lieux de Mémoire*. Defined as places, institutions, and organizations that commemorate memory, the idea of sites of memory is particularly applicable to the Civil War as described in Pierre Nora, "Between Memory and History: *Les Lieux de Mémoire*," *Representations* 26 (Spring 1989): 7–24. For Nora's broader studies and the application of these concepts to French history, see Pierre Nora and Lawrence D. Krtitzman, eds., *Realms of Memory: Rethinking the French Past*, 3 vols., trans. by Arthur Goldhammer (1996–1998); Pierre Nora and David P. Jordan, eds., *Rethinking France: Les Lieux Des Mémoire*, 4 vols., trans. by Mary Trouille (2001–2010). Works discussing Nora's application to United States history include Geneviève Fabre and Robert O'Meally, eds., *History and Memory in African-American Culture* (1994).

While Europeans' work often rely on the notion of a unitary national memory, Michel Foucault's theory of counter memory—a concept that emphasized contested memory—may also contribute to understanding Civil War memory. Works that explain this concept include Michel Foucault, *Language, Counter-Memory, Practice: Selected Essays and Interviews,* ed. by Donald F. Bouchard, trans. by Donald F. Bouchard and Sherry Simon (1977). For application of Foucault's theory, see a series of essays in "Memory and Counter-Memory," *Representations* 26 (Spring 1989): 1–149. Memory studies have prompted a number of historical journals to publish special sections examining various aspects of memory, see AHR Forum, "History and Memory," *American Historical Review* 102 (December 1997): 1371–1412; and Round Table, "The Uses of Memory," *Journal of American History* 85 (September 1998): 409–465.

To understand how memory theory has been applied to one particular subject, see seminal works of World War I memory including Paul Fussell, *The Great War and Modern Memory* (1975); Jay Winter, *Sites of Memory, Sites of Mourning: The Great War in European Cultural History* (1995), and *Remembering War: The Great War between Memory and History in the Twentieth Century* (2006). Some books that do not seem to be about memory and yet are all about it include Benedict Anderson, *Imagined Communities: Reflections on the Origin and Spread of Nationalism* (1983) and Eric Hobsbawm and Terence Ranger, eds., *The Invention of Tradition* (1983).

While these studies examine European history, the seminal works in American memory include Michael Kammen, *Mystic Chords of Memory: The Transformation of Tradition in American Culture* (1991). David Thelen has made a number of valuable contributions to understanding memory; among the most valuable for understanding Civil War memory include Roy Rosenzweig and David Thelen, *The Presence of the Past: Popular Uses of History in American Life* (1998) and David Thelen, *Memory and American History* (1990). In addition to these studies, Thelen edited and introduced a collections of articles that remain seminal in American memory studies, see David Thelen, ed., "Memory and American History," *The Journal of American History* 75 (March 1989): 1117–1280; among the essays in this collection, see David W. Blight, "'For Something beyond the Battlefield': Frederick Douglass and the Struggle for the Memory of the Civil War," 1156–1178.

David W. Blight stands above all other contemporary American scholars in his collected works on Civil War memory including his award-winning *Race and Reunion: The Civil War in American Memory* (2001). In this study, Blight made the critical connection between racial attitudes and Civil War memory, particularly their relationship with national reunion. In turn, he connected these to the dismal political and social status of African American at the end of the nineteenth century. He suggested a relationship between forgetting slavery and emancipation as the cause and consequence of the Civil War and the rise of Jim Crow and disenfranchisement. Like all seminal work, he has been challenged by other scholars including Caroline E. Janney, *Remembering the Civil War: Reunion and the Limits of Reconciliation* (2013). While she recognizes race as central to understanding Civil War memory, she argued that Union mattered very much, if not more, to the Unionist Civil War generation. It is not that they forgot slavery, they remembered it; however, emancipation meant that they had achieved a critical war aim that saved the Union. In contrast, true Union, a successful sectional reunion, was still uncertain in the decades after Appomattox. As a result, these men and women embraced indications that the Union had truly been restored and perceived reunion with former enemies as indicative of the triumph of the Union Cause.

While the Union was restored, cultural sectionalism remained based on the notion of a distinct Southern (white) society within a larger United States. A number of distinguished scholars of the American South have addressed how memory shaped this identity including David Goldfield, *Still Fighting the Civil War: The American South and Southern History* (2002) and W. Fitzhugh Brundage, *The Southern Past: A Clash of Race and Memory* (2005).

Given the importance of Civil War memory to Southern history it is no surprise that the first pioneering studies of Civil War memory involved the Lost Cause. The classics that initiated the entire subfield include Rollin G. Osterweis, *The Myth of the Lost Cause, 1865–1900* (1973); Thomas L. Connelly and Barbara L. Bellows, *God and General Longstreet: The Lost Cause and the Southern Mind* (1982); Charles Reagan Wilson, *Baptized in Blood: The Religion of the Lost Cause, 1865–1920* (1980); Gaines M. Foster, *Ghosts of the Confederacy: Defeat, the Lost Cause, and the Emergence of the New South, 1865–1913* (1987). More recent studies include Gary W. Gallagher and Alan T. Nolan, eds., *The Myth of the Lost Cause and Civil War History* (2000) and

William C. Davis, *The Cause Lost: Myths and Realities of the Confederacy* (1996). Unlike many aspects of history, women were central to Civil War memory studies, particularly their role advancing the Lost Cause; see Caroline E. Janney, *Burying the Dead but Not the Past: Ladies' Memorial Association and the Lost Cause* (2008) and Karen L. Cox, *Dixie's Daughters: The United Daughters of the Confederacy and the Preservation of Confederate Culture* (2003). One notion that the United Daughters of the Confederacy wanted forgotten was the horrific nature of slavery. In this they had help from historians who studied slavery; see John David Smith, *An Old Creed for the New South: Proslavery Ideology and Historiography, 1865–1918* (1985) and *Slavery, Race, and American History: Historical Conflict, Trends, and Method, 1866–1953* (1999). For changes in how historians viewed slavery after the Civil Rights movement, see Peter J. Parish, *Slavery: History and Historians* (1989).

Though the Lost Cause dominated memory studies, the Union Cause received some attention in the twenty-first century including John R. Neff, *Honoring the Civil War Dead: Commemoration and the Problem of Reconciliation* (2005); Barbara A. Gannon, *The Won Cause: Black and White Comradeship in the Grand Army of the Republic* (2011); and Robert Hunt, *The Good Men Who Won the War: Army of the Cumberland Veterans and Emancipation Memory* (2010). Studies of African American memory represent a critical element in understanding the Union cause including Martin H. Blatt, Thomas J. Brown, and Donald Yacovone, eds., *Hope and Glory: Essays on the Legacy of the 54th Massachusetts Regiment* (2001); David W. Blight, *Beyond the Battlefield: Race, Memory, and the American Civil War* (2002); Mitch Kachun, *Festivals of Freedom: Memory and Meaning in African American Emancipation Celebrations, 1808–1915* (2003); William A. Blair, *Cities of the Dead: Contesting the Memory of the Civil War in the South, 1865–1914* (2004); and Kathleen Ann Clark, *Defining Moments: African American Commemoration & Political Culture in the South, 1863–1913* (2005). Women advocates of the Union cause have received less attention than their Confederate counterparts. Cecilia Elizabeth O'Leary's *To Die For: The Paradox of American Patriotism* (1999) examines Northern women as part of a broader study on American nationalism. The price of victory for the Union cause was high; in some cases, black soldiers were murdered. The studies that remind Americans of these crimes include John Cimprich, *Fort Pillow, a Civil War Massacre, and Public Memory* (2005) and Kevin M. Levin, *Remembering the Battle of the Crater: War as Murder* (2012).

Civil War battlefields are rarely associated with murder; among the best books for understanding how and why they are memorialized include Edward Tabor Linenthal, *Sacred Ground: Americans and Their Battlefields* (1991); Carol Reardon, *Pickett's Charge in History and Memory* (1997); Timothy B. Smith, *This Great Battlefield of Shiloh: History, Memory, and the Establishment of a Civil War National Military Park* (2004) and *The Golden Age of Battlefield Preservation: The Decade of the 1890s and the Establishment of America's First Five Military Parks* (2008); Jim Weeks, *Gettysburg: Memory, Market, and an American Shrine* (2003); and Jennifer M. Murray, *On a Great Battlefield: The Making, Management, and Memory of Gettysburg National Military Park 1933–2013* (2014).

The Civil War landscape goes beyond the battlefield as explained by Kirk Savage, *Standing Soldiers, Kneeling Slaves: Race, War, and Monument in Nineteenth-Century America* (1997); Paul A. Shackel, *Memory in Black and White: Race, Commemoration and the Post-Bellum Landscape* (2003); and Cynthia Mills and Pamela H. Simpson, eds., *Monuments to the Lost Cause: Women, Art, and Landscapes of Southern Memory* (2003). Essential studies in the Civil War memory's imaginary landscape include Nina Silber, *The Romance of Reunion: Northerners and the South, 1865–1900* (1993); Tony Horwitz, *Confederates in the Attic: Dispatches from the Unfinished Civil War* (1998); Gary W. Gallagher, *Causes Won, Lost, and Forgotten: How Hollywood and Popular Art Shape What We Know about the Civil War* (2008); and Brian Steel Wills, *Gone with the Glory: The History of the Civil War in Cinema* (2007).

Confederate leadership was not kept in the attic. A number of studies examine Robert E. Lee and his cohort including Gary W. Gallagher, *Lee and His Generals in War and Memory* (1998); Alan T. Nolan, *Lee Considered: General Robert E. Lee and Civil War History* (1991); William Garrett Piston, *Lee's Tarnished Lieutenant: James Longstreet and His Place in Southern History* (1987); Brian Craig Miller, *John Bell Hood and the Fight for Civil War Memory* (2010); Wallace Hettle, *Inventing Stonewall Jackson* (2011); Paul Ashdown and Edward Caudill, *The Mosby Myth* (2002) and *The Myth of Nathan Bedford Forrest* (2006).

Union leadership fared poorly in memory. Grant went from national idol to national idiot as chronicled by Joan Waugh, *U. S. Grant: American Hero, American Myth* (2009). The title of Wesley Moody, *Demon of the Lost Cause: Sherman and Civil War History* (2011), summarizes Sherman's memory. Finally, Thomas J. Rowland, *George B. McClellan and Civil War History: In the Shadow of Grant and Sherman* (1998) examined someone who has been considered a demon of the Union cause for his wartime inaction.

In contrast, the man who fired McClellan, Abraham Lincoln, has been studied by scholars at length including Merrill D. Peterson, *Lincoln in American Memory* (1994); Barry Schwartz, *Abraham Lincoln and the Forge of National Memory* (2000) and *Abraham Lincoln in the Post-Heroic Era: History and Memory in Late Twentieth-Century America* (2008). In contrast, much less has been written about his Confederate counterpart in memory; Donald E. Collins, *The Death and Resurrection of Jefferson Davis* chronicled how his reputation evolved in the decades after the war.

Lincoln and Davis were both born in the border state of Kentucky. The memory studies on this region include Anne E. Marshall, *Creating a Confederate Kentucky: The Lost Cause and Civil War Memory in a Border State* (2010); John C. Inscoe, *Race,*

War, and Remembrance in the Appalachian South (2008). Border Appalachia experienced some of the most brutal type of unconventional warfare, another forgotten aspect of the Civil War. Recently, scholars have attempted to correct this amnesia in studies, see Matthew C. Hulbert, *The Ghosts of Guerilla Memory: How Civil War Bushwhackers Became Gunslingers in the American West* (2016).

Few remembered guerilla war at the centennial. Studies that examine memory at the Civil War's one-hundredth-anniversary include Robert J. Cook, *Troubled Commemoration: The American Civil War Centennial, 1961–1965* (2007); David W. Blight, *American Oracle: The Civil War in the Civil Rights Era* (2011); Robert Penn Warren, *The Legacy of the Civil War: Meditations on the Centennial* (1961). Warren's meditations are also an artifact of Civil War memory. Another relic of memory, the Confederate battle flag, remains a contested symbol as discussed in John M. Coski, *The Confederate Battle Flag: America's Most Embattled Emblem* (2005).

A number of authors have examined disparate though critical aspects of Civil War memory. Surprisingly, it took a long time for someone to assess the memory of prisons; see Benjamin G. Cloyd, *Haunted by Atrocity: Civil War Prisons in American Memory* (2010). Similarly, the memory of the various ethnic groups who served each side has only recently been studied. For those interested in German Unionists see, Christian B. Keller, *Chancellorsville and the Germans: Nativism, Ethnicity, and Civil War Memory* (2007). David T. Gleeson, *The Green and the Gray: The Irish in the Confederate States of America* (2013) assesses the memory of Irishmen who served the Confederacy in its final chapter.

Veterans of all ethnicities remember the war. Studies examining former soldiers and memory include Stuart McConnell, *Glorious Contentment: The Grand Army of the Republic, 1865–1900* (1992); R. B. Rosenburg, *Living Monuments: Confederate Soldiers' Homes in the New South* (1993); M. Keith Harris, *Across the Bloody Chasm: The Culture of Commemoration among Civil War Veterans* (2014). African American veterans remembered including those chronicled in W. Fitzhugh Brundage, "Race, Memory, and Masculinity: Black Veterans Recall the Civil War," in *The War Was You and Me: Civilians in the American Civil War,* ed. Joan E. Cashin (2002): 136–156.

Often the most seminal memory work is found in essay collections including Alice Fahs and Joan Waugh, eds., *The Memory of the Civil War in American Culture* (2004); Susan-Mary Grant and Peter J. Parish, eds., *Legacy of Disunion: The Enduring Significance of the American Civil War* (2003); and Joan Waugh and Gary W. Gallagher, eds., *Wars within a War: Controversy and Conflict over the American Civil War* (2009). The contribution of essay collections to this historiography, as opposed to full-length studies, suggests that there are critical aspects of Civil War memory that represent a gap in our understanding of this important phenomenon. First and foremost, recently scholars have challenged the unitary nature of loyalty in the Civil War; the next step should be to look at Civil War memory of these dissidents. Different allegiances during the war would lead to a different memory afterwards. Moreover, Lost Cause memory has been defined almost exclusively as a province of elites. Did the common Confederate soldier have nothing to say about how the war should be remembered? Second, there is a great deal of work to be done on the Union Cause. Assessments of African American memory remain scattered in articles, essays, and chapters in larger studies, but this subject has not received a comprehensive analysis. Similarly, Unionist women's memory needs a systematic examination. Merging these ideas, a study of African American women and Civil War memory represents a significant gap in understanding the war's aftermath.

Third, there are large gaps in the twentieth century after World War I; most studies go only as far as the 1920s. The next period of interest is the centennial in the 1960s. An entire book could be dedicated to Civil War memory in the second half of the twentieth century. In this era, it might be popular memory, including television, that shaped Americans' Civil War memory, or perhaps it was textbooks. Examining Civil War memory in the places most Americans learn about the Civil War—school books—represents another significant gap in understanding how Americans remember the Civil War.

Finally, and perhaps most critical of all, we need to understand how people remembered, or more properly forgot, the war's true horror. Moreover, for its survivors the war was not just a memory; wounds still ached, families still grieved, and soldiers remained traumatized by their wartime experiences. The Civil War generation's memory work reflected their desperate need for solace as they coped with the price that both sections paid for the national sin of slavery.

INDEX

Note: page numbers in italics indicate photos.

Aaron, Daniel, 103
Abolitionism, 34, 74; radical, 111
Abolitionists, 34–36, 57–58, 73, 111; blamed for war, 2, 64; fanatical, 40, 41; radical, xvi, 34; villain, 129
Academics and Civil War Memory, 50, 62, 114, 125–26, 130
African Americans (black Americans): abolitionists, 34, 75; challenging racism, 58–59; Civil War Centennial, 71–72; Civil War generation, xvii, 28; Civil War Memorial, 85–86, 86; Civil War memorialization, 87; Civil War memory, xvii, 129; collective memory, 20, 26–27; commemoration, 27; disenfranchised, 38; as historians, 28, 65–67; illness during the War, 116; Jim Crow, 83; and Lincoln, 45; mammy stereotype, 90; movie audiences ignored, 107; and Sherman's March, 12; Unionism, 35, 65; as voters, 44; women, 7, 20, 23, 26–27, 81
African American soldiers, xviii, 28, 29, 33, 40, 41, 65, 79, 85, 90, 92, 98, 112, 114, 127; commemorated, 89–92, 96–97
Agrarianism, 69
Agrarian society, xvii, 54
American Historical Association (AHA), 51
American military heroism (Union and Confederate) 29, 38
American nationalism, 35, 47, 51, 70, 106
Amputees, xiv, 25, 120
Andersonville, 117–18; *The Andersonville Trial* (Play and Television program) 118
Antebellum religion, 4
Antebellum romanticism, 3–4

Antietam, 77, 92
Anti-imperialists, 47
Anti-reunionism, 24
Antiwar sentiments and Civil War memory, 38, 50, 63, 109, 114, 115, 121, 129; Antimilitarism, 109. *See also* Revisionism
Anxieties, xv, 43, 44, 83, 101; gendered, 38, 43, 101; nationalist, 38 nineteenth-century, 104
Appomattox, ix, 1, 8, 41, 43, 105, 114, 129; surrender, 31–32, 37
Archives (Civil War Memory), xv, 9, 26, 70, 80
Arlington National Cemetery, 26, 90–91
Army of Northern Virginia, 8, 10, 14
Army of Tennessee, 10, 78
Aunt Jemima, stereotype, 90

Battlefield parks, xviii, 92–93, 95, 97
Battlefield preservation, xviii, 92–94, 96
Beard, Charles A., 54–55, 56, 57, 63, 68
Beard, Mary, 54–55, 56, 57, 63
Begin, Menachem, 96
Bierce, Ambrose, 103
"Black Confederates," 127–28
Bledsoe, Albert Taylor, 14
Blight, David W., 26, 38, 52, 71, 72, 83, 84, 90, 109
"Blundering generation," 57
Bodnar, John, xviii, 85, 87
Border States, 32, 122
Bowdoin College, xiii, 105
Brown, John, 33, 96
Brown, Williams Wells, 28
Brownson, Orestes A., 36
Buck, Paul H., 56
Burial of Latané, 105
Burns, Ken, 100, 111
Bush, George W., 114

Carter, James E. (Jimmy), 96
Catholics, 17, 125
Catton, Bruce, 37–38

Cause Victorious, 19, 21. *See also* Union Cause
Centennial of the Civil War, 50, 62, 70–72, 74, 95, 102
Century "Battles and Leaders" series, 29–30
Chamberlain, Joshua Lawrence, 102, 105
Chancellorsville, 34, 123
Channing, Edward, 53–54
Charleston, SC, 2, 17, 71, 113
Charleston Naval Base, 71
Charleston shooting (2015), xiii, xviii–xx, 85, 112, 113, 131
Chickamauga Battlefield, 92–93
Children's Civil War, 125
Children's literature, 104
Civil rights, 38, 70–72, 75, 83, 95, 100
Civil Rights acts, 58
Civil Rights Act and improving race relations, 74
Civil rights movement, xv–xvii, xix, 37, 59, 61, 62, 66, 67, 69–71, 74, 75, 84, 90, 95–96, 102, 110
Civil War: Centennial Commission (CWCC), 71–72; children's literature, 104; commemorations, 26–27, 47; dead, 5, 21, 114; fiction, 119; literature, 100, 102–3; popular culture, 100, 106; popular memory, 100; public memory, xviii, 87
Class and Civil War Memory, 9, 27, 43–44, 54, 63–64, 80–81, 86, 101, 111, 116, 125, 126
Cold War, xvii, 59, 62–64, 66, 71
Collective memory, xiv–xvii, xix, 1, 3–6, 11, 14–15, 16, 17, 19–20, 25–26, 28–31, 33–36, 39, 48–50, 114, 118–19
Colonization, 57, 127
Common soldiers, 14, 17, 57, 76–77, 124
Communism, xvii, 59, 62–63, 66, 67, 75
Concentration camps, 63, 68
Confederacy, 1, 4, 9, 11, 17, 32, 39, 42, 48, 52, 70, 71, 72, 76, 97–98, 121

Confederate: amputees, 120; army, 8, 10, 18, 40, 123, 127–28; Battle Flag, 70, 105; identity, 32, 70–71, 105, 123
Confederate monuments, 32, 88–89, 95
Confederate nationalism, 121
Confederates, xvi, xviii–xix, 2, 5–7, 13–14, 16–18, 20, 29, 31–34, 39, 90, 97–98, 102, 104, 107
Confederate soldiers, 1, 3, 8, 11, 24, 41, 43, 76–77, 90, 97–98, 116, 120, 127
Confederate States, 17–18, 123, 130; former, 3, 6, 15, 27, 41, 87
Confederate States Centennial Conference, 71
Confederate supporters, xv–xvii, 2–3, 5, 12, 15, 17, 20, 23, 50–51, 85–86, 94, 101, 105, 127, 129; contemporary, 6; modern, 128; sympathizers, xix
Confederate Veteran magazine, 14
Confederate women, 6, 27, 80, 129; admired, 43; monument to, 90; memory efforts, 20
Consensus history, 67–70
Conservatism and Civil War Memory, 4, 12, 15, 48, 49, 71, 113
Contested memories, 33, 49
Context, cultural, xiv, 3
Cook, Robert J., 70
Copperheads, 32
Corruption and Civil War Memory, 51, 74
Counterculture movement, 1960s, 75
Crane, Stephen, 101, 104
Craven, Avery O., 57–58, 62, 65, 115
Crossroads (blog), 130
Cuba, 44, 101
Cyberspace, 114, 130

Davis, Jefferson, 11, 31
Day-Lewis, Daniel, 126
Democratic Party, 32, 49, 56, 66–67, 75
Democrats, 16, 31–32, 49
Dixiecrat Party, 67
Douglass, Frederick, 26

Du Bois, William Edward Burghardt (W.E.B.), 65–67, 78
Dunning, William, 55

Early, Jubal, 8, 11, 78
East Tennessee Unionism, 33
Elkins, Stanley, 68–69
El Sadat, Anwar, 96
Emancipation, 20–21, 23–26, 29, 31–33, 36, 47–49, 54–55, 57, 62, 64, 66, 73–74, 87, 109–12, 121, 128; amnesia about, 20; Cause, 108; commemoration, 71; Day, 7, 26–27; emphasized, 40; Memorial, 87; memory, 23, 46, 111; rejected, 20, 32, 113
Emancipationist vision, 26
Emancipation Proclamation, 53, 71–72, 122, 125–26
Environmental history, 123–24

Faubus, Orval, 73
Faulkner, William, xiii, 103
Federal government, xviii–xix, 5, 13, 19–20, 25, 34, 36, 53, 87, 92, 100, 102, 126
Federal power, increased, 123
Fifty-Fourth Massachusetts Infantry Regiment, 29, 79, 89, 99
Film industry, 129
Filmmakers, 98, 100, 106–7, 109
Films, 13, 79, 100, 106–9, 129
First Gulf War, 82
Flying Dutchmen, 35
Foote, Shelby, 112, 124
Forrest, Nathan Bedford, 112
Fort Fisher, 98
Fort Pillow, 97, 127
Fort Sumter, 1, 20, 65, 68
Fort Sumter attack commemoration (centennial), 71
Fort Sumter Attack commemoration in 1865, *2*
Fort Wagner, 79, 97

Foster, Gaines M., 4, 14, 42, 50
Franklin, John Hope, 71
Fredericksburg, 93, 125
Freeman, Douglas Southall, 49

Gender, 6, 7, 15, 16, 43, 81–82, 124–26
Generations, xv–xix, 34–36; Civil War, 15,
    19–20, 23, 30–31, 35, 39, 41, 45, 77,
    118; conservative, 34; depression, 48;
    new, 43, 50, 100; post–Civil War, 5, 10,
    39, 100, 114–15
Gettysburg, 9–10, 51–52, 92–96, 101,
    112; Battlefield Monument Association,
    95; Cyclorama, 95; Eternal Light Peace
    Memorial, 94–95; fiftieth anniversary
    encampment, 52; preservation efforts,
    94; seventy-fifth reunion, 51
Grand Army of the Republic, 20–23, 41,
    108, 118, 163; posts, all-black, 22; posts
    integrated, 22
Grant, Ulysses S., 9, 29–30, 105; in
    memory, 30
Grant, Ulysses S., III (grandson of Civil
    War general), 71, 78
Gray Ghost, television program, 110
Great Depression, xv, 48, 49, 69, 84,
    100–101
Guerilla warfare, 18, 103, 117

Haley, Alex, 111
Hampton, Wade, 16
Higginson, Thomas Wentworth, 28,
    33–34, 40
Historians, xv, xvii–xix, 13–14, 18, 28–29,
    35, 50–52, 54–55, 57–58, 62–63,
    66–67, 76–77, 79–83, 116, 121
Historical memory, xiv–xv, xvii–xviii, xix,
    4–5, 9–11, 13, 15, 18, 23, 25, 30–33,
    35–36, 38–39, 49–50, 70, 72, 77, 83,
    96, 101
Hofstadter, Richard, 67
Holocaust, 59, 118
Home front, 8, 105, 124, 129

"I Have a Dream Speech," Martin Luther
    King Jr., 72
Immigrants, xvii, 17, 34–35, 122–23;
    German, 34–35, 123; Irish
    Confederates, 17, 18, 123; Irish Union,
    123
Imperialism and Civil War memory, 46
Individual memory, xiv, 1, 4–5, 17, 20, 35,
    93, 96–97
Industrialization, xv, xvii, 38, 41–42, 54,
    94, 101
Insurgency, 8, 13, 44, 117
Integration, 22, 48, 74, 79
Internet, xix, 29, 106, 130
Iraq, 119
Irish Volunteer Memorial in Charleston, 17

Jackson, Thomas J. "Stonewall," 3, 8, 11,
    20, 35, 83, 105, 128–29

Kennedy, John F., 71, 75
Kennedy, Robert F., 75
Killer Angels, 9, 101, 105
King, Martin Luther Jr., 72, 75
Ku Klux Klan, 107, 112

Labor: activism, 47; agricultural, 52; free,
    42, 54, 58, 111; Unions, 44; wage, 47
Ladies' Memorial Associations (LMAs), 6,
    26, 39, 90, 104
Ladies of the Grand Army of the Republic
    (LGAR), 25–26
Lee, Robert E., 1, 3, 5, 8–11, 30–31, 49,
    73, 78, 90, 92, 101–2, 105, 126–27,
    129; army, 31; associates, 9; death, 10;
    farewell at Appomattox, 1; mythic Lee,
    78; popularity, 50
Lincoln, Abraham, 19–20, 30–31, 48–50,
    51, 58, 71, 73, 78, 87, 98, 100, 105,
    122, 126; image, 31; memorial, 72;
    in memory, 31, 48–49; policies, 32;
    presidency, 114; pro tax war, 130;
    racism, 127

Longstreet, James, 9, 11
Lost Cause (Confederate Memory), xiii–xix, 1–18, 29, 32–33, 36–43, 47–51, 53–59, 62–66, 69–70, 72–74, 76, 78, 87, 99, 104–5, 107, 109–14, 122–24; attraction, 43; commemorations, 7–8; conservatives prefer, 15; in literature, 103; official memory, 86, 92; popular memory, 100; in public spaces, 112; reunionism, 62; success of, 37, 50; vernacular memory, 86, 87, 96; white supremacy, 3
Lynch, John R., 51

Mahone, William, 16
Mammy stereotype, 90
"Marble Man" (Robert E. Lee), 10, 49, 78
Masculinity, 43, 81, 82, 104, 124; manhood, 15, 43, 104, 120, 124
Massacres, 122, 127
Maxwell, Ronald F., 129
McKinley, William, 43–44
Memorial Day, *6*, 21, 23, 26, 33, 45–46
Memory, xiii–xix, 3–4, 8, 10–35, 47–52, 68–70, 78, 82–83, 87, 92, 94–96, 98–102, 104, 106–8, 125–27; abolitionist, 34; battle over Civil War, 2, 105; competing collective, xv; contested Civil War, 108; emancipationist, 23, 46; guerilla war, 117; official Civil War, xviii, 86–87, 92, 94–97; popular Civil War, 109, 129; reconiliationist, 93; studies, 50, 68, 125; theory, xix, 4, 27, 31; unitary Civil War, xvii, 16, 20; white Civil War, 72
Mexican Civil War, 121
Military history, 8, 77, 125
Mitchell, Margaret, 101, 104
Modernity, 42
Monument Avenue in Richmond, 90
Monuments, xiv, xviii, 26, 31, 40–41, 79, 84–85, 87, 89–90, 92, 97, 99, 130; Confederate, Laurens, SC, *88*; Union,

Brooklyn, NY, *89*; Union, Indianapolis, IN, *88*
Moody, Dwight Lyman, 35
Morgan, John H., *40*
Mosby, John Singleton, 110; reunion of his command, *110*
Movies, xiv, xviii, 49, 79, 84, 98–100, 105–9, 129–30; *Cold Mountain*, 129; *Copperheads*, 129; *Field of Lost Shoes*, 129; *Gangs of New York*, 129; *Gettysburg*, 105; *Glory*, xix, 79, 89, 99–100, 108–9, 126; *Gods and Generals*, 11, 129; *Lincoln*, 98, 126; *Shenandoah*, 109
Myth and memory, 3–4, 12, 15, 21, 64, 76, 107, 130

National Association for the Advancement of Colored People (NAACP), 66, 108
Nationalism, 34, 41, 44, 51, 58, 64, 65, 104, 106, 109, 121; competing, 61
Nationalists (historical school), 50
National Park Service (NPS), 94–96
National unity, and Civil War memory, xix, 44, 47, 62–63; cemented, 44; served, 37
Nativism, 34, 123
Nazi regime (Germany), 63
Neoabolitionist, 61
Neo-revisionism, 113
Nevins, Allan, 64, 71
New Deal, 49
New South, 4, 41–42, 50, 86, 101
"New Women," 39, 101
New York Times, 125, 128
Northerners, xix, 10–13, 25, 31, 38, 42–44, 47, 53, 67, 73, 83, 89, 93–94, 102, 120; amnesia on war, 35; amputees, 25; antiwar, 32; memory, 73
Novels (Civil War), 99–101, 107, 119

Oates, William C., 16–17
Obama, Barack H., 113–14, 126

Official Records of the War of the Rebellion,
    28–29, 80
"Old South," 4, 6, 10, 15, 42, 81
Olustee, Battlefield, 97
Optic, Oliver, 104
Osterweis, Rollin G., 4, 76
Owsley, Frank L., 56–57

Peace interpretation memory, 35
Peninsula Campaign, 77, 125
Petersburg, 16, 92–93
Pickett's Charge (Gettysburg), 9, 94–95,
    102
Pollard, Edward A., 1
Popular culture, xiv, xviii, 84, 99–100, 103,
    105–7, 125
Popular memory, xiv, xviii, xx, 13, 98–102,
    104, 106, 111
Populists, 16, 44, 64
Port Hudson, 97
Post-traumatic stress disorder, 118
Post-Vietnam America, 100, 110, 118
Potter, David M., 64
Prisoners of War (POWs), 108, 114,
    117–18. *See also* Andersonville
Progressive Americans, 34, 38–39, 47, 54,
    63, 80; and Lincoln's memory, 48
Puck magazine, *42, 45, 46*

Race, xv, xvii, xix, 21–22, 26, 28, 33–35,
    38, 71, 73, 80–81, 83–84, 103, 107,
    111–14, 121, 125, 129
Racial attitudes, xvii, 55–56, 66, 68, 74, 83,
    113; changing, 62, 63, 67, 87, 100
Racism, xvii, xx, 32, 38, 44, 47, 51, 56, 58,
    59, 64, 65, 68, 73, 75
Ramsdell, Charles W., 56
Randall, James G., 57
Rebellion, xvi, 11, 13, 28–30, 41, 80
Reconciliation, 5–6, 21, 24, 26, 29–30,
    32, 35, 41–42, 44, 47, 49–51, 92,
    93, 95–96, 109, 111; Cause, 108–9;
    narrative, xix

Reconstruction, 6–7, 12, 26, 41, 44, 50–51,
    55–56, 95, 101–2, 107, 109, 116, 122,
    129; radical, 26
Reconstruction memory, 51, 55
Red Badge of Courage, 101, 119
Reenactors, 98
Religion, 3, 4, 11, 15, 35, 105, 115,
    124–25; Civil Religion (Lost Cause), 4
Repressible Conflict, Civil War as, 57
Republican Party, 16, 19, 22, 30, 31–32,
    43–44, 49, 54, 58, 75, 113, 115
Reunion, 6, 26, 38, 41, 43–44, 47, 50–53,
    53, 62–63, 70, 83–84, 93, 95, 99, 101,
    103, 106, 109–13, 129; facilitated, 24,
    51, 102; rejected, 24
Revisionism, 56, 57, 64, 67–69, 113, 129;
    neo-, 113–14, 115, 121
Rhodes, James F., 50–51, 55; revived, 64
Romance, 4, 6, 7, 8, 38, 43, 99, 100, 101,
    103, 105–7, 109, 111, 124
Romantic melodrama, xviii, 99
Roosevelt, Franklin D., administration
    of, 66
Roosevelt, Theodore, 44
Roots, television program, 111
Ryan, Father Abram J., 17

Sadat, Anwar L., 96
Saint-Gaudens, Augustus, 90
Sculpture, 85, 90
Secession, xvi, 2, 5, 8, 11, 13–15, 23, 32,
    36, 41, 44, 51, 73, 95, 108, 122, 129;
    crisis, 19, 67–68
Sectional, 31, 65, 70; bloodletting, 24,
    100; differences, 42, 104; divisions, 65,
    100, 106; harmony, 70; periodicals, 32;
    prejudices, 29; (sectional) ism, xviii, 64,
    128
Segregation, xv, 22, 67, 69, 72, 79
Segregationists, 70
Selznick, David O., 99
Sesquicentennial, xvi, 84, 85, 111, 113,
    114, 126, 128, 129

Shaara, Michael, 101

Shaw, Robert Gould, 79; image, 89

Shaw Memorial (Boston), 96

Sherman, William Tecumseh, 12–13, 82, 83, 102; March 12–13, 82–83

Shiloh, 78, 92–93, 108

Slave owners, 19, 26, 32–33, 52, 55, 67, 72, 101, 111; unionist, 32

Slavery, xv–xix, 2–3, 6–7, 13–14, 19–21, 23–24, 26–31, 38, 50–58, 64–65, 67–69, 72–75, 81, 111–12, 121–22, 126–29; benevolence, xvii, 74; defended, 58, 68, 70; disparaged, 51; expansion, 56; fate of, 61; memory of, 6, 29, 51, 68–69, 111; paternalism, 69; portrayed, 52, 55, 58, 111; rejected, 54; religion, 69; resist, 69; studies, 68–69; white, 47

Slaves, 20, 23, 45, 47–48, 52–55, 57–58, 65, 67–69, 73–75, 87, 90, 105, 107–8, 111, 114, 127; emancipated, 116; freed, 32; loyal, 40; mammy, 90; narratives, 80; well-fed, 58

Slave trade: domestic, 75; internal, 67; trader, 112

Social media, xix, 113–14, 130

Sons of Confederate Veterans (SCV), 127

Southern: identity, xix; identity defined as white, 3, 50, 69; manhood, 43; memory, 89; military prowess, 109; mythmaking, 41; narratives, 104; nationalism, 80; textbooks, 41, 128; white women, 6, 8, 39, 43, 81, 104

Southern Historical Papers, 14–15

Southern Historical Society, 4, 9–10, 49, 70, 80

Southern History, 9, 68–69, 130

Spanish-American War, 17, 34, 42, 44–45, 47, 93, 101, 107

Stampp, Kenneth M., 67–69

Stephens, Alexander, 13, 34, 40

Stone Mountain, xiii

Stones River, 93

Suffrage: African American, 51; women's, 47

Tariffs, 126, 128

Television, xiv, 99–100, 110, 118, 124

Television programs, xviii, xix, 84, 100, 110

Texas, 128

Textbooks, 39, 40–41, 53, 55, 74, 106, 128; college, 55

Theater of operations: Eastern, 9–10, 18; Western, 10, 78

Thirteenth Amendment, 126

Trauma, 16, 27, 28, 120

Treason, 11, 13, 20; committed, 13–14

Trotter, William Monroe, 108

Truman, Harry S., 67

Trump, Donald J., 114

United Daughters of the Confederacy (UDC), xviii, 4, 6, 26, 39–40, *40*, 43, 47, 50, 58, 90, 97, 104; caring for indigent confederate veterans, 39

Ulysses (Homer), 131

Union Army, 6, 24, 32, 37, 78–79, 83, 85, 104, 110, 111, 116, 122, 123–24, 127, 163; Navy, 104

Union Cause, xiv–xix, 2, 7, 16, 18–21, 23–26, 29–35, 38, 44, 47–48, 52–54, 61–64, 70, 72–76, 78, 84, 92, 99–100, 105–6, 108–9, 111–14, 120–22, 125–27, 129–30

Unionists, 5, 20–21, 23–25, 47, 94, 117; black, xvii; white southern, 6, 33, 45, 91

Union Soldiers, 22, 24, 44, 52, 76–77, 88, 97, 105, 121, 123

Union Soldiers and Sailors Memorial Arch, *89*

United Confederate Veterans (UCV), 4–5, 14, 47, 91, 118

United Sons of Confederate Veterans, 15

United States Colored Troops (USCT), 97, 127, 130

Vernacular memory, xviii, 85, 87, 94
Veterans, xiv, 14–15, 20, *22*, 22–25, 27,
    29, 31–32, 46, 92–94, 103, 108, 114,
    118–20; amputees, 25; black Union, 22,
    23, 28; Confederate, 4–5, 14, 43, 47,
    91, 118, 120; Union, 20–21, 22, 24, 43,
    45, 118, 119–20
Vietnam War, 13, 62–63, 75–77, 82, 83,
    100–101, 102, 107, 109; veterans, 118
Virginia Military Institute, 129
Virginia textbooks, 128

Wakeman, Sarah, 82
War for Southern Independence, 54
Warren, Robert Penn, 1, 72
Website, 97, 130
White supremacy, xiii, 3, 32, 33, 49, 51,
    83; maintaining, 3
White women, 7–8, 20, 27, 40, 47, 80, 90;
    upper-class southern, 6
Williams, George Washington, 28, 65
Wilson, Joseph T., 28
Wilson, Woodrow, xv, 51

Womanhood, 15, 81; idealized Confederate,
    101
Woman's Relief Corps (WRC), 25–26, 47
Women, xiii–xviii, 3, 5–8, 19–21, 23–27,
    29–34, 38–39, 48, 54–56, 69, 80–82,
    89–90, 104–5, 114–16, 124–25; elite,
    39; enslaved, 116; loyal, 25, 105;
    middle-class, 116; northern, 20, 43,
    125
Women's clubs, 39
Women writers, 104
Won Cause, 19, 23. *See also* Union Cause
Woodson, Carter G., 65
Works Progress Administration (WPA),
    69, 80
World War, 12, 38, 41, 47, 50, 57–58, 63,
    102, 113
World War I, xv, xvii, 47–49, 56–57, 59,
    62, 67, 102, 106–7
World War II, xvii, 48, 58, 62–63, 67–68,
    79, 82–83, 97, 100, 106–7, 118

Yuma, Johnny, 110

ABOUT THE AUTHOR

BARBARA A. GANNON is currently an associate professor of history at the University of Central Florida (UCF). She received her BA from Emory University in Atlanta, an MA from George Washington University in Washington, D.C., and a PhD from the Pennsylvania State University. She is the author of *The Won Cause: Black and White Comradeship in the Grand Army of the Republic*, an examination of the black and white members of the Union Army's largest veterans' organization. This book received the Wiley-Silver Prize (University of Mississippi) for the best first book on the Civil War, was recognized with an honorable mention by the Lincoln Prize Committee 2012 (Gilder Lehrman Institute), and was a finalist for the Jefferson Davis Prize (American Civil War Museum).